TOM FLETCHER was born in Kent, and studied at Harvey Grammar School and Oxford University, graduating with a First in Modern History. He is a Visiting Professor at New York University, an honorary fellow at Oxford University, and a campaigner on global education and the UK's creative industries. He was Britain's Ambassador to Lebanon from 2011 to 2015, and was awarded the Companion of St Michael and St George (CMG) in 2011 for services to the prime minister. He is married to Dr Louise Fletcher and they have two sons, Charlie and Theo.

'A brilliant book'   *Times Literary Supplement*

'A cavalier diplomat using the best of new technology to tackle the toughest of old challenges: T. E. Lawrence with a smartphone'
BARONESS VALERIE AMOS,
former UN Assistant Secretary General;
President of School of Oriental and African Studies

'A call for us all to reconsider our place in society and in our interconnected world. It urges us to be brave, creative, involved and connected. Diplomacy, he insists, is too important to be left to diplomats and he calls on us "citizen diplomats" to engage with it, to wield power ... As the pages turned, I thought this read increasingly as a new manifesto, and I finished it thinking how unsurprised I would be if Fletcher ended up running the Foreign Office, or the country'   *Observer*

'The UK's creative diplomat par excellence'   JOHN KAMPFNER

'An irrepressible and irresistible optimist'   *L'Hebdo*

'When people ask how Lebanon held it together while the region was in flames, the first name they mention is Tom Fletcher'

NAJIB MIKATI,
Prime Minister of Lebanon 2011–14

'Fletcher confronted a society riven with dysfunctional politics and facing threats at its borders ... Fletcher's charisma and energy helped Lebanon defend its borders and stave off terrorism, and built a stronger and more resilient UK position in the region'

Foreign Affairs Magazine

'That sound you hear is the massed ranks of long-departed British ambassadors turning in their graves. Some of us, alive but retired, have had to reach for our smelling salts. Step forward our former man in Beirut, Tom Fletcher'

SIR CHRISTOPHER MEYER,
former UK Ambassador to Washington

TOM FLETCHER
THE NAKED DIPLOMAT

Understanding Power and Politics
in the Digital Age

WILLIAM
COLLINS

William Collins
An imprint of HarperCollins*Publishers*
1 London Bridge Street
London SE1 9GF
www.WilliamCollinsBooks.com

First published in Great Britain as *Naked Diplomacy* by William Collins in 2016
This William Collins paperback edition published 2017

1

'The Embassy' ('Sonnets from China XV'), from *Collected Poems* by
W. H. Auden copyright © 1976 the Estate of W. H. Auden, by permission
of Random House Inc. and Curtis Brown Ltd.
Extracts from *Yes, Minister* and *Yes, Prime Minister* copyright © 1980 Jonathan
Lynn and Antony Jay, by permission of Alan Brodie Representation Ltd,
www.alanbrodie.com

A catalogue record for this book is
available from the British Library

ISBN 978-0-00-812758-9

Printed and bound in Great Britain by
Clays Ltd, St Ives plc

MIX
Paper from
responsible sources
FSC® C007454

To Louise, without whom this book would never have been written.

To Charlie, Theo and Twitter, without whom it would have been written much faster.

And to the colleagues who march towards the sound of gunfire, in order to try to stop it.

Contents

PART ONE
Glad-handing on the Shoulders of Giants:
A Short History of Diplomacy

PART TWO
Statecraft and Streetcraft:
Power and Diplomacy in a Connected World

PART THREE
What Next?

As evening fell the day's oppression lifted;
Tall peaks came into focus; it had rained:
Across wide lawns and cultured flowers drifted
The conversation of the highly trained.

Thin gardeners watched them pass and priced their shoes;
A chauffeur waited, reading in the drive,
For them to finish their exchange of views:
It looked a picture of the way to live.

Far off, no matter what good they intended,
Two armies waited for a verbal error
With well-made implements for causing pain,

And on the issue of their charm depended
A land laid waste with all its young men slain,
Its women weeping, and its towns in terror.

W. H. Auden, 'The Embassy'

INTRODUCTION TO THE
PAPERBACK EDITION

I would obviously like to claim that 2016 proved this book right. After all, in a post-truth world, we can all claim anything. In my favour, it was a year in which many of the themes of *The Naked Diplomat* – truth and lies online and offline; coexistence versus wall building; open versus closed societies; the implications of our inability to reach angry and frustrated parts of our societies – have been thrust into centre stage.

But nobody really called 2016. I predicted that of the United Nations, US, France and the UK, two would be run by women in 2017. I may have got the wrong two. It has been a logic-defying, irrational year, in which three acronyms officially entered the dictionary – 'LOL', 'OMG' and 'WTF'. And many began to worry that liberalism could be confined to the dictionary.

Among the many ironies of 2016, Germany emerged as the bulwark against Fascism; the Pope emerged as the leading spokesman for freedom; China emerged as the defender of the Davos consensus; and a TV celebrity billionaire emerged as the voice of the ordinary American. Empowered citizens voted for policies they knew would make them poorer; for liars to clean up politics; and to take back control by reducing their global influence. And experts responded to accusations that they were no longer needed by being consistently wrong. Meanwhile, Russia bombed Syrian civilians to save them from terror. George Orwell, take a bow.

The beginning and end of chapters in history books can be pretty arbitrary. But 2016 is the end of the chapter that started in 1989, or maybe even 1945 or 1789. It could be the end of the American Age. It might mark the (hopefully temporary) resignation of America as a driving force for liberty throughout the world. Donald Trump's election created a vacancy for leader of the free world. For the first time in my life, we can take nothing about the next year for granted, let alone the next decade: because 2016 is the new normal. We are in new and uncertain terrain.

I think three themes run through Brexit, the rise of Trump and the polarisation of political debate that we have seen.

Firstly, the West is in an Age of Distrust. Authority is one more devalued currency. The UK parliamentary vote on military action in Syria in 2013 was rejected because Iraq had destroyed confidence in the establishment's ability to make sound foreign policy. Likewise, many rejected staying in the EU because MPs' expenses, the banking crisis and EU mismanagement had destroyed confidence in Westminster, the Square Mile and Brussels. And – ironically for a tycoon and TV personality – Trump is a rejection of the establishment and mainstream media. YouGov report that public trust is plummeting not just in politics, the media and the banks, but also in teachers, doctors and the police.

So, institutions traditionally based on consent, deference and trust are failing, and politics is failing. For the first time in recent history, the challenge is not states with too much power, but too little. Declining powers such as Russia are more disruptive than rising ones. And the great powers don't seem to want to exert great power. Meanwhile, a Europe used to summits where it discussed other countries as problems – Afghanistan/Pakistan, the Middle East, North Korea – is now finding itself on the agenda.

On the global balance sheet, it has moved from being an exporter of solutions to an exporter of problems. And, as US Senator Mike Enzi says, 'if you're not at the table, you're on the menu'.

Facing this new context, leaders and politicians are struggling to connect, to get their message through. As Shelley is quoted as saying of a rival, 'he had lost the art of communication, but not alas the gift of speech'. And the politicians know it. One recent European leader told me: 'We no longer think it is just the past that is another country. It is now the present that is another country.' We all feel better connected but less well informed. For the first time, our problem is too much information, not too little. Being more in touch has reduced our ability to 'reach out and touch people'.[1] Hence the distrust.

Secondly, we have been reminded of Mark Twain's nifty observation that history rhymes.* After economic downturns, nations turn inwards at the moment they should look outwards (and this was, of course, happening before Trump). They become nationalist when they should be internationalist. I now understand why we spent so much time at school studying the Weimar Republic. The consequences of the crash of 2008–9 could be as great as those after the crash of 1929.

And thirdly, as the first edition of this book argued, the flux we are experiencing is just the initial implications of the Internet. How humans interact socially and economically is changing at a faster pace than at any time in history. So how we interact politically is going to change too, as we are seeing in elections throughout the West. Look at the impact of the printing press and scale it up. There will be many losers. At a time of massive prosperity, inequality continues to rise, unleashing the spasms of anger we

---

* Perhaps it is appropriate in a post-truth year that there is no strong evidence that either Twain or Shelley actually made these observations.

are seeing at the ballot box and that we will increasingly see on our streets. It was not American poverty that generated Trump but American prosperity.

I have a confession to make: I was on Trump's mailing list. It started out gently. I took his questionnaire on media bias, just to disagree with it. But then I was sucked further in, like a potential terrorist being slowly radicalised. I received several emails a day addressing me as his key supporter. More questionnaires. I had one asking for debate advice – I suggested a greater focus on tolerance. One from Newt Gingrich asked for personal advice on how to win in November – 'Change the candidate,' I offered. So much for experts.

But thanks to my fascination with how his campaign pitched their world view to those they thought shared it – aggressive, macho, divisive, dishonest – I did not unsubscribe from this deluge of direct engagement. It reminded me of two personal experiences as a communicator. Firstly, my Indiana summer selling door to door in the Midwest – 'Everyone's buying it,' we would repeat like a mantra. And secondly, the online arguments with extremists in the Middle East that this book describes. They and the Trump campaign used the same rhetorical and political devices – 'us and them', find someone to blame, we can make you great again.

Let's be honest with ourselves. Many of us have an inner Trump somewhere. The bit of us that is too prone to boastfulness, to anger, that seeks constant competition and that hits out at those we think are weaker than ourselves.

But the difference is that, for most of us, this is not something we're proud of. And it is something we spend our lives finding ways to contain and restrain. Most people manage to do that at some point between the ages of three and five. But we work at it, and almost all of us get there – we contain our inner Trump. We evolve.

I worked in Downing Street during previous transitions of power – going from the Gordon Brown to the David Cameron era was like trying to master dressage after rodeo. But I also observed close-up four transitions of the crucial and often misunderstood relationship between US president and UK prime minister: Blair/Bush to Bush/Brown to Brown/Obama to Obama/Cameron. They are moments of opportunity and excitement. But they also require great sensitivity and care. Leaders have a sixth sense about political capital, and who has it or doesn't have it.

When Senator Obama visited Downing Street some months before the 2008 election, he had it in buckets. He was keen to give a suitably presidential statement outside the famous black door. One of my jobs was to keep him in No. 10 as long as possible, so that everyone would see how good the personal rapport was with Prime Minister Brown. So I took him to Margaret Thatcher's old study to look at the particles of moon rock that President Richard Nixon had gifted Prime Minister Harold Wilson in January 1970. As I showed him these extraordinary and inspiring souvenirs of a more ambitious age, I hoped for a moment of reflection, maybe even an unforgettable piece of Obama rhetoric on America's future. Instead, the senator recoiled. All day I wondered why – was it mention of Nixon? Was he overwhelmed by the moment? Only later did I realise that my tie had taken some friendly fire while I was changing my son's nappy that morning. The future leader of the free world had not had the ideal introduction to British hygiene. I hope the special relationship did not suffer too much as a result.[2]

I think President Obama is a humble man with much to be arrogant about. We will find out whether President Trump is the opposite. Whether he can learn to restrain his inner Trump. And whether we really are set for a period in which the most powerful nation in the world is led by a blond Berlusconi.[3] Ironically, we are left hoping that he is a politician who doesn't follow through on his election promises.

More importantly, we will learn fast whether society has evolved, has learnt from history how to contain its own inner Trump. Humankind's story is one of the gradual – albeit with bad years, and sometimes bad decades – evolution of reason over craziness, expertise over instinct, community over tyranny, and honesty over lies. Painstakingly and with great sacrifices, we built political systems to restrain the dangerous individual who believes that only he – and almost always *he* – has the answers. As a species, our strength is that we know we are a work in progress.

So we need to remind ourselves how to restrain tyrants. Basic dictatorship is not complicated. It tends to follow very similar patterns: an economic crash, blamed by the aspiring tyrant on elites, minorities and his opponents; the promise of greatness, of bread and circuses (or cookouts and reality TV in the modern version); the gradual undermining of institutions; intimidation of the independent media; the reward (not confined to dictatorships, of course) of loyalty over competence; holding enemies close; the building of a personality cult; and the systematic removal of checks and balances.

At each of those moments, the dictator hopes that we stay silent, argue among ourselves, or become distracted. In the period ahead, we are going to find out if the checks and balances created over centuries to constrain our inner Trumps are being simply tested, or tested to destruction. The painful lessons of the twenty-first century stand before the firing squad, wondering if they will hear the first shot.

*

And what about Brexit – depending on where you stand, either Independence Day, a 'quiet revolution', or a suicide note.

The UK's role in the twenty-first century will not be defined by the EU referendum itself, but how the British respond to it. The period ahead will require a sense of collective purpose that we have not had since the Second World War.

I spent much of 2016 in places that have entered an uncertain time because of the referendum: Dublin, Belfast, Barcelona, Gibraltar, Berlin, London, Cyprus. The decision of the UK people to leave the EU may have been based largely on local factors, but it is the best example of how decisions in one country now affect everyone. Ironically, our localism made the case for internationalism, because it has placed us in the position of needing to work harder on our international partnerships. It is also part of an even greater irony – a worldwide campaign against globalisation.

These are moments of peril for Europe more widely. For the first time since the Second World War, people are leaving the European centre at an alarming rate, and parties that have dominated are not just losing but being wiped out. W. B. Yeats saw it well at a time of similar upheaval in 1919:

Turning and turning in the widening gyre
The falcon cannot hear the falconer;
Things fall apart; the centre cannot hold;
Mere anarchy is loosed upon the world,
The blood-dimmed tide is loosed, and everywhere
The ceremony of innocence is drowned;
The best lack all conviction, while the worst
Are full of passionate intensity.[4]

That passionate intensity is at the heart of the third symptom of twenty-first-century change, and a theme of much of this book – the polarisation of debate and the consequent rise of extremism.

As later chapters describe, I was ambassador in Beirut when the Syria conflict began, and lived through the four years in which it developed into the worst war of the twenty-first century. Let's remember that the Assad killing machine has no pause button. Industrial terror is its factory setting, and it survives only through brutality. I will spend much of my life trying to explain how and why we let it happen on our watch. And much of my time now is spent trying to ensure that Syrian children denied education do not pay the price. They deserve better than the choice between a barrel-bombing tyrant, the box-office barbarity of ISIL, and the perils of a Mediterranean raft. They deserve more than the suicide vest or life jacket. The closing chapters of this book argue for a return to our humanitarian responsibilities.

But we cannot understand the wider challenges facing the world without looking at Syria. There is such a strong connection between breakdown in the Middle East and the polarisation of debate in our own societies. And Syria is the grimmest example of what happens when the international order fails – you get carnage, great power conflicts, and a Petri dish for extremism.

And that extremism will continue to have consequences for all of us. I describe in this book how the three cities in which I have spent most of my adult life – Paris, Beirut and Nairobi – have been victims of terror. The sociopaths with smartphones have reawakened our own versions of extremism. It is a vicious cycle in which those who want to radicalise communities in the West and the Middle East feed off each other's messages.

So, the scaffolding put up around the twentieth century's global order is fragile. We are still building the driverless car but seem to have achieved a driverless world. An age of austerity has combined with an age of migration and an age of massive technological change. This brings the mix of immigration, insecurity and inequality that fuels nationalism and extremism.

As a result, I believe we will see new battles in the twenty-first century. Not, like the twentieth century, between East and West, North and South, men and women, black and white, or Islam and Christianity.

Instead we will see four new dividing lines.

Firstly, between coexisters (like the caveman in my first chapter) and wall builders. The target of Islamist extremists is often the 'greyzone' – places where people interact across communities and races. This places them on the same side as Western extremists, on the wrong side of the twenty-first-century's key argument: between those who want to live together and those who don't. Their publicity machine thrives on Donald Trump, burkini bans, and any measure that makes Western claims of openness, tolerance and respect seem a sham. In the battle for modern Islam, we rely heavily on the moderate voices prevailing. Yet too often we undermine their message by not sticking to our deeply held values. There isn't a twenty-first-century problem to which the answer is another brick in the wall. Post-US election, there is a bigger battle at stake for all of us: to ensure that it is harder for the next Trump to weaponise intolerance in the way he has.

Secondly, we will see a division between libertarians and control freaks. This will pit the prophets of complete freedom against those who argue we need secrets, in our personal lives and as governments. So we have Julian Assange and WikiLeaks at one end of the spectrum and the North Koreans at the other. Most of us will find our position, issue by issue. But there will be surprises too. Former Commander of Joint Special Operations Command Stan McChrystal is right that it is now more dangerous to share too little information than too much. Governments are beginning to recognise that without opening up they cannot establish the trust necessary to govern. Chapter 8 looks in more detail at this balance between security and liberty.

Thirdly, the line will be between those who want to make the problem bigger and those who want to make it smaller. This book argues that technology has created a significant shift in the power balance between global, regional, national, local and individual. All the talk in Britain at the moment is about our relationship as a nation with Europe. Yet these two entities – the superstate and the nation state – are the two that are going to lose power fastest in the twenty-first century. We'll need better global systems; more powerful local systems; and we'll want more individual control. That doesn't leave the nation state or regional organisation with much. We will need to make the case to a more sceptical public that it is sometimes in the national interest to pool sovereignty.

Finally, we will see a growing chasm between 'on demand' winners and 'on demand' losers. Many of us are going to love the 'on demand' economy. We'll get more of what we want when we need it. But it will take a lot of people to service that. Their time will be on demand so that ours can be our own. Make that gap between winners and losers too wide, and we create peril. Growing inequality is the biggest geopolitical risk today.[5] If displaced people had a country, it would be the twenty-first largest in the world.[6]

We better mind that gap.

So how do we survive the twenty-first century as businesses, individuals and countries?

We can start by getting out of our echo chamber. I only realised the day after the US election that my Twitter timeline had no

Trump supporters on it – maybe that's a sign I'm pretty closed-minded too. One of the ironies of the final twenty-four hours of the campaign was seeing Hillary Clinton's team singing along to 'Livin' On a Prayer' – I fear Gina and Tommy voted Trump.

Maybe the silver lining of 2016 is that more good people will become activists. As the murder of the inspirational British MP Jo Cox reminded us, we have to defend the progress and freedoms we took for granted with greater urgency and passion.

So the most influential generation in history, empowered by access to information and networks previous generations could never have imagined, will need to summon up fresh will to protect what my generation took for granted. They will need to establish checks and balances on the new emperors, from tech giants to tyrants, just as we learnt to do on the old ones.

Second, we can thrive by investing in education. If America changes tack on climate change, the life expectancy of the next generation just got shorter. Instead we need to better equip them with curiosity, creativity and courage. And kindness. Let's not forget kindness. For moral and pragmatic reasons, our greatest challenge now is making more people less poor. And an individual's freedom of opportunity should not be defined by where they are born. Right now it is easier to destroy than to build. But we need to build a global education system that can reach the seventy-five million children not in school, and give everyone equal access to the best we can teach them. Someone needs to write the first global curriculum, with global citizenship at its heart – now there's an idea ...

Third, we can survive by shifting our mindset from maps and chaps to networks and coalitions. If our world view is shaped and defined by hierarchies, organograms and titles, we need to see the world afresh. I tried to apply these lessons in a review of the UK Foreign Office, released by the government in April 2016. Much media reaction focused on a suggestion from one envoy that diplomats should become more like the characters in *24* or *Spooks*. Hacks imagined an army of social media-savvy, digitally literate e-nvoys, new Internet pioneers putting the OMG into HMG.

But the more important message of the review was that in the Digital Age we need to move our organisations away from prioritising competences, hierarchy and inputs and towards those based on skills, networks and outputs. I hope the future Foreign Office will be less male and pale, more digital, more expert, and more flexible. The buccaneering diplomats on the walls of King Charles Street will soon be joined by portraits of pioneering modern diplomats: the first female and minority ambassadors; the local staff who keep embassies running when events force UK colleagues to flee; the consular staff who rescue Brits in the most difficult of circumstances.

I am now trying to apply similar lessons to innovation at the United Nations. How can we use solar drones for better peacekeeping and provision of education? How can we create digital citizenship to increase security and reduce identity fraud and international crime? How can we use social media to engage and build a new generation of global citizens? How do we build the online rights to match the offline rights we have codified? How do we overhaul the global system for humanitarian giving? How do we respond to the challenges and opportunities of artificial intelligence? We need to find new ways to make the huge amounts of great work done by the UN more meaningful and accessible to the public. That takes more than a hashtag and a civil society side event. And leaders need to get much better at executing global policy, not simply announcing it.

Fourth, a successful century depends on us winning the argument for openness. There will be a temptation to pull up the drawbridge and focus purely on domestic security or nationalist politics. Let's be in no doubt: a retreat from the world is the path to irrelevance and drift. Our national interest now depends on our internationalism. Countries are strongest when outward-looking, pioneering, exploring, welcoming. So we must marshal our best national instincts and values, and not our worst. In the battle with more isolationist and intolerant opponents, we have to show that our societies have not themselves become intolerant or isolationist.

This is not just posturing. We need a world view based on actually viewing the world, because our ability to keep pace with the dangerous political and social implications of technological change depends on our brightest minds coming up with ingenious solutions to problems, from climate change to economic instability. We should be unashamedly backing freedom of the Internet, so that the smartest people in the world can create together the extraordinary ideas that we don't yet know we need. We should be proud when our countries are magnetic, and smart enough to recognise the economic potential of migrants and refugees, from Einstein to Jobs. We were all migrants once, and the twenty-first century might make us migrants again. This will be a century of people on the move: improved communications, the Internet, climate change and conflict will create more migration than any previous era. So we need to learn how to absorb, assimilate, coexist.

However insecure we will feel at times in the coming period, the answer to modern security threats is in fact more liberty, equality, fraternity. Not less. Or as Benjamin Franklin put it at a time of similiar uncertainty: "those who would give up essential *Liberty*, to purchase a little temporary Safety, deserve neither *Liberty* nor Safety."

*

The gadgets we marvel at today will not seem marvellous for long. The changes we wonder at won't seem wonderful for long. The predictions we think are crazy won't seem crazy for long. At moments in 2016, it appeared that technology had disrupted democracy. But used properly it still gives us the means to tackle inequality, improve cyber and economic security, outsmart the extremists, ensure that artificial intelligence helps not harms us, and make it easier for citizens to be part of government.

But that all depends on us – whether we are just connected to technology or can truly connect with each other through that technology. Because Facebook and Twitter didn't create our desire to connect. Our desire to connect created Facebook and Twitter.

Progress zigzagged in 2016. So what can citizen diplomats[7] do in response?

We can build networks in a time of institutional failure; consensus in a time of arguments; and bridges in a time of walls.

We can strive for expertise, patience, perspective and judgement in a time of fake news, sound bites and echo chambers.

We can aspire to be courageously calm, tolerant and honest in a time of outrage, intolerance and post-truth politics.

We can be internationalist in a time of nationalism, and open-minded in a time of closed minds.

Above all, we must remain curious in a time of too much certainty.

I'm now an ex-Excellency, a recovering ambassador. But I stand by my original conclusion – we need to forge a renewed spirit of global citizenship.

Diplomats will play our part. But naked diplomacy is too important just to leave to diplomats.

PREFACE

The Diplomat Who Arrived Too Late

Shen Weiqin was the diplomatic adviser to Emperor Qin Er Shi during China's Qin dynasty. It was a pretty cushy job, with steady access to the many pleasures of the royal court, a fair amount of arduous but interesting travel, and long periods of relative peace in which to study, opine and schmooze.

Shen knew his master's mind and his master's foibles, and was well suited to the role we now call a 'sherpa', the key adviser who helps the leader prepare for diplomatic summits. In modern statecraft, the sherpa's assistant is called the yak, a metaphor that would also have meant something to His Excellency Shen Weiqin. The modern yak carries the mountains of paper generated and required by any modern diplomatic negotiation. Shen's carried him.

Shen must have anticipated a routine month's work as he set out for the Congress of the Tribes in Xianyang in 208 BC. His emperor's armies had soundly thrashed the Chu tribe, burying alive all those who surrendered. This is what we now call hard power, though the Geneva Convention discourages such treatment of defeated opponents.

The victory left the field open for a strong peace treaty that would give Qin increased taxes and land rights, and the opportunity to recruit any remaining Chu warriors to fight for him. This would have been straightforward and probably routine business for Shen, who by this time had negotiated three such deals with the unburied survivors of other defeated clans.

Making peace is easier when you have shown you can make war. As he carried out his restorative and silver-tongued victor's diplomacy, Shen was an early example of the statecraft that President Theodore Roosevelt aspired to many centuries later: 'Speak softly and carry a big stick.' Only the choice of weapon was more deadly.

But Shen was to be rudely awakened from his diplomatic comfort zone. The envoys representing the Chu tribe had developed a new and innovative means of passing messages quickly, by positioning rested horses along the key trade routes. This was the third-century BC equivalent of a decent social media account. As a result, they had gathered intelligence of an uprising in the west and of disquiet within Emperor Qin's ranks, caused by the despotism of his favourite and most intimate adviser, the flamboyant eunuch Zhao Gao (who deserves his own book). Shen's diplomatic opponents were able to use this crucial information to hold out for a much better deal than they would otherwise have got.

Shen had been outmanoeuvred at his own game. In modern language, his diplomacy had been disrupted. The chastened and no doubt increasingly saddle-sore envoy returned with trepidation to his master to report the bad news.

As is probably already evident, Emperor Qin was no shrinking violet. The previous year he had tricked his elder brother, the rightful heir to the Qin dynasty, into committing suicide. Mercy had not got him his throne, and was not going to help him keep it.

In this case, Qin decided to punish poor execution with slow execution. Shen was tied to a wooden frame and 'slow-sliced', a particularly gruesome demise involving the methodical removal of 999 body parts in random order as drawn from a hat: death by a thousand cuts, give or take. The process, '*lingchi*', literally means 'ascending a mountain slowly', a metaphor that resonated with his pre-summit diplomacy in a way that Shen was presumably unable to relish. His diplomatic failure was classified by the emperor as an act of treason, and so no opium was administered to ease the pain.

It is not recorded at what point in the three-day process Shen passed away. But his grisly exit provided evidence for Lu You, one of history's first human rights activists, to argue in 1198 for the abolition of *lingchi*, which is the only reason we now know about the case. Again, probably no consolation to poor old Shen.

Shen discovered the hardest way that diplomacy is Darwinian: its practitioners need to evolve to survive.

In today's diplomatic services, the consequences for poor performers are more time-consuming yet less draconian than they were for Qin. But given that the alternative to peacemaking is often war, our diplomatic failures and mistakes can still have the gravest fallout.

It matters that we get it right.

Historical tales of grisly deaths aside, formal diplomatic encounters with contemporary Asian governments are friendly but often fairly dry affairs. Perhaps it is the heat, the time difference, or the lengthy delays caused by translation. With our Chinese interlocutors it was often striking that the army of note-takers stopped writing when their leader spoke – not only out of deference, but because they already knew exactly what he was going to say. They would tell me that they found it odd that our prime ministers were so much less well disciplined.

So I was perplexed at one of these heavily choreographed exchanges to see several counterparts on the other side of the table stifling uncharacteristic giggles and passing notes. My diplomatic antennae were well attuned to spotting potential gaffes, especially those that would appeal to our mischievous travelling press lobby, ever ravenous for stories of incompetence – working with the UK media for the UK government is often like playing for a football team whose own fans have decided should be relegated.

Trying not to disturb my prime minister as he made a complex case through a flustered translator for the rebalancing of the global economy, I scoured the room for evidence of a problem, without success. Eventually I called over one of the embassy experts, who after some deliberation pointed out that it was my name plate in front of me (the wording of which was of course visible to everyone except myself) that had caused such confusion and hilarity. Someone had translated my job title – Private Secretary to the Prime Minister for Foreign Affairs – as 'Intimate Typist for the Prime Minister's Affairs Overseas'.

There are many, too many, bureaucratic positions around the average modern leader, but few leaders have an official to type out their love letters.

I spent four years in 10 Downing Street in the role of Private Secretary for Foreign Affairs, under three very different prime ministers: Tony Blair, Gordon Brown and David Cameron. I also helped to advise Deputy Prime Minister Nick Clegg in his first months in the role, giving me experience of the unholy trinity of major UK political parties.

Though the job involved little intimate typing, it did include briefing the prime minister, joining his official meetings, and circulating an account for ministries and embassies to digest and act on. The unofficial motto of the Private Secretary should be that 'my job will be done when historians have read what I think he thinks he ought to have said'.

In reality, writing these records was only cover for the real job: a combination of policy adviser, journalist, negotiator, bag carrier and relationship manager. Occasionally I was also a therapist, administering reassurance and encouragement at tougher moments, or urging humility at better ones. Sometimes I was a translator, who could follow a prime minister and a French president to places that the female interpreter could not reach (no doubt happily for her). I was a recruitment consultant, who suddenly found senior ambassadors awaiting news of their next position to be very friendly. And even a bodyguard, as when Zimbabwean despot Robert Mugabe emerged from a dark corner of a United Nations summit to seek a handshake with Gordon Brown. I wrote speeches, dreamt up policy initiatives, and procured ProPlus for David Cameron from President Obama during a long summit session when two European Commission leaders had droned on for even longer than usual. I was once job-shadowed by a prince.

Few jobs in government are more gruelling than that of Private Secretary. The first voice I heard each morning, and the last each night, was the relentlessly cheerful No. 10 switchboard. The operators could gently ruin another weekend with skills that would be the envy of the smoothest diplomat. The hours meant that I would often bath my son in the Downing Street flat, and once took him to a Top Secret meeting I was chairing – he was only three, so I hope that no official secrets were compromised. During one demanding period, my wife interrupted a long weekend conference call between the prime minister and a head of state to inform us all in undiplomatic language of how fed up she was that I was still on the line. After an awkward moment to digest this, the PM suggested gently that it was probably time to end the call.

But it is worth it. Jobs in Downing Street give you a ringside seat, and often a place in the ring. Having watched the US election result alone in Gordon Brown's office in the early hours of the morning, I woke him to tell him of President Obama's victory. I was in the car with Gordon Brown as he left the prime minister's official country house at Chequers for the last time, and with David Cameron as he arrived there for the first time. I listened in to President Obama's farewell call to Gordon Brown as I walked to David Cameron's study to brief Cameron on his imminent congratulatory call from the White House.

Few jobs can be as exciting, and such a privilege. They give you an extraordinary insight into moments of history, and the characters who shape them.

But this is not a book about my time in Downing Street, and nor is it one in which I talk about private conversations between leaders or the confidential issues on which I have worked as a diplomat – I don't believe that public servants should write 'kiss and tell' books, which undermine trust between future leaders and their advisers. The anecdotes I use are purely illustrative, and the tip of the iceberg. The 'Private' is more important than the 'Secretary'.

This is also not a book about foreign policy or international relations in the traditional sense of wars and treaties, maps and chaps, big powers and bigger egos. There are plenty of those written by much smarter and more knowledgeable people, and they won't enjoy this one much. It is not a classic diplomatic memoir, in which the retired statesman – armed with hindsight, disappointment and accumulated grievance – explains why the world would be a better place if only all the pesky politicians, foreigners or fellow diplomats had listened to him more. Nor is this a classic book on diplomacy written by a leader either anxious to shape or defend their historical record,* or to burnish their statesperson credentials prior to a run for office.

Instead, I want to explain why diplomacy matters *more than ever* in the Digital Age, and not just to diplomats.

During my time as Private Secretary I saw technology changing statecraft. I worked for the last paper-and-pen prime minister, Tony Blair; the first email prime minister,† Gordon Brown; and the first iPad prime minister, David Cameron.[1] When I started, we had to consider how policy would look on the Sky News ticker at the bottom of the screen: 140 words. By the time I left, we were judging how it would look on Twitter: 140 characters.

This shift represents wider tectonic shifts in communications, and therefore society. The iGeneration has more opportunity than any generation before it to understand their world, to engage with it and to shape it. In the years since 9/11 the globe has been transformed more by American geeks in dorms than al-Qaeda operatives in caves. Mark Zuckerberg will be remembered long after Osama Bin Laden.

But it has been citizens from Tunis to Kiev who took the ability to network that those geeks created and turned it into something extraordinary. In years to come, people may say that the most powerful weapon in this period of the twenty-first century was not sarin gas or the nuclear bomb, but the smartphone. We have seen the power of the best of old ideas allied with the best of new technology. Regimes can ban iPhones, but the freedom and innovation that they represent will get through in the end.

---

* As Churchill said, 'History will be kind to me, because I intend to write it.'

† I once received an email from Gordon Brown at 3.45 a.m. Another time I showed him a document on my BlackBerry. I was pleased when he commented 'This is good.' But not for long. He clarified – 'Not your paper, that's hopeless, the scroll function.'

This new context changes everything. Increasingly, it matters less what a prime minister or diplomat says is 'our policy' on an issue – it matters what the users of Google, Facebook or Twitter decide that it is. Set-piece events are being replaced by more fluid, open interaction with the people whose interests we are there to represent.

So, escaping the politics, thrills and tensions of Downing Street, there was only one place to go to maintain the adrenalin. In 2011, I moved to the epicentre of many of the earthquakes shaking the Middle East: Beirut.

My nineteenth-century predecessors as ambassadors to Lebanon went by horse, traversing the Levant region at a civilised pace that modern Lebanese traffic jams try to recreate. My twentieth-century predecessors went by air and road – one, Edward Spears, landed during the Second World War and commandeered at gunpoint the first car he saw.

By the time I got there, communication was digital. Living on the Road to Damascus, I anticipated revelations. From the beginning of my stay, it was clear to me that if we couldn't win the argument for democracy, politics and coexistence in a country like Lebanon, we'd lose it closer to home. And that social media was a new and vital tool for us in fighting that battle, just as it was a tool for our opponents. We would need to go toe to toe, tweet by tweet.

Celebrity cook Jamie Oliver, as the Naked Chef, sought to pare back cooking to the essentials. In Lebanon, I came to realise that the diplomat needs to do the same (perhaps with an iPad to protect his modesty), while preserving the skills that have always been essential to the role: an open mind, political savvy, and a thick skin. I moved from being an intimate typist to being a Naked Diplomat.

Like the best traditional diplomacy, iDiplomacy is raw and human. The 'tweeting Talleyrands'[2] need to interact, not transmit. They will learn the language of this new terrain in the way they have learnt Mandarin or Arabic.

Equipped with the right kit, and the right courage, diplomats should be among the pioneers of the new digital terrain. They are already writers, advocates and analysts, albeit for a rarefied audience. They must now become digital interventionists. The most important thing social media does for us is not information management, or even engagement. It is that, for the first time, we have the means to influence the countries we work in on a massive scale, not just through elites.

This is exciting, challenging and subversive. Getting it wrong could start a war: imagine if a diplomat mistakenly tweeted a link to an offensive anti-Islam film. Getting it right has the potential to rewrite the diplomatic rulebook. A digital démarche,* involving tens of thousands, will be more effective than the traditional démarche by a single ambassador, because it can mobilise public opinion to change another country's policy.

The Internet brings non-state actors into the conversation. That's part of the point. Those we engage with will be a mix of the influential, curious, eccentric and hostile. Once they're in, they can't be ignored. Diplomacy is action not reportage, so diplomats will need to show that they can use these new tools to change the world, not just describe how it looks.

I ask colleagues who are not convinced about the power of these new digital tools to imagine an enormous diplomatic reception with all their key contacts. No serious diplomat would delegate such an event, as some delegate their Twitter accounts. None would stand in the corner shouting platitudes about warm bilateral relations, as do too many people via official social media

---

* French term for a formal diplomatic meeting, in which the ambassador passes on messages from his capital.

channels. No one would turn up but lurk silently in the corner, as do too many on digital accounts. Better to be in the mix, sharing information in order to get information, hearing the best of the new ideas and confronting the worst. With or without the Ferrero Rocher.

When the way the world communicates changes, so must its diplomats. They transformed the profession when the ground was cultivated, when the stirrup was invented, when sea routes opened up, when empires rose and fell, and when the telephone came along. Someone once said that you could replace diplomats with the fax. They saw off the fax, and – in more recent years – the telegram. (Yes, in that order for the British Foreign Office.)

Now we have to prove that you can't replace diplomats with Wikipedia, just because it knows more facts. You can't replace diplomats with Skype, just because you can now speak to far-flung places over a broadband line. And you can't replace diplomats with Twitter, just because you no longer need to shout from a real balcony to reach crowds of people. Diplomats must adapt their business and their mindset to these extraordinary and revolutionary new digital tools.

Many of us have made mistakes on social media, but the biggest mistake is not to be on it. It is survival of the digitally fittest.

We need to seize our smartphones.

But are we already too late?

INTRODUCTION TO THE FIRST EDITION

Here Lies Diplomacy, RIP?

> 'Now listen, Mother dear,' said Basil, 'the Foreign Service
> has had its day – enjoyable while it lasted, no doubt,
> but over now. The privileged being of the future is
> the travel agent.'
>
> Nancy Mitford, 'Don't Tell Alfred' (1960)

New York Times columnist Roger Cohen has declared that 'diplomacy – the kind that produced Nixon's breakthrough with China, an end to the Cold War on American terms, the Dayton peace accord in Bosnia – is dead'.[1] He is not alone. Should diplomats be packing up their diplomatic bags and finding something more productive to do?

Diplomacy is easy when you are a country on the up. Representatives of other countries answer your telephone calls, seek you out, expand their embassies and trade delegations. Magazines put you on the cover and talk up your rise. Your leader gets invited to the country houses of his counterparts, keen to bask in his reflected vigour and success. Your business lounges fill up. You have the wind in your sails.

Diplomacy is easy when you have won on the battlefield. Your rivals or opponents are more inclined to see things your way, and your allies to cut you some slack. You can flex your muscles and set the terms.

Diplomacy is easy when your people are in a pioneering mindset. The diplomats who manage empires aren't the people who build them. They are preceded by traders, explorers, innovators. The great civilisations were all built on great start-ups. Countries succeed when they have a magnetic quality, and an openness to the world around them: when they invest more in bridges than walls. When their world view is formed by having actually viewed the world.

Diplomacy is easy when the rules are clear, when nations are all playing on the same chess board. The subtle dance between the nineteenth century's great European states had moments of great jeopardy, and in the end could not contain the shifts in the underlying tectonics of power. But, post-Napoleon, the key players all felt a shared interest in preserving a status quo. They spoke the same language, literally and metaphorically – they even ensured with touching but shrewd generosity that it was the language of the vanquished party. There was an elaborate code to their collective work, albeit surrounded by lashings of protocol, gallons of alcohol, fiendishly delicate etiquette, and the occasional deadly duel.

But diplomacy is *hard* when you are a nation or a region in real or perceived decline, when it becomes more difficult to get that White House meeting, or to schedule that telephone call. Or when your 'podiums and president' press conference is downgraded to a brief 'pool spray' photo-op. Or worse, a 'grip and grin'. When the eyes of the world's leaders flicker over your shoulder at the more hungry or vigorous new powers on the block.

Diplomacy is hard when your military power is on the wane, either because austerity is biting, or because your citizens are less willing to make great sacrifices to impose the nation's interests, extend its influence or intimidate its opponents. 'Gunboat diplomacy' does not get you far without a gunboat. Or aircraft carrier. Threats of military force lose their potency when the dictator being threatened knows that your red lines* are easily erased.

Diplomacy is hard when you are competing with players with greater pioneering zeal, when your nation loses its creative edge or hunger for innovation. Diplomacy is hard when a lack of resources or confidence leads to an introspective national mindset rather than a drive to find new ideas, markets and sources of renewal. When your agenda is set by demagogues and tabloids. When even some on your own side want to throw in the towel and decline quietly and unobtrusively in a corner. When visitors to your embassy or ministry smell the faint whiff of genteel decay.

Diplomacy is hard is when the rules of the game are in flux, when there are players willing to turn the chess board over, when the international system is being disrupted from outside, or degraded from within. It is hard when tyrants and terrorists, pirates and persecutors, are setting the agenda. Diplomacy is hard in the periods when rival sources of power think that diplomacy doesn't matter.

Yet the periods when diplomacy is hardest are also the periods when it matters most.

Much of the West is therefore in a phase of hard diplomacy. Diplomacy that wears out the soles of your shoes, runs up the air miles and telephone bills, forces you to innovate and adapt. During such periods of change and peril, we don't need diplomats who arrive on a yak when the opposition has been and gone by horse.

---

* The origin of the phrase is a 1928 agreement on oil drilling rights as the Ottoman empire collapsed. The French have their own version, the yellow line.

Those who want to hammer the last nails into the coffin of diplomacy fall into three camps: diplomats no longer represent anything; diplomacy has been disrupted by technology; diplomacy has failed.

There are elements of truth in each of these arguments. If Google is more important than many states, is it not more important to be a Google ambassador than a national one? Aren't diplomats simply courtiers, moving between hierarchies without recognising they are part of the past? Can't diplomats be replaced by sentiment analysts with Skype accounts? If diplomats did not exist, why would we need to invent them in the twenty-first century?

Diplomacy does indeed face a crisis of legitimacy and trust.

Traditionally, representation was the main point of diplomats.[2] If you were your prince's person in a rival court, it mattered less what you did than what you were: the symbol of power and prestige. An ambassador's legitimacy and power depended on the support of a small number of people in his ruling elite, sometimes just one.

In the era of growing democracy in the West – the last 200 years or so – that elite grew, but not dramatically. A British ambassador making pre-posting calls, getting his marching orders, would not need to step outside Westminster.

When states become weaker, so do those who represent and derive authority from them. As the trend continues towards global decision-making for the big global issues on the one hand, and greater localisation and individualisation on the other, where does a state's representative fit in?

But the reality is that governments and states are not finished yet. Although they no longer have overwhelming dominance of information or even knowledge, they do remain the means through which questions of national interest are determined. As long as we have states, we will still need diplomats to mediate between them. They still have a niche.

So diplomats will need to redefine their legitimacy, and reconnect to the new sources of power. I was proud to be Her Majesty's Ambassador in Lebanon, and put the letter saying so on the wall. But I also felt that I was Her Majesty's *Government*'s Ambassador. And even the Ambassador of the British People. When there were monarchies, diplomats represented kings and queens. When there were great states, they represented great states. Now, with the dispersal of power, can they more credibly claim to represent the people of their countries?

We don't yet know whether people will respond to the threats of the twenty-first century with more nationalism or less. Diplomats who derive their legitimacy solely from states must secretly hope for the former. Diplomats who see themselves as embodying something more must hope for the latter.

The role of diplomats is being transformed faster than at any point in history. But no one has come up with a better idea. Diplomacy existed before states, and will exist after they have ceased to be the principal form of geographical power. We are in uncharted waters – but we always have been. This book will try to make the case for diplomats to remain on the boat.

The second critique also has elements of truth. Diplomacy does indeed face disruption, by technology, and by others who can do diplomacy more effectively. Being in office no longer means being in power.

Digital technology will transform the way that governments engage with citizens. But while the Internet defies boundaries, most governments find it hard to escape the confines of national responses. Data is not sufficiently shared and regulation struggles to keep pace.³ Governments have not yet tackled the big questions on the balance between privacy and transparency, or found the right formula to nurture innovation.

Who disrupts diplomacy? Many analysts, businesses, commentators are already well under way.

Traditionally, diplomats divided their rivals into three groups. First, the obviously hostile, such as great power rivals or aggressor states. In periods such as the run-up to the Congress of Vienna or the Cold War, this was straightforward and neat. We had clear enemies, definable nemeses. You could chart them on a map. You could kill them in a Bond film.

Secondly, the apparently friendly states, such as great power allies, who were nevertheless competing to get a bigger slice of the cake. For the UK, Europe has fallen into this category since the Second World War. We have vastly similar values and objectives, yet still contest resources and influence, and argue over the decisions where we need to pool sovereignty. *Je t'aime, moi non plus*.

Third, the local rivals for authority and influence – in the case of many ministries of foreign affairs, this was usually the Treasury or the prime minister's office.

No country faces permanent enemies or can count on permanent allies. The first, most hostile, group are now more likely to be transnational, non-traditional actors – terrorists, renegade states or information anarchists. This could be the throat cutters and concert bombers of the self-proclaimed Islamic State, the despots in North Korea, Syria and Zimbabwe, or Julian Assange.

The apparently friendly second group are now more likely to be those competing for business or security influence, including the media, NGOs and multinationals. They will be the disruptors – think tanks, big data analysts, social media gurus – who are replacing diplomats in their ability to analyse or shape foreign policy. A proliferation of organisations now compete with diplomats by selling geopolitical analysis. The best are the Brookings Institution, Chatham House and Carnegie.[4] Or the service providers who are moving ahead so fast with the way they respond to customer needs that they make government efforts – passports, visas, commercial introductions – look hopeless. I'd also include the new technology companies, with whom governments will increasingly contest key ground.

The local contenders are probably still the Treasury.

Diplomats need to understand those groups of rivals, the tools available to them, and why and how they are deploying them. They need to use social media more effectively than terrorists. They need to understand JPMorgan Chase or Google's diplomatic machinery in the way that they understand China's. They should be competing with the best technology they can lay their hands on. They should be on a digital war footing.

I often ask people who they think will have the greatest influence on the twenty-first century – Google or Britain? Increasingly, most say Google. I want to show in this book how they can be proved wrong. Google has been a technological superpower for a decade. Britain has been one for at least 250 years.

There will be many times when digital media feel to professional diplomats an obstacle to traditional diplomacy. We saw over the August 2013 debate on whether to strike Assad for using chemical weapons the way that digital debate makes it harder to play diplomatic poker, with the UK and subsequently US positions shifted as a result of online and offline disagreement. Governments are already much more restrained than a century ago, particularly when it comes to going to war. That is a good thing, but it makes it harder to make the threats necessary to stop our opponents taking territory or killing civilians. Our bluff is too easily called.

New digital media will also create different and sometimes uncomfortable oversight of what diplomats do, including the difficult compromises made in the heat of a negotiation. That's good. But they will further empower rival sources of influence and power. Digital media will make it harder to gain the consent of those whom diplomats claim to represent, and easier to lose it.

To gain the trust needed to avoid extinction, diplomats will need humility as to the limits of their authority, and a readiness to be more accountable to and more representative of the populations for whom they work.

Technology and society are being transformed, with or without diplomats. This presents threats as well as opportunities. But so did the printing press, the telephone, air travel. Now that anyone can be a diplomat, we have to show that you can't live without diplomats. When I became an ambassador at the age of thirty-six, some people asked me if I was too young to do the job. Looking at the way the region (and the world) was changing, I sometimes wonder if I was too old.

Yet we still need experts who can really understand the countries with which we are dealing, people who can help us to respond to global changes, to see where the next opportunities are, and from where the next challenges will come. Diplomats, if they are doing their jobs well, are an essential part of that. Technology should enhance rather than diminish that role.

The third argument against traditional diplomacy is that diplomats are not proving to be very good at it.

In this narrative, diplomats lack the skills and resources to put in the hard hours and tough negotiations that are needed to do real diplomacy. America's inwardness, increased popular and media oversight, and Western public revulsion at military engagement make it harder still.

Diplomacy has always struggled to keep up with events. It has woefully failed to reform the international system it inherited after the Second World War. There has been a lack of collective international graft and realism in fixing some of today's major conflicts, not least Syria and Israel/Palestine, both abject failures of the UN Security Council.

But for every diplomatic failure – the 2009 Copenhagen climate change summit, the Middle East Peace Process – there are successes such as the Iran nuclear deal or the Dayton peace accords. It is in the nature of diplomacy, an effort to deal with an unpredictable and complex world, that diplomats won't always get it right. It is not a reason not to keep trying.

There is a pivotal moment in David Puttnam's brilliant 1981 film *Chariots of Fire* when sprinter Harold Abrahams is reprimanded, in a typically understated but caustic upper-class English way, by the Master of Trinity College. His crime? Having employed a professional coach to prepare for the 1924 Olympics. The fiercely ambitious Abrahams is having none of this amateurishness. 'I believe in the pursuit of excellence. And I will carry the future with me.' He storms out, storms the race, and wins Olympic gold.

Political life, including diplomacy, faces a similar moment. There is a thirst for authenticity and authentic leaders. People feel disconnected from politics, authority, governments and decision-making. We are in an era of distrust, disconnection and detachment. Diplomacy finds itself ill-equipped for this new context. And it faces greater competition than ever before. Like many industries based on institutional authority, diplomacy insufficiently reflects the realities of a world in which the balance of power between citizens, business and government is shifting from hierarchies to networks. It too often prioritises pumping out a message over changing society.[5] Much of its procedural method – summits and communiqués – was designed in 1815 for an age of monarchies and great states.

There is little that you cannot learn about government from the British sitcoms *Yes, Minister* and *Yes, Prime Minister*. In one episode, senior civil servant Sir Humphrey Appleby is asked by his prime minister how they should react to a bellicose speech by a foreign leader. 'In practical terms we have the usual six options,' replies Sir Humphrey. 'One: do nothing. Two: issue a statement deploring the scene. Three: launch an official protest. Four: cut off aid. Five: break off diplomatic relations. And six: declare war.' So what to do? 'Well if we do nothing we implicitly agree with the speech. Two, if we issue a statement we just look foolish. Three, if we lodge a protest it will be ignored. Four, we can't cut off aid because we don't give them any. Five, if we break off diplomatic relations we can't negotiate the oil contracts. And six, if we declare war it might just look as if we're overreacting.' In one exchange, Sir Humphrey punctures the utter futility of much modern diplomatic communication, and captures why so many people are simply zoning out of political discourse.

Harold Abrahams would have recognised that while you can respect the competition, you must use it to improve. With power shifting unpredictably, so must the diplomats of the Digital Age. Diplomatic service – the clue is in the name; like the rest of the political class, diplomats have to find news ways to connect with the public they serve. Of course, international relations are much more than simply public relations, but diplomacy is not yet as social, progressive or democratic as it needs to become. It is not yet connected to the new sources of power. Like Harold Abrahams, diplomats no longer have the luxury of being amateurs.

Despite what for some looks like an increasing distance between foreign ministries and the public they represent, I think that there remains an energising, purposeful and revitalising argument in favour of diplomacy.

Diplomats were instruments of the prince when the Florentine diplomat and political theorist Niccolò Machiavelli was writing of Renaissance city-state diplomacy, and then servants of the state when Talleyrand and his peers were establishing European interests without the irritating interference of emperors. But Harold Nicolson, writing in 1961, sought a higher cause for his profession: 'there does exist such a thing as international morality. Its boundaries are not visibly defined nor its frontiers demarcated; yet we all know where it is.'

We need to find it again.

Without doubt, many diplomats throughout history have been driven by something more than realpolitik. They have rarely accepted that their only role is to advance the naked interests of their states. They see themselves as representing the idea of peace – the words for messenger in both Greek (*angelos*) and Hebrew (*mal'ach*) have sacred connotations. Bernard du Rosier, a Renaissance Archbishop of Toulouse and commentator on diplomacy, declared that the 'business of the ambassador was peace' and that he was 'sacred because he acted in the general welfare'.[6] Diplomacy needs to reconnect to this more idealistic sense of collective diplomatic purpose: the promotion of global co-existence.

The sense of a moral dimension to foreign policy was what lay behind former British Foreign Secretary Robin Cook's much derided effort towards an 'ethical foreign policy'. The problem of his government's approach was not the aspiration but the execution. The public do not believe that the ethics survived the sands of Iraq.

Diplomats help states to surrender the bits of their authority that need to be surrendered if we are to transition to a system that has more chance of survival. That is never going to be popular, but it is as important a task as ever. Diplomats lubricate the interaction of power, ideas and change to make it as peaceful as possible.

Diplomats have always tried to shape world developments for the better, and we can do so again. We can now connect, understand, engage and influence in ways our predecessors never could. But we also need to understand the rival and disruptive forces that are competing with the efforts to coexist.

Diplomacy needs to reconnect with its sense of optimism, opportunity and idealism. We need diplomats more than ever because the implications of diplomatic failure are more catastrophic than ever. The need is not for something to replace diplomacy, but for better diplomacy.

Many would say that the best era in which to have been a diplomat was the period around 1815, when elite diplomats strutted the halls of Vienna, reshaping Europe. I'd say it is 2016. But two centuries on, someone needs to write the new version of the Vienna Convention, to give fresh shape and purpose to this old business, and to make it fit for a new world.

To do so, we first need to understand what it was that made diplomacy so distinctive and important over the years. What can we learn from the cast of sometimes colourful and often colourless characters who strutted and pranced, connived and blustered on the diplomatic stage? How were their roles changed by previous waves of innovation – language, the printing press, or the plane?

We need to go back to where it all began.

PART ONE

Glad-handing on the Shoulders of Giants: A Short History of Diplomacy

1

Early Diplomacy:
From Cavemen to Consuls

> While other sciences have advanced, that of government is at
> a standstill – little better practised now than three or four
> thousand years ago.

John Adams, 1813

We don't know the name of the first diplomat, but let's call him Ug.

At some point, Ug – perhaps slower or smaller than his peers (diplomats often are) – persuaded a fellow Neanderthal to stop clubbing him over the head for long enough to work together against a common rival. A survival instinct in Ug prioritised co-operation over conflict. He was, probably literally, a naked diplomat.

And so diplomacy is almost as old as humanity.

Centuries later, one of Ug's many descendants – for Ug had found that diplomacy increased the survival prospects of his otherwise feeble genes – found the beginnings of language. He and his fellow palaeohumans began to communicate sufficiently to begin to create basic societies. The most primitive of these communities quickly developed systems to guarantee freedom of movement for messengers to avoid them being bludgeoned or eaten.[1] Around 4000 BC they developed basic forms of writing to help divide resources, especially grain and beer. Diplomacy was under way, and alcohol was already playing its part.

The most important difference between humans and the rest of the animal world is that we can cooperate flexibly in large groups.[2] And not just to feed or protect ourselves. That's why, for better or worse, we run the globe. Outside of Disney films, the animal kingdom doesn't do big conferences. There is no Security Council for owls and dolphins. There is no Lion King. We, not the fish, design the treaties on fishing quotas. We have dramatically reduced the threat from our fellow species (bar the mosquito, though thanks to Bill Gates we are getting there too).

Part of our vital biological make-up as humans is that we can cooperate with people we don't know, or who share little of our DNA. And part of our survival instinct is that there are people able to make the case, not necessarily always true, that cooperation is better for us than killing each other. That means that there is a biological case for diplomacy. All Ug was saying, long before and (slightly) less melodically than Lennon, was give peace a chance. Diplomatic uniforms, titles, protocol and platitudes aside, the basic concept since Ug's first grunts and gestures has not changed as much as we might think.

Technological innovation always precedes political change and diplomacy. The sickle and plough allowed settled living, and the domestication of animals. Social structure and a basic rule of law followed, creating more space and time for innovation. The invention of the wheel and of writing, several thousand years BC, made diplomacy both more necessary and more possible. Both took place, ironically, in the graveyard of much modern diplomacy, Iraq. Some of the earliest traces of more formal diplomacy are from the bureaucratic records of imperial China, where poor Shen Weiqin plied his trade before he was so slowly sliced up.

In the third century BC, Chanakya, the key adviser to the founder of the Indian Maurya dynasty, wrote in Sanskrit the oldest detailed guide to diplomacy: *Arthashastra*, or *The Science of Politics*.[3] His advice on diplomacy and espionage is pretty robust: violence, torture and spying dominate the text. The best way to deal with neighbouring countries is to appease, bribe, divide, punish, deceive, ignore or bluff, a set of approaches that have dominated Anglo-French relations for most of history. But Chanakya also sees part of the diplomat's role as preservation of wildlife and the rule of law, an idea retained in much diplomatic work today. In sage advice that could equally apply to modern spies dodging honeytraps, he advises envoys to 'always sleep alone', and to avoid strong liquor and hunting.

Diplomacy also started to take root elsewhere. In Egypt, following the battle of Kadesh in 1274 BC, Pharaoh Rameses II and ruler of the Hittite empire Hattusili III created the first known international peace treaties, on stone tablets.[4] Some of the covenants in these early treaties bear a strong similarity to the Ten Commandments that Moses was given, probably between the fourteenth and twelfth centuries BC – a fairly one-sided diplomatic treaty between God and Man. The messenger was not always welcome. The Bible records envoys of King David having their heads shaved and buttocks exposed by an unimpressed monarch – a punishment self-imposed by many modern football fans when travelling overseas.

Rival Chinese states in the first millennium BC started to draft more detailed treaties to enforce conquest and avoid unnecessary conflict. Others in Asia, such as the Japanese and Koreans, drew from this example, including by establishing temporary embassies. Records remain of Chinese Song dynasty ambassadors who were able to outfox opponents through guile and cunning rather than force. Theories of human interaction, such as Sun Tzu's *The Art of War*, demonstrate how leaders spent an increased amount of time considering how to subdue their enemies without the cost in blood and treasure of fighting them. As the Chinese empire expanded by sea from the second to thirteenth centuries AD, they sent resident envoys as far afield as India, Persia, Egypt and Africa, often despatching two – as they did to Japan in 653 – in case one never arrived, as was all too often the case. It must have been interesting when both did.

By the time the Chinese invented gunpowder in 900, they had already used diplomacy to create an empire so large that they did not have to use the gunpowder as an instrument of warfare and statecraft. If they had done so, as the Europeans started to do to such devastating effect in the fourteenth century, all our treaties and diplomatic language might now be in Chinese.

In Europe, meanwhile, the first Greek city states also found a need for diplomats to negotiate with rivals and allies. The basic rules and conduct of diplomacy they adopted in the Congress of Sparta in 432 BC were a template for much of the diplomacy of the next twenty-two centuries until the aftermath of Waterloo. The Spartans, in a sign of extreme confidence, even invited the adversaries – the Athenians – that they were considering attacking.

The Greeks tended to send diplomats on short missions rather than making them resident in other countries. Heralds would venture out to pass messages and to report back, if they had not been executed, on the quality of the reception they received. The forefather of the modern consul, often a resident of the city who happens to have a particular link to another, can be found in the Greek *proxenos*, who acted as informal sources of information and message carriers.

It was the Mongols who first put diplomacy on a more sophisticated footing. In 1287, Prince Arghun sent the first embassy to the West under Rabban Sauma, an elderly monk turned diplomat, as part of his effort to form an anti-Muslim alliance against Syria and Egypt. He promised the French the city of Jerusalem, and generously suggested that he would be 'very willing to accept any samples of French opulence that you care to burden your messengers with'. He even tried to broker an accord with the distant Edward I of England. But Europe, or the Vatican at least, was clearly well behind their Mongol visitors – Sauma reported back that he was underwhelmed by the 'lack of worldly intelligence among the cardinals of Rome'.[5]

As communication, travel and trade developed, it became necessary to establish rules for diplomatic interaction that went beyond protocols on exchanges of gifts. Like the Japanese, the Byzantine and Sasanian (modern Iran) leaders took the precaution of sending messages with two envoys in case one was lost or misplaced in unforgiving new environments. In the thirteenth century, the Mongols took this idea further and developed a new form of diplomatic passport, granting their envoys special status and protection. Genghis Khan, a historical figure usually more associated with ending rather than protecting lives, introduced diplomatic immunity. For messengers to do their job, it helped that they occasionally returned intact. That principle remains in place today, thankfully.

Six hundred years ago, it was the East that could claim to be the centre of diplomatic understanding and political power. But an unknown goldsmith in Strasbourg was about to change everything.

2

Diplomacy By Sea:
From Columbus to Copyboys

At the beginning of the age of European maritime discovery, the Chinese were ahead of the West in almost every respect, not just diplomacy. In 1492, Christopher Columbus set off to discover the Americas with ninety men in three ships. His closest Chinese equivalent, the intrepid eunuch Admiral Zheng He, had an armada of 300 ships, a compass and 27,000 men (including 180 doctors and several envoys). Columbus's biggest hull was barely twice the length of one of Zheng's rudders.[1] This hard-power advantage meant that many of the earliest diplomatic protocols and customs were more Eastern than Western. To this day, diplomats are scathing of colleagues seen as 'kowtowing', a deep and humble bow, to representatives of other nations.

Despite this head start for China, Europe took the lead in the centuries that followed, in diplomacy as in harder power. Maybe peninsulas made it easier for small kingdoms to hold out against potential conquerors.[2] Europe might have had an advantage in this era of climate, topography, resources, culture, politics or religion. Or perhaps it was simply down to short-term accident and chance.[3]

The Chinese had invented the first newspaper in 748. But German inventor Johannes Gutenberg's creation of the movable-type printing press in the 1440s allowed humans to capture more accurately and share more widely the most important lessons of their ancestors. We no longer relied on oral histories alone. This created an extraordinary platform for innovation, and more time to explore and create. Gutenberg was the Tim Berners-Lee of his age, generating unprecedented access to knowledge.

Within two generations, Columbus and others were leading the Age of Discovery. When Columbus returned from the Bahamas, eleven print editions of his journey spread around Europe. Within twenty-five years, sailors had circumnavigated the globe, and the Reformation was under way, on the back of the production and distribution of millions of Martin Luther's pamphlets. Merchants and farmers alike began to question the absolute rule of monarchs, and the political fundamentals of society. There was a new thirst for knowledge, stimulating the Enlightenment, the American Revolution and free-market capitalism. This print revolution contributed to the formation of modern nation states, and therefore the diplomats to represent them. The spread of information in shared languages stimulated the emergence of common and competing national identities. These new European nations – Germany, France, Austria, Russia – needed people to understand their differences, and to mediate between them.

As the Europeans closed the gap on their global competitors, they sought new ways to protect and project their advantage. One manifestation of power was the man on the spot. The first more permanent embassies, expressions of ambition and influence, were started by the states of northern Italy during the Renaissance, with Milan the trailblazer. Cosimo de' Medici (1389–1464) became the first semi-permanent ambassador of the city in 1450. Backed by enormous personal wealth, he helped to create a balance of power between his native Florence and the leading Italian city states. He even took his own bank with him, a luxury sadly but sensibly denied by modern treasuries to their diplomats.

Wars are of course another powerful tool for domination, and the Renaissance had plenty of them. But they are also disruptive and costly for leaders. Increasingly, princes wanted people who could build their influence in other ways. They needed local intelligence, and eyes and ears on the ground. Milan sent the first ambassador to the French court, in 1455, and Spain despatched the first permanent representative, to London in 1487. These tended to be noblemen, able to finance the lavish lifestyle meant to come with the territory. An embassy came to mean a physical presence rather than a formal visit.

Advisers such as Machiavelli began to build a theory of power around this work. These early envoy roles were sought-after positions held by the talented innovators and explorers of the age. Men such as Dante, Petrarch and Boccaccio were among the first envoys of Florence. This is like making Damien Hirst, Sebastian Faulks and Ian McEwan Britain's ambassadors today. For these early envoys, diplomacy was not a career but a pursuit, one that reinforced their social position and cultural instincts. Early forms of the word 'ambassador' – *ambaxade*, *ambasciatore*, *ambaxada* – seem to have derived from *ambactia*, meaning charge or office. Or perhaps *ambactus*, servant. Even at its well-heeled origins, I like to think that there was a sense of public service to the description.

Inevitably, an informal network of travellers and messengers became more structured. Leaders needed to know that the man in front of them – and of course in this era it always was a man – was really representing his prince. So the tradition of presenting credentials on arrival, which continues to this day, began.

Many diplomats are still communicating with their host government and their own capital using these gloriously archaic instruments. On arrival in a country, the ambassador is not meant to meet anyone officially until he has presented his credentials to the head of state, a process that can often undermine his impact during the most important period. While the private sector focuses on the first ninety days of a CEO's tenure, the ambassador often spends their first weeks marooned in their house, unpacking and waiting for permission to hand over a piece of paper. When it comes, the ceremony can be moving and memorable – the hairs on the back of my neck stood up when I listened to the British national anthem at the president's summer palace high in the Shouf mountains of Lebanon in August 2011. But the protocol gets in the way of real diplomacy.

Much of the language remains more Renaissance than Digital Age. Here is an extract from my credentials, which perhaps shows that modern diplomats have not travelled as far from our lace-cuffed predecessors as the smartphones in our pockets suggest:

To All and Singular to whom these Presents shall come, Greeting!
  Whereas it appears to Us expedient to nominate some Person of approved Wisdom, Loyalty, Diligence and Circumspection to represent Us in the character of Our Ambassador Extraordinary and Plenipotentiary at Beirut; Now Know Ye that We, reposing especial trust and confidence in the discretion and faithfulness of Our Trusty and Well-beloved Thomas Fletcher, Companion of our Most Distinguished Order of St Michael and St George, have nominated, constituted and appointed as we do by these

Presents nominate, constitute and appoint the said Thomas Fletcher to be Our Ambassador Extraordinary and Plenipotentiary at Beirut as foresaid.

Giving and granting him in that character all Power and Authority to do and perform all proper acts, matters and things which may be desirable or necessary for the promotion of relations of friendship, good understanding and harmonious intercourse between Our Realm and the Republic of Lebanon and for the protection and furtherance of the interests confided to his care; by the diligent and discreet accomplishment of which acts, matters and things aforementioned he shall gain Our approval and show himself worthy of Our high confidence.

Terrific stuff, but hard to tweet.

The letter of credence was established to show that an envoy was genuinely representing his state, when there were not other ways to check thoroughly. That's now easier to establish. Credentials can be replaced by a Google search.

Not every historical leader appreciated the new customs either. When Anthony Jenkinson, a sixteenth-century trader, traveller and envoy of Elizabeth I, tried to present credentials to the cosmopolitan Persian emperor Shah Tahmasp, he failed to wear the slippers offered to cover his infidel feet, was thrown out of Isfahan and his footprints back to the port covered in sand. He was Photoshopped out of Persian history.

As the number of diplomats attached to royal courts grew, they inevitably began to compete for attention and influence. With their masters jostling for power and prestige, diplomats in European capitals were ranked on the basis of the power of their monarchs, a fiendishly complex and contested process. This rivalry consumed much of their energies, and would strike terror in the heart of the modern diplomat less used to having to compete so overtly for attention and influence.

According to Samuel Pepys, the Spanish and French embassies in London frequently came to blows in the 1660s over breaches of such protocol and ranking. Asked where he would like to sit at a dinner with the English king, Charles II, the French ambassador answered: 'Discover where the Spaniard desires to sit, then toss him out and put me in his place.' I admit that I have attended many diplomatic dinners where such dark thoughts have crossed my mind. But fortunately for less adversarial modern diplomats, ranking is now based on your date of arrival in post.

Another account describes how, during the 1661 arrival of a new Swedish ambassador to London, the French coach (with 150 men, forty of them armed) clashed with that of the Spanish ambassador, similarly tooled up. The Spaniards killed a Frenchman and took down two French horses, forcing the French to reluctantly cede the second position in the procession. Louis XIV of France was so incensed that he told his Spanish counterpart that he would declare war if there were ever to be another such breach of protocol.

But such clashes continued – in 1768, the Russian and French ambassadors to London duelled following a dispute over who should sit where in the diplomatic box at the opera. The modern equivalent is the competition to be seated next to the US president at international summits. Alphabetical orderings can often be the most diplomatic solution. At these moments, British diplomats tend to favour the use of 'United Kingdom' over 'Great Britain'. It gets the leader closer to their American counterpart, and safely clear of the difficult group of countries whose names begin with 'I'.

Diplomacy can both thrive and suffer in times of intrigue and change. The cold war that followed the Reformation set back the process of statecraft, with Catholic or Protestant ambassadors frequently seen, with some justification, as the centres of intrigue and espionage in rival courts. Yet it forced those envoys still allowed to lurk behind the curtains of those courts to make their communication with their capitals more cunning, and increased their value to their masters.[4] In the 1630s, Cardinal Richelieu, one of Louis XIII's most infamous and effective ministers, wrote of the need for ceaseless negotiation, even when – in fact especially when – no fruits are reaped. After 1626, he established a Ministry of External Affairs to centralise the management of foreign relations under a single roof, and – perhaps most importantly to him – to control the information reaching his king. The practice was soon followed all over Europe. A picture of the 'Red Eminence' should be on the wall of every modern ministry of foreign affairs.

Maritime expansion by the early European empires created the need for further rules and negotiation, not least because failure to observe increasingly complex protocol could trigger conflict. Elizabeth I was clearly a sharp and perceptive observer of diplomatic vanity, and banned her ambassadors from accepting awards or insignia from other nations – 'I would not have my sheep branded by any mark but my own.' The tradition continues to this day, though it is explained to sensitive diplomats in gentler terms.

Diplomacy was increasingly the arena in which to play out wider competition for respect, with failure to observe basic courtesies taken as great insults to a monarch's dignity. When the Spanish ambassador to the English court of James I refused to dip his colours to his host in the early seventeenth century, the ensuing diplomatic furore nearly triggered a second armada.

Most European envoys sent east had a more commercial brief. British diplomat Anthony Jenkinson, having recovered from his undignified exit from Persia, reported back to Elizabeth I that his 1557 Christmas dinner with Tsar Ivan IV Vasilyevich had laid the foundations for a potentially lucrative trading relationship. Clearly there was no Elizabethan human rights lobby to suggest that emperors who called themselves 'Terrible' and had been executing rivals since the age of thirteen might not be appropriate commercial partners. Another envoy, Thomas Roe, recorded having avoided offending the Mogul of India by accepting an attractive female concubine for the duration of his stay, 'in order to comply with custom' (an excuse that probably would not work today). Competition between these early European merchant envoys was fierce and the penalties severe – the Dutch tortured eighteen British traders to death in the East Indies in 1623.

Yet, necessary concubines aside, the job of Elizabethan envoys was in many ways recognisable. Sir Jeremy Bowes was the ambassador sent by Elizabeth I to the court of Ivan the Terrible following Jenkinson's convivial, and clearly successful, Christmas lunch. Apart from staying alive, he had three jobs: to assert the authority of his queen as the equal of the tsar, to obtain important commercial contracts for British merchants, and to establish a commercial office in Vologda. His successors in Moscow today are working on similar projects. Bowes also had to free a British widow whose Dutch husband had been roasted to death, a consular case that is happily less likely to arise in today's embassy.

The first pioneering diplomats were not setting out across continents on some kind of grand tour or glorified gap year, but to seek new resources and trading opportunities. In the age of maritime diplomacy, consuls would mediate between ships from their countries and port authorities to ensure market advantage. Schoolchildren still learn that 'trade follows the flag'. But diplomatic history also suggests that the flag often follows trade – the business lobby needed a British embassy in Constantinople in the sixteenth century, and so the Levant Company funded it, an association that continued until the early nineteenth century.

Diplomacy has always had a strong mercantile core, although in recent decades commercial work has tended to come in and out of diplomatic fashion. It was placed at the centre of the British Foreign Office's priorities after the First World War and in the 1970s. The British post credited with making the best commercial effort in the 1970s was Tehran. They responded to instructions to focus embassy time and resources on supporting business links with Iran. This came at a cost: they were late to spot the warning signs of the overthrow of the shah.

Diplomats tend to enjoy trade promotion because it is more tangible than other elements of their roles. It is hard to measure warm bilateral relations, or the extent to which lobbying on climate change shifts a host government's position. But a contract with numbers stands out.

So what do businesses want from diplomats? They want hard and relevant political analysis, a good contact book, and the willingness to use it. Businesses know that diplomats can get the right people around the table.

But there are also risks. Diplomats can lose their objectivity about where the national interest lies, and the balance between commercial priorities and our wider equities. This particularly applies to diplomats who would like to make some money themselves at some point, as many will increasingly need to do. Traditionally, the revolving door was more of an exit door. Senior diplomats left their foreign ministries to get highly paid jobs on the boards of oil companies, banks and arms manufacturers.

Increasingly that model will change – diplomats will more often leave in mid career, harassed by spouses angry at the impact of regular moves on family life; needing a financial cushion; and seeking new experiences and oxygen. This is healthy, increasing the pool of diplomats who have tried other professions, and who are flexible and marketable enough to adapt, learn and return. The downside is that it will undermine the sense of diplomats as a cadre, and blur the lines of accountability further. As austerity bites and diplomats get paid less, they risk becoming more reliant on business to keep the ship afloat. This is not easy for modern diplomats, any more than it would have been for the British consul in sixteenth-century Constantinople.

An awkward but unavoidable question for diplomats will be the extent to which we sell our services. The British Foreign Office already hires out ambassadors for commercial events. I've made speeches on subjects ranging from ceramic water filters to ornamental garden gnomes. It is a small jump from this system to one where we offer a commercial service for our insights. None of us would want to see diplomacy become too mercantilist or commercial, but the economic realities may dictate that there is no choice.

Diplomats gradually developed a sense of their own craft. As diplomacy took root as a profession, it was codified, analysed and described, mainly by French diplomats. In 1603, Jean Hotman de Villiers (1552–1632), an Oxford professor who led diplomatic missions for Henri IV, produced a guidebook for ambassadors, *De la Charge et Dignité de l'Ambassadeur*. Abraham de Wicquefort (1598–1682) was a Dutch envoy and spy who, after playing a central role in producing the Treaty of Westphalia, was found guilty of treason. Imprisoned in the water castle of Loevestein, he wrote the huge *L'Ambassadeur et ses Fonctions* in 1681. This became the handbook for seventeenth- and eighteenth-century diplomacy, and was based on real-world examples of his craft. Much of it stands the test of the time, including his advice that ambassadors need to combine the theatre of their public role with the discretion and often secrecy of their private negotiations. Loevestein was clearly a good place to think big. Another political prisoner was Hugo Grotius, often seen as the father of modern international law. More notable, for diplomats anyway, he went on to become Swedish ambassador to France. François de Callières (1645–1717), a diplomat for Louis XIV, analysed European diplomacy in his 1716 book *De la Manière de Négocier avec les Souverains*. He agreed with de Wicquefort that the ambassador had to be a good actor.

Diplomats also needed to stay in closer contact with their capitals. When envoys began to create too much information to pass by hand or official messenger, they instigated a mail service for handwritten correspondence, and a Postal Convention (of 1674) to try to protect confidentiality. Documents began to be transported by the more formal system still in use today, the diplomatic bag. This was meant to guarantee that messages between an embassy and its capital could not be interfered with by the curious or hostile. Naturally, this was usually ignored in the atmosphere of intrigue and mistrust surrounding the wars of religion.

The diplomatic bag still exists virtually unchanged today.

The bag has always been dogged by controversy. It is meant to be sealed and inviolate, but that has rarely been the case. Cardinal Wolsey, an adviser to Henry VIII, was a serial violator of its confidentiality, in order to supervise the intrigues of the increasing number of foreign envoys appointed to London. As late as the end of the nineteenth century, the ambassador Lord Curzon exploded with fury when the Turks searched his bags, 'and condemned them to a thousand hells of eternal fire'. In 1964, Italian authorities violated an Egyptian bag, having heard moans from inside it, to discover a kidnapped Israeli. In the early twenty-first century, British minister Peter Hain described the violation of the bag by Robert Mugabe's officials in Zimbabwe as 'not the actions of a civilised country'. (In fact, opening a diplomatic bag was probably one of the more civilised actions undertaken by Mugabe.) I was involved in another African drama when a diplomatic bag seeping blood was found to be carrying bush meat, meant to arrive in London in advance of the visit of a head of state. He was clearly no fan of British cuisine.

With electronic communications more secure, there can be few items that really require such an elaborate means of despatch. (I suspect the modern diplomatic bag is normally filled with orders of DVD box sets.) The diplomatic bag has an important history. But it can be replaced by an email.

Meanwhile, diplomats from the great European states also developed a continental system of rules and processes to match the new confidence and structures of their states. The Treaty of Westphalia, hammered out in Münster and Osnabrück between the Habsburgs, French, Spanish, Swedish and Dutch in 1648, ended the Thirty Years War and explicitly recognised the existence of separate sovereignties. Diplomats and aristocrats – most were still both – from 140 imperial states took part. The treaty drew the new boundaries of Europe, allowed for freedom of worship, and established the principle of non-interference in the domestic affairs of other states.

Not everyone was happy with a system that prioritised national over transnational rights, especially those who derived their authority from other sources of power – in full flow, Pope Innocent X called the treaty 'null, void, iniquitous, invalid, unjust, invaluable, reprobate, damnable, inane, empty of meaning and effect for all time'. Diplomacy was never meant to be easy or uncontroversial.

Gradually, like all good bureaucrats, envoys involved in such negotiations built up entourages and embassies. And, to manage the networks of egos and prima donnas, capitals had to expand the foreign ministries from Richelieu's dingy back offices into grander and more impressive buildings. The beginnings of empire brought their own demands. In 1660, Britain established a Council of Foreign Plantations, which grew in the eighteenth century into the Colonial Office. Ernest Satow's massive *Guide to Diplomatic Practice*, first published against the undiplomatic backdrop of 1917, traces the first uses of the word diplomacy to mid-eighteenth-century Vienna, and in England in the 1787 *Annual Register*. But an English satire, *The Chinese Spy*, was unimpressed by these stirrings of activity: 'The diplomatic body, as it is called, was at this ball, but without distinguishing itself to any great advantage.'

Nevertheless, the British Foreign Office was established in 1782, the year that the steam engine was invented, one of the building blocks of the British empire. Charles James Fox, the first Foreign Secretary, was backed up by a staff of twelve: 'nine male clerks, two chamber keepers and a "necessary woman"'. This is roughly the size of the current Foreign Secretary's Private Office, although the gender balance is now improved.

Dating from this period, many ministries of foreign affairs insist that formal communication between the ambassador and the host government is by a verbose letter covered in stamps and seals: the *note verbale*. A typical one might run: 'The embassy of Tajikistan presents its esteemed compliments to the Foreign Ministry of Mali. The embassy respectfully requests that the ambassador be permitted to park his official vehicle in the main courtyard of the esteemed foreign ministry on his next visit. The embassy of Tajikistan takes this opportunity to share its respect and warmest regards with the distinguished ministry.'

Mostly, a *note verbale* is these days sent by fax, and therefore disappears without trace. An embassy will normally spend a great deal of time on the telephone, checking whether they have arrived and when a reply is likely. The average embassy is also expected to send such a note when the ambassador leaves the country, even temporarily. Many ambassadors even convey such earth-shattering news to their fellow diplomatic colleagues. In Beirut, I regularly received faxes telling me that ambassadors I had never met would be out of the country for three days.

Clearly this is all bonkers. The *note verbale* can be replaced by a text message.

The US was not far behind Britain. A Cabinet-level Department of Foreign Affairs was created in 1789 by the First Congress. It was later renamed the Department of State and changed the title of its top job from Secretary for Foreign Affairs to Secretary of State. Thomas Jefferson returned from a France in the grip of revolutionary fervour, where he had planted American sweet potatoes and corn on the Champs-Élysées, to take the position. Jefferson would have been staggered by the pace of modern communication, finding it harder to keep his diplomats on a short leash: 'For two years we have not heard from our ambassador in Spain; if we again do not hear from him this year, we should write him a letter.' At this point, the US foreign service had just two diplomatic posts and ten consular posts, so the silence of their envoy to Madrid must have been deafening.*

Gunboat diplomacy could be pretty ambitious, and remained high risk. Not everyone took envoys as seriously as they themselves had started to do. In 1793, Lord George Macartney led a doomed mission of 700 British diplomats and businessmen to try to establish permanent diplomatic relations with the Chinese emperor Qianlong. He failed because Qianlong could not accept the idea of diplomatic relations with a representative rather than the monarch himself. George III's gifts were accepted merely as tribute, and Macartney was sent home with his tail between his stockinged legs.

Some decided that the whole business was too fraught with peril to be worthwhile. In his 1796 farewell message, US president George Washington counselled his successors against European entanglements: 'hence therefore it must be unwise in us to implicate ourselves, by artificial ties, in the ordinary vicissitudes of her politics, or the ordinary combinations and collisions of her friendships, or enmities. Our detached and distant situation invites and enables us to pursue a different course.' Many current US politicians make the same argument for disengagement and splendid isolation.

---

* I recently found letters from my nineteenth-century predecessor in Beirut, George Wood, demonstrating the way that envoys, like Jefferson's in Madrid, took advantage of this distance from the capital to freelance. Wood consulted his Foreign Secretary about arming the local Druze sect, and had done so with gusto by the time the terse reply reached him telling him not to proceed under any circumstances, so as not to annoy the Turks. By then the 1860 civil war was over. Every modern ambassador to whom I have told this story longs wistfully for the days when diplomacy was less burdened by swift communication with the centre.

Some American diplomats struck out nonetheless. Benjamin Franklin challenged protocol in his own way, shocking contemporary society by being the first diplomat to attend the king without a hat when he was received by Louis XVI at Versailles in 1778. He also invented bifocals in order to lip-read the asides and intrigues of his French interlocutors. But Washington's instincts about dastardly Europeans were also proved right in 1798, when the French demanded that American diplomats pay huge bribes in order to see their foreign minister. The Americans rejected this preposterous offer, and have been making European statesmen pay ever since.

The French had more success elsewhere. In the eighteenth century, French took over from Latin as the language of diplomacy, a position it held until the Second World War. Much traditional diplomatic language is still in French – for example, démarche, chargé d'affaires and entente. The French also seemed to particularly enjoy the physical trappings of diplomacy more than most. Lord Gower, the British ambassador in Paris at the end of the eighteenth century, lamented the local requirement to bow three times to fellow ambassadors and twice to a chargé d'affaires. (Extraordinarily, in some southern European foreign ministries the practice of bowing to colleagues of ambassadorial rank continues to this day.)

Of course, bureaucracies feed themselves, and foreign ministries gradually expanded their back offices. The Duke of Wellington lamented the consequences. In 1812, while commanding the British army against Napoleon in Spain, he sent an exasperated note, loaded with sarcasm, back to the Foreign Office. It would strike a chord with many modern diplomats:

I have dispatched reports on the character, wit and spleen of every officer. Each item and every farthing has been accounted for, with two regrettable exceptions for which I beg your indulgence. Unfortunately the sum of one shilling and nine pence remains unaccounted for in one battalion's petty cash and there has been a hideous confusion as to the number of jars of raspberry jam issued to one cavalry regiment during a sandstorm in western Spain.

This reprehensible carelessness may be related to the pressure of circumstance, since we are at war with France, a fact that may come as a bit of a surprise to you gentlemen in Whitehall.

This brings me to my present purpose, which is to request elucidation of my instructions from Her Majesty's Government so that I may better understand why I am dragging an army over these barren plains. I construe that perforce it must be one of two alternative duties. I shall pursue either one with the best of my ability, but I cannot do both. Is it 1) To train an army of uniformed British clerks in Spain for the benefit of accountants and copyboys in London, or perchance 2) To see to it that the forces of Napoleon are driven out of Spain?[5]

The answer from the copyboys is not recorded.

3

Diplomacy's Finest Century

The nation state ... is not a quaint and anachronistic holdover
but a compromise written in blood that just about managed in
the second half of the last century to bind the demons that
attend power to a peaceful and progressive policy.

Chris Patten, *What Next? Surviving the Twenty-First Century* (2008)

Wellington might have been exasperated by the bureaucratic and
penny-pinching procedures of the Foreign Service. But the
hundred years that followed the Congress of Vienna of 1815,
while ending in the diplomatic failure of the First World War,
were European diplomacy's finest century.

Only with the continent at peace could European powers
expand their global reach and build their empires. Armies
provided the blood that established the era of the nation state.
Diplomats provided the compromises. Less of a sacrifice, but no
less important.

As ever, technological innovation spurred diplomatic changes.
A Frenchman, Claude Chappe, had invented the semaphore in
1791. In 1819, the first steamship crossed the Atlantic. In 1837,
Brits William Cooke and Charles Wheatstone invented the telegraph (using just twenty letters, which must have been awkward

for diplomats in Quebec or Yugoslavia). All were to play their part in the evolution of statecraft.

This was the period in which the word 'diplomacy', from the Greek term for a twice-folded document, began to be used more frequently. This reminds us that there was a sense of purpose to diplomacy. It was not just about a discussion, relationship management or information-gathering, but about an outcome – the 'diploma' on which an agreement was written, or what we now often call the 'deliverable'. Diplomacy had a point.

When backed up by force, diplomacy could deliver even quicker results than in the past – the British government could 'change the balance of the Eastern question by sending a few frigates to Besika Bay'.[1] Foreign Secretary Viscount Palmerston ordered the British fleet to blockade a Greek port in 1850 because a British subject, Don Pacifico, had been insufficiently compensated for his imprisonment. Defending his actions in Parliament, Palmerston claimed that 'a British subject, in whatever land he may be, shall feel confident that the watchful eye and the strong arm of England will protect him from injustice and wrong'.[2] Modern consular support is less dramatic, and our resources less intimidating, but the principle still applies.

This willingness to project power helped Europe become the centre of international gravity in this period. Diplomatic procedures and standards were developed and exported. Negotiation became more constant, not just based on a division of the spoils after each war. The habits of diplomacy – more frequent conferences and summits, more exchanges of envoys – took root. The great powers used statecraft and diplomatic craft as they jostled for mastery in Europe.

Political change once again increased the need for new rules to govern diplomats and diplomatic interactions. Diplomats started to take themselves even more seriously, and grant themselves new titles.

Diplomacy has retained many of the titles of this era. I frequently observed the frisson which some fellow Ambassadors Extraordinary and Plenipotentiary (to give them their full title, as some prefer to do) felt when addressed as 'Your Excellency'. Very few who rely so heavily on the title are particularly excellent. Indeed, my standard rule is that the more a colleague tells people of their excellence, the less excellent they are likely to be. When in Downing Street, I dropped the practice of including the full titles of ambassadors (e.g. Sir Crispian Penfold-Thwaite-Penfold GCMG*) on standard records and minutes of meetings, halving the length of the average distribution list but pricking the vanity of some grander and more impressively titled colleagues.

The Civil Service still retains more confusing job titles from the nineteenth century than most. Hence the mix-up over my role as the prime minister's intimate typist. I once tried to explain the title 'Permanent Undersecretary', the head of the Foreign Office, when introducing the last incumbent, Sir Simon Fraser, to a reception in Beirut. It was the least accurate title I could imagine – Simon was neither permanent, nor under anyone, nor indeed a secretary. Increasingly, we will discover that over-doing the titles acts as a further barrier to communication with those we represent, and therefore to our continued usefulness and relevance.

Once again, *Yes, Minister*'s Sir Humphrey bursts the balloon when explaining to his new minister the job titles in his ministry:

----

* Within the FCO, the honour of CMG is known as 'Call Me God', and KCMG is 'Kindly Call Me God'. GCMG is of course 'God Calls Me God'.

'Briefly, sir, I am the Permanent Undersecretary of State, known as the Permanent Secretary. Woolley here is your Principal Private Secretary. I, too, have a Principal Private Secretary, and he is the Principal Private Secretary to the Permanent Secretary. Directly responsible to me are ten Deputy Secretaries, eighty-seven Undersecretaries and two hundred and nineteen assistant secretaries. Directly responsible to the Principal Private Secretaries are Plain Private Secretaries, and the Prime Minister will be appointing two Parliamentary Undersecretaries and you will be appointing your own Parliamentary Private Secretary.' 'Can they all type?' asks his mystified minister. 'None of us can type, Minister,' replies Sir Humphrey, 'Mrs McKay types – she is your secretary.'

The demands of nineteenth-century diplomacy also meant that protocol was further codified, and treaties became longer. Rules were even needed to keep the diplomats apart. Foreign Secretary George Canning duelled with his Cabinet rival Lord Castlereagh in 1809, making today's National Security Council debates seem somewhat tame. A gifted poet, songwriter and speechwriter, Canning had also shown himself an accomplished warmaker, whose belief that 'we are hated throughout Europe, and that hate must be cured by fear' would gladden the hearts of many modern Eurosceptics.[3] Napoleon had also been happy to ignore the gentlemanly codes of diplomatic immunity and throw British envoys in jail for espionage. But after his fall, the Congress of Vienna of 1815 established a more robust system, for the first time regulating a profession of diplomacy that was distinct from politics and statecraft.

The congress took place against an inauspicious backdrop. Russian Cossacks were on the Champs-Élysées, trying to prevent

Napoleon from making another comeback. His reckless ambitions had shattered borders and destroyed institutions. Europe was threatened by decades of conflict and uncertainty, so the powers that had defeated him – Russia, Great Britain, Austria and Prussia – invited the other states of Europe to send their representatives to Vienna. All despatched heavyweight statesmen, the titan diplomats of their age who had spent, or were to spend, decades at the top of the international system.

Austria fielded Prince Klemens von Metternich, a former ambassador to Prussia and France. By this stage diplomacy was firmly established as a sound profession for the upwardly mobile nobility – Metternich's father and son were also in the family business. Metternich's relationship with Napoleon must have been complex – he had arranged Napoleon's marriage to an Austrian princess, but also made the career-threatening mistake of publicly arguing with him at Napoleon's thirty-ninth birthday party. He also numbered Napoleon's sister Caroline Murat among his numerous lovers, their trysts taking place in what is now the British ambassador's Residence in Paris, then home of her more scandalous sister Pauline.* Metternich had previously entered a bizarre agreement barring him from diplomacy while his father-in-law was alive. I suspect this is unique among pre-nuptial deals. Like many diplomats of the age, he spoke better French than his native language, and left illegitimate offspring in most of the capitals in which he served.

Britain sent Lord Castlereagh (who had wounded Canning in the thigh in their duel, but escaped unscathed himself). His destructive tendencies were not limited to Cabinet colleagues – he would slice his own throat several years later, after suffering from

---

* Pauline's breast cup, in which she offered drinks to suitors, is still on display in the ambassador's Residence, thus prompting many an awkward silence at drinks receptions.

a mental breakdown and gout. Castlereagh was a principal architect of the system of rolling congresses agreed at Vienna. He
divided people in death as in life, prompting Lord Byron to pen the
poisonous epitaph 'Posterity will ne'er survey, A nobler grave
than this: Here lie the bones of Castlereagh, Stop, traveller, and
piss.'

Prussia sent Karl August von Hardenberg, a former chancellor,
more austere perhaps than some of the other rogues around the
table, and seen by his contemporaries as too regularly outfoxed by
Metternich. Tsar Alexander I, a manipulative autocrat who had
succeeded his assassinated father at the age of twenty-three,
represented Russia himself, not trusting anyone else to defend his
corner. Like George W. Bush almost 200 years later, he would
hold prayer meetings with his foreign policy advisers before
taking key decisions.

France, the defeated power, sent Charles Maurice de Talleyrand-
Périgord, who was to be the star of the show. A former bishop
with a justified reputation as a womaniser, he had been prevented
from taking his family birthright because of the social embarrass-
ment of a deformed leg. Instead he turned his restless talents to
statecraft, with zeal. He had managed by hook or by crook to
serve Napoleon and the regime he had deposed, making him
ideally suited to the intrigue and drama of the congress. At
Vienna, through diplomatic cunning, he prevented the partition
of France and repositioned himself in French politics as the
saviour of his country.

Talleyrand also saw commercial and personal opportunity – he
demanded payment from other states for his services, employed
the celebrity chefs of his day, and ate and drank prodigiously. He
used to hold meetings in his bedroom so that he could press the
advantage of his warm bed over his cold, standing interlocutors.
Through guile and skill he turned a weak hand into an advan-

tage. When the king of Saxony challenged France as 'one of those who have betrayed the cause of Europe', Talleyrand countered with panache, 'That, sire, is a question of dates.'

This eclectic array of characters gathered at the end of summer 1814 to reorganise the internal boundaries of Europe, and establish a common position on the abolition of the slave trade, the role of royal families across the continent, navigation of rivers and a new German confederation. A massive agenda, by any standards. There cannot ever have been such a colourful and scandalous cast list at any international conference in history, until perhaps the Big Three summits that Churchill, Stalin and Roosevelt bestrode at the end of the Second World War. Few could have survived the media spotlight of the twenty-first century. They make modern diplomatic events seem particularly lame, austere and genteel.

There is no collective noun for diplomats, though people might think up a few when cities are clogged by motorcades, or in Vienna's case cavalcades. Inevitably, matters of diplomatic precedence and protocol featured heavily in their deliberations. Seating plans alone were feverishly contested, as the leaders competed for influence and power. Hundreds of representatives, and a supporting cast of mistresses and flunkies, were lavishly entertained for months in the capital. To complicate their task, Napoleon escaped from his exile in spring 1815 to retake the French throne, and the powers had to break off their deliberations in order to defeat him again and despatch the vanquished autocrat to distant St Helena.

The negotiations were tortuous. The British wanted to retain the 'balance of power' of the preceding century, to ensure future Napoleons could not disturb the equilibrium, and to protect their domination of the seas. Prussia wanted more territory. Austria needed to play off the allies against each other, in order to contain the Russian threat. Russia wanted to use religion to bolster the positions of the continent's monarchs and to keep the Turkish sultan in check.

Coming to decisions in this context was hard work. Voting was out of the question, given the belief of most royal participants that they had a divine right to be there, and that there could be no question of sharing sovereignty. In reality, as with so many conferences, the key players had stitched up the process in advance. Britain, Russia, Austria and Prussia agreed to form an inner circle of negotiations, with other players consulted when necessary, and ideally not at all. Talleyrand saw the danger, and put himself vociferously at the head of those excluded, managing to delay the start of the conference with his histrionic protests of injustice. All four of the big players calculated that they could use France as a counterbalance to their opponents within the inner circle, and so expanded their core group to include the wily Frenchman. Once in the gang, Talleyrand dropped all his demands for issues to be tackled in a larger group, and converted elegantly to the concept of a great-powers deal. This was realpolitik at its most brazen and effective.

Recognising the advantage of being pen-holder, much treasured to this day in the British and French missions to the United Nations and European Union, Castlereagh drafted the most important clause, a mutual-support pact in the face of revolution. Through a conference that lasted months, a new European order was born, with key business now to be managed by the five great powers – Great Britain, Russia, France, Prussia and Austria. This big-power stitch-up was the forefather of the modern United Nations Security Council, where China and the United States have replaced Prussia and Austria.

Unlike previous peace conferences, the architects of the 1815 congress were less concerned with punishing the transgressor –

in this case France – than setting in place structures to manage the status quo and reduce the potential for further military conflict. It was a recognition by the monarchies of Europe, shocked by the French Revolution and the insurgent rise of Napoleon, that united they stood, divided they would fall. It was also a response to Napoleon's abuse of the existing and unnecessarily complex diplomatic procedures to filibuster the Congress of Prague a year earlier.

In many ways the outcomes of the Congress of Vienna were backward-looking – the shoring up of a status quo of elites, reactionary regimes and monarchs. But the diplomatic process that underpinned the decisions was ingenious and creative, and created a system of interdependence that prevented continent-wide conflict for a century. Given its context, it was a supreme act of diplomacy.

The congress also laid the basis for the fastest expansion of diplomacy in history. At the beginning of Queen Victoria's reign in 1837, she had permanent ambassadors only in Paris, Constantinople and St Petersburg; by the end, she had almost a hundred.

This was the era of aristocratic diplomacy, 'outdoor relief for the upper classes'.[4] Looking back in the second edition of his guide to diplomacy in 1922, Ernest Satow wrote that 'a good diplomat must in short be an English gentleman. The higher the grade the greater the need for private income.'[5] Some of those gentlemen, such as Sir Richard Burton, would disappear for months on end, charging around unexplored territories on camel or horseback. Their snug-trousered portraits stare down disapprovingly from the Foreign Office's walls at today's diplomats as they complete their risk assessments.

To add to the theatre, diplomatic uniforms were adopted – Lord Curzon later gave meticulous thought to the outfit in which he would call on the emir of Afghanistan, including wellingtons, fake medals, spurs, a cocked hat, and, deliciously, 'the most gigantic and swashbuckling sword I could find'. He would not have got through the door of today's diplomatic assessment and recruitment centres, which tend to frown on swashbuckling swords. But such swaggering Flashman diplomats set out to study, adventure and conquer.

The Industrial Revolution was the engine for this Western expansion, giving Europe another surge forward. British entrepreneurs unleashed the power of steam and coal. Factories and gunboats, then later computers and nukes, allowed them to build economic muscle, project power and influence, and strike out.

In 1500, Europe's future imperial powers – Britain, France, Spain, Portugal – controlled 10% of the world's territories and generated just over 40% of its wealth. By 1913, at the height of empire, the West controlled almost 60% of the territories, which generated almost 80% of the wealth. While competition and scientific and technological advantage were key to success, the diplomats of the nineteenth century would have added another reason: the ability to spot opportunities, to negotiate a profitable peace, and to hold it together. They knew how to take that technology and turn it into raw power.

The job was still not of course without its dangers. British diplomat Alexander Burnes, a Hindi- and Persian-speaking Scot with a roving eye, was hacked to death by a mob of jealous husbands in Afghanistan in 1841. His colleague Charles Stoddart was imprisoned and executed for spying in Bukhara in 1842, following a failed mission to persuade the emir to free Russian slaves. Bertie Mitford, the grandfather of the famous sisters, was made to watch ritual disembowelment on arrival in Japan as ambassador in 1868 (perhaps it was this that prompted his granddaughter Nancy to ascribe to a character in one of her novels the opinion that 'abroad is unutterably bloody and foreigners are fiends',[6] a view shared by her father David – and some modern politicians). The entire diplomatic corps was placed under siege during the Boxer Rebellion in China in 1900. Diplomatic papers record seventeen deaths among the English 'King's Messengers', who transported the diplomatic bag, in the first thirty years of the nineteenth century.

The expectation of diplomatic hospitality also created its own challenges – 14,000 Persian merchants took up uninvited residence at the British legation in Tehran in 1906 as part of their effort to secure constitutional reform. Earlier, 300 of the shah's wives and eunuchs had made a similar request for sanctuary. Sir Mortimer Durand, the British representative, was, he reported to London, 'somewhat staggered'.

New rules gave a sense of greater purpose and historical context to diplomats, who could now make war as well as peace at the stroke of a pen. The Prussian chancellor Bismarck famously edited out the diplomatic niceties from a telegram from his emperor Wilhelm I to Napoleon III, thereby leaving its recipient furious, and triggering the Franco-Prussian War of 1870. Future diplomats who could spend days negotiating the positioning of a comma in the Maastricht Treaty would have cooed with admiration at Bismarck's later drafting success, following days of negotiation, in establishing his master as 'German emperor' rather than Wilhelm's preferred 'emperor of Germany'.

Diplomats and their masters also began to have to take much greater account of public opinion. Advisers started to offer judgements to their leaders as to which of their mistakes the public could accept, and which were unforgivable. These were not always well received by capitals. In 1919, Foreign Secretary Lord Curzon responded furiously to one such missive from his ambassador to Paris, saying, 'I have always known you to be a cad, I now know you to be a liar.'[7] It has never been easy for envoys to speak truth unto power.

By the end of the nineteenth century, there was a new and increasingly influential player on the block. America began investing heavily in innovative naval technology. Steam-powered battleships with powerful armaments bought real-world diplomatic clout. They could also drag the new nation into war. When its battleship the USS *Maine* exploded for undetermined reasons in the harbour of Havana, the American press stoked war fever and blamed Spain. This gave a pretext for America to replace Spain as the dominant power in its own backyard, in countries such as Cuba, Puerto Rico, the Philippines and Guam. America had arrived as a global power to rival the European states that had entrenched their positions at the Congress of Vienna.

Yet America's ambitions remained opaque. As president, Thomas Jefferson wanted it both ways, to 'enjoy the fruits of power without falling victim to the normal consequences of its exercise'.[8] Or as John Quincy Adams, Secretary of State in 1821, put it, America 'goes not abroad, in search of monsters to destroy. She is the well wisher to the freedom and independence of all. She is the champion and vindicator only of her own.'[9] This dilemma at the heart of American foreign policy continues to this day.

The diplomatic system in 1815 – constructed with such care and swagger – looked robust enough on the eve of the First World War. Surveying regional tensions, diplomats assessed that there would need to be some accommodations to acknowledge shifts in power, but did not anticipate that conflict would shatter the genteel assumptions that underpinned their interactions. European diplomacy had got fat, entitled, and complacent.

So the British ambassador in Berlin continued his yachting expedition with the German kaiser even after Archduke Franz Ferdinand was assassinated in 1914, triggering the Great War.

The ambassador visited key ministers after the outbreak of conflict, and dined as usual that evening at his Residence in Berlin. When his meal was briefly disrupted by pesky protesters, his staff judged that the German emperor's apology for the inconvenience was tardy. Having not arrived until ten the next morning, it 'served to show what we had thought, that the emperor was not a gentleman'.[10]

After diplomacy's finest century it was one thing to declare war, but quite another to misjudge diplomatic etiquette.

From Telephone to Television

> The telephone is a dangerous little instrument,
> unfit for diplomacy.
>
> Harold Nicolson, *On Diplomacy* (1961)

While the diplomats were sat in lengthy and bucolic congresses trying to prevent their leaders from tipping Europe back into war, a period of massive technological innovation was once again to rip through their trade. In 1876, Alexander Graham Bell had invented the telephone. In 1903, the Wright brothers had made the first flight, lasting just under a minute. American Reginald Fessenden made the first radio broadcast on Christmas Eve 1906. In 1926, John Logie Baird invented the first mechanical TV. Their inventions were to transform diplomacy in the twentieth century.

The Great War that followed diplomacy's finest century was obviously a fallow period for diplomacy, as military logic – and much military illogic – prevailed over efforts to end the conflict. Once the world's armies had exhausted themselves in the mud of France and Belgium, the victors imposed the tough Versailles Treaty on their defeated rivals. It took six months to negotiate, and hammered Germany with disarmament and massive reparations. Seventy diplomats from twenty-seven nations grappled with its clauses and subclauses. Many had themselves fought in the conflict, and all would have lost friends and relatives – this would not have felt like an academic exercise.

As at Vienna, the real business was of course done by the big powers – in this case Britain, the US and France. Unlike at Vienna, the major defeated power, Germany, was not given a privileged place at the table. The treaty's signature took place in the spectacular Hall of Mirrors at Versailles. But it did not pass the test of time, nor gain the endorsement of the street. An unknown Austrian corporal called Adolf Hitler was not alone in feeling humiliated by its terms. The best diplomacy cannot be based purely on who has the strongest cards at the time. A test for any treaty must be 'how will this look in twenty years?' For every game-changing treaty, there have been plenty that screwed up.

The diplomats had another try in Switzerland and London in 1925. The Locarno Treaty might have been the British Foreign Office's most important moment. Signed with great fanfare in the room there that still bears its name, it welcomed Germany back into the community of nations, put in place non-aggression pacts on Germany's western borders, and established the British empire as the largest in history, with mandates in Palestine, Iraq and Transjordan. As ever, all of that was secondary in British eyes to the need to clip the wings of the French.

They might not have realised it in the corridors and grand halls of Europe, but big-ship diplomacy had already accelerated the entry of the new great power that was to dominate twentieth-century diplomacy, including in Europe. The Atlantic had just got smaller.

Internationalists in the US – Theodore Roosevelt, Henry Cabot Lodge, Woodrow Wilson – had long argued that the US had to become, in Roosevelt's words, 'the balance of power of the whole globe'. In the aftermath of the First World War, President Wilson warned Americans that the world would be 'absolutely in despair if America deserts it'. In 1919 he helped to create the League of Nations, an idealistic stab at a new liberal order, underpinned by US power. Wilson aimed to replace the nineteenth-century European balance of power diplomacy with a global consensus against misuse of arbitrary power, backed up by collective mechanisms for preventing nations from stepping out of line. For the first time, international players defined and established a response to 'unethical' behaviour by world powers. The league was the first international mission whose main objective was to preserve peace rather than simply to carve up power. It was the beginning of a more idealistic statecraft. The Kellogg–Briand Pact of 1928 even tried to make war illegal.

This was noble ambition indeed, but – like much declaratory diplomacy – easier to agree than to enforce. Italian dictator Mussolini was later to dismiss the league as 'very well when sparrows shout, but no good at all when eagles fall out'.[1] But the principles that lay behind it have underpinned much American and international foreign policy philosophy since. Goldsworthy Lowes Dickinson, a contemporary British political scientist, saw in it the potential of growing democratisation – 'the impossibility of war would be increased in proportion as the issues of foreign policy should be known and controlled by public opinion'.[2] He was wrong in his century, but I will argue later that he may be right in ours.

Despite this progress, the two decades that followed, under both Democrat and Republican presidents, were a period of American retreat from world affairs. It was Hitler's rise that panicked President Franklin Roosevelt to make the case afresh for US re-engagement in Europe on more idealistic grounds, in defence of the endangered 'institutions of democracy'. He concluded that the US was no longer best secured through detachment, and that the US economy was now more dependent on the global economy. 'The world problem cannot be solved if America does not accept its full share of responsibility in solving it.'[3] The language of the US debates of the 1930s is strikingly similar to the US debates of the 2010s.

The Second World War was further evidence of the need for a new world order, and the failure of the League of Nations to deliver collective security. Europe's nineteenth-century diplomatic structures had proved insufficient for the twentieth century. But the period that ended the conflict was also a high point in big-ship diplomacy. Churchill would spend months overseas, determined to establish a new world order through personal relationships with the leaders of the great powers, fuelled by epic dinners.[4] The Yalta Summit of 1945 was the ultimate in the great-power projection of authority, washed down with gallons of vodka, wine and rich food. World leaders had never been able to get to know each other as intimately.

Yet this was the swansong for this kind of 'maps and chaps' statecraft. Its energy sapped by conflict and overstretch, Britain accelerated the painful process of shutting down an empire it could no longer defend – militarily or ideologically. Meanwhile, Asia was back as a serious player in international relations – before 1919, fifteen of the sixteen most active diplomatic states on the world stage were European. After 1919, that number was twenty-two out of forty-seven.[5] The United States needed a new and more effective global architecture, which recognised this recalibration of global power away from Europe.

So, under heavy US pressure, the United Nations was formed. Fifty nations met in San Francisco in 1945. The victorious powers – US, Russia, Britain, France and China – were able to lock in their diplomatic clout by establishing themselves as permanent members of the Security Council with veto powers, a neat formula (for them at least) that continues to this day. For the first time, the world had a permanent forum for diplomatic horse-trading that was indisputably uncontested. Behind the protocol and preening, the tedium and tantrums, the hot air and hot rooms, that forum still matters. The United Nations had fifty-one members in 1945, eighty-one in 1959, and 191 by 2004. It is far from perfect, but no one has yet come up with a better idea for the pursuit of global coexistence.

So much for managing the politics. The US also needed a system for managing the global economy. In July 1944 the 'Bretton Woods' institutions, the World Bank and International Monetary Fund, were hammered out, the first effort to pool key decisions on global economic sovereignty on such a scale. Terminally ill British economist John Maynard Keynes and the American Harry Dexter White grappled over their foundations in 'the summit to top the lot, a raucous, rollicking, exhausting, even death-dealing experience ... a rancid stew'.[6] Over 700 delegates and 500 journalists consumed huge amounts of alcohol while the structures of the modern global economy were put in place.[7]

Meanwhile, the US turned more firmly towards what we now call soft power, starting with a programme of global radio (and later TV) broadcasts to take on the propaganda coming out of the Soviet Union. Of course, the Soviets might have described it in opposite terms. The hard power still of course underpinned this. America was now able to operate militarily as both a European and Asian force, giving it a unique global advantage.

As in previous eras, diplomats decided that one consequence of the changes in the way that power was arbitrated was that their positions should be enhanced. Protection for diplomats, such a concern for that unexpected hero of diplomacy Genghis Khan, was further codified in the 1961 Vienna Convention on Diplomatic Relations. As a result, diplomats cannot be tried for crimes in the countries in which they are serving, though they can be declared *persona non grata* (or PNG'd, in the shorthand). Hence the massive number of parking tickets incurred by embassies in London, with the US the serial offender. Under the Vienna Convention, ambassadors can also be 'recalled for consultations', usually a sign of a frost in relations rather than any ambassadorial misdemeanour. Expulsion of diplomats, often tit for tat, remains another straightforward way to let off a bit of diplomatic steam.

When Samuel Morse sent the first telegram on 24 May 1844, from Washington to Baltimore, the daughter of a friend chose the biblical message – 'What hath God wrought?' Not everyone in diplomacy was impressed by this more immediate form of communication. On receiving his first telegram in the 1860s, Palmerston is reported to have spluttered, 'My God, this is the end of diplomacy.'[8]

Maybe not the end of diplomacy. But he was right that it was indeed the beginning of the end of nineteenth-century diplomacy. Statecraft in the second half of the twentieth century was transformed by the spread of the telephone. For the first time, it was possible for leaders to speak to each other directly and immediately, without the services of intermediaries and envoys. The Cuban missile crisis showed the power of this direct communication to stop wars. And to start them – in 2003, the Iraq War was the first to be planned by secure videoconference.

Many diplomats must have wondered if this infernal new instrument meant the end of their privileged role as carrier and keeper of the message, with the skills associated with delivering it in the most effective way – normally smooth delivery, a vat of soft soap and a head for alcohol. Why have a foreign ministry or diplomats in the field when leaders can talk to each other directly?

But diplomats need not have worried. Every time a new form of communication develops, espionage accelerates in order to monitor and disrupt it. The sophistication of electronic eavesdropping quickly made telephone calls extremely vulnerable. At a New Year party in the British embassy in 1960s Moscow, diplomats wondered aloud how the KGB was celebrating. A phone rang in the corner of the room. The diplomat who picked it up listened in bemused incredulity to the sound of a champagne cork popping and two glasses clinking before the line went dead. The KGB wanted to let the Brits know that they were celebrating too. Even eavesdroppers can let their guard down occasionally.

One of my jobs in Downing Street was to listen to all of the prime minister's telephone calls with his foreign counterparts, in order to produce an official record – the average such call has up to five declared people listening in on their mobile telephones via the Downing Street switchboard. I've listened to thousands of them, including at times in playgrounds, pubs, while cooking and on mountains. This mass participation, even muted, tends to act as a brake on candour.

Telephone diplomacy, like all diplomacy, inevitably gets mired in protocol. When calls between heads of state are set up by their advisers, it is harder to establish who called whom. I've been on numerous calls where one leader has slammed the phone down because he believes he is being kept waiting by his counterpart. Leaders rarely if ever 'cold call' their opposite numbers. In my four years in No. 10, we did it only once, during the financial crisis when Gordon Brown wanted to bounce Nicolas Sarkozy into a deal on 'naked short-selling'. With no warning of the call, we could not arrange a decent translator, ensuring huge confusion when 'naked short-selling' was rendered into hesitant French as 'short, nude sales'. Sarkozy was understandably perplexed.

Few leaders are good at establishing rapport on the telephone, making really effective communication ever harder. To get round this, some leaders have turned to videoconferences. In No. 10 we established secure video communications with US, French and German leaders, sometimes simultaneously. Tony Blair and Gordon Brown used to have long videoconferences with George W. Bush, with Vice President Dick Cheney ever present (normally looming large in the frame, and drinking Coke through a straw), but always silent. Like traditional diplomatic meetings, videoconferences tend to be heavily choreographed. US advisers gave us a very hard time when Gordon Brown chose to neglect the carefully constructed agenda and talk about what was actually on his mind (normally the world economy).

After the Second World War, women made a long-overdue appearance on the diplomatic stage. Lucile Atcherson was the first to join the US State Department, in 1922. But it was not until 1953 that Frances Willis became the first female US ambassador, in her case to Switzerland.

In the 1930s, one British ambassador in Berne had written that it was 'unthinkable that diplomats should produce babies', as inane an idea as it is biologically unsound.[9] The ambassador in Bucharest, turning a blind eye to the prodigious quantities of alcohol consumed by male diplomats, wrote of the danger of women diplomats who would 'breakfast on an ether cocktail and will abandon the chancery for the playing field'.[10] But the many roles undertaken by British women during the Second World War broke down the traditional prejudices that had caused diplomats to question whether women could manage the role, and a small band of pioneering women started to break through in London too. In 1946, women were at last allowed to join the Diplomatic Service, with Cicely Mayhew the first. Having helped crack the Enigma code at Bletchley Park during the war, she was surprised to be patronised as 'our new lamb' by her colleagues. In 1972, the infamous Diplomatic Service Regulation Number 5, which made it necessary for women diplomats to resign if they married, was finally abolished.[11] Anne Warburton became Britain's first woman ambassador, to Denmark in 1976. Yet even in 1965, the Foreign Office could still give its diplomats guidelines on when women should leave the dinner table once the food was finished: 'after an interval of not more than 20 minutes, as it is horrible if the interval goes on too long'.[12]

Outside the monarchy and swinging, there are few vocations where a spouse is still expected to be part of the package. Yet traditionally, the diplomatic partner has been exploited. In popular eyes, he – or still more often she – is a trailing spouse, offering tea parties and living a comfortable life. In reality, she – although increasingly he – is someone who has sacrificed their almost certainly more lucrative career to follow their partner. They tolerate their family home being a hotel, entertaining space and public place. They accept the professional obligation on the diplomat – EU employment law notwithstanding – to be on duty 24/7.

Until 1992, British foreign ministry spouses were even appraised for their ability to support their husband's role. As well as offering advice on how to talk to ladies at dinner, R. G. Feltham's *Diplomatic Handbook*, first published in 1970, suggested to new (naturally assumed to be male) diplomats that 'Your wife should develop a pursuit, such as tennis, to give her a wider conversational reach beyond servants and the weather.' Oh dear.[13]

*

More than the arrival of television itself, the advent of 24/7 news coverage disrupted the diplomat's ability to shape the reporting of events for his or her capital. As former UK Foreign Secretary David Miliband puts it, 'Global, real-time news-gathering, distribution and analysis has rendered useless a lot of traditional diplomatic reporting. Foreign ministers can read the latest resignations, opinion polls and GDP figures in the media before diplomats can tell them.'[14] Game-changing events such as the fall of the Berlin Wall could be watched in real time by leaders, rather than relying on the despatches from their representatives. Diplomats were no longer in the business of reportage.

Keeping the public vaguely informed about what they were doing has only really been an issue for diplomats over the last century. Not until after the First World War did the Colonial Office feel it necessary to establish an information service, with Winston Churchill – a man who knew something about connecting with the public – the first Secretary of State to take a keen interest. The Second World War dramatically accelerated this process, as the totalitarian states demonstrated the power of what we used to call propaganda, but now call public diplomacy. But in 1964 the parliamentary Ploden Report still fiercely criticised the UK Foreign Office's information work for not being linked to the national interest.

After the Second World War, diplomacy was further reshaped by the increased ability of leaders and diplomats to meet in person. Roads were the arteries by which power and influence spread in the twentieth century, just as railways had been in the nineteenth century. US Secretary of State Henry Kissinger was the first great practitioner of a more direct, personal interaction between statesmen, heralding the age of 'Concorde Diplomacy'.[15] Planes were to accelerate diplomacy just as trains and automobiles had.

In advance of the 2009 G20 summit, I was part of the team that covered an exhausting three continents in three days with Gordon Brown, and was unfortunately pictured by the *Financial Times* asleep behind him at one meeting. Hillary Clinton visited 112 countries and ramped up almost a million miles of air travel in her term as Secretary of State. Barack Obama and David Cameron bonded during a flight on the president's Marine Force One helicopter in July 2010 – we noticed that the Americans did not wear seat belts. The ability to cope with weeks in the air every year is highly prized. When I applied to be Private Secretary to Valerie Amos, then the minister for Africa, her first question was, 'Do you dribble on flights?'

There is also a danger that diplomacy is reduced to a test of stamina. The fact that European leaders can meet relatively easily once a month should not be a reason for them to meet once a month. There is now a serious imbalance in European international engagement as a result, with too little time spent on the other four continents, and too much time squabbling over issues that should be settled at lower levels. In my experience, the more a European country needs baling out, the more likely it is that its diplomats travel in business class. During the aftermath of the 2008–9 financial crisis, I once took a flight with EU colleagues where only my German colleague and I were in economy.

Bleary-eyed leaders now often swap stories of how far they have travelled, normally over weekends and at night. Some have an advantage, having developed more sophisticated private planes in order to deliver some form of normality and to stay in touch. Others compete to ensure they have the biggest plane on the runway at international summits – the Italian former prime minister Silvio Berlusconi and the Russian president Vladimir Putin usually won that contest. We once had a race with President Sarkozy from Sharm el-Sheikh to Tel Aviv by plane in the knowledge that there was only time for one leader to have a bilateral with Ehud Olmert, the Israeli prime minister. We Brits got there first – despite (or maybe because of) the fact that we had a French aircrew.

In the game of competitive planes, though, the UK tended to lose. Fear of a media backlash prevented Tony Blair from purchasing a prime-ministerial plane – dubbed 'Blair Force One' by the press. As a result, until an aircraft was finally bought in 2015, we still spent significant time and money getting our leaders to summits in less comfort and style than any other country. The nadir for me was arriving at one summit with the prime minister on a plane that had been used by Led Zeppelin and the Dallas Cowboys. The plane had an orange on its side. We had wipe-down seats. The media had their story.

As a result of the ease with which leaders can travel, the pace of international diplomacy has quickened. Many diplomats assume that the answer to most global challenges is a conference. At a 'three-shirter' European Union budget discussion or climate change summit, I would often long for the days when Winston Churchill's Private Secretary, Jock Colville, could write in his diary: 'war declared, rode on Hampstead Heath for three hours'.[16]

All of this travel and immediacy did not, however, sound the death knell for diplomats. The modern periods of US/Soviet Union rivalry and US unipolarity relied as heavily on diplomacy as other eras. The weapons were more destructive, but the underlying rivalries and power plays would have been familiar to the early diplomats of the Italian city states. In many ways, the 1962

Cuban missile crisis resembled the stand-off between James I and the Spanish ambassador that I described earlier – great-power brinkmanship and muscle-flexing as power ebbed and flowed. Superpower summits such as Geneva in 1955 were the successors of the great-power conferences that established Europe's Westphalian system, carefully balancing the powers of the new states in the seventeenth century.

The modern summit is not unrecognisable from those of previous centuries. Most disappoint participants and observers. As Oxfam said of the 2005 Gleneagles G8 summit (actually one of the best twenty-first-century summits for moving the argument on poverty and debt forgiveness), 'If that was a summit, I'd hate to see a valley.' At a moment when every profession is facing massive transformation, diplomats still find themselves carrying far too much of this cumbersome diplomatic baggage. They retain many of the customs and practices that were first constructed around the diplomatic encounters of the Renaissance and would have seemed very familiar to Talleyrand and Co.

When he wasn't stitching up the Congress of Vienna or charging American diplomats for meetings with him, Talleyrand opined that 'only a fool mocks etiquette, it simplifies life'.[17]

Most of history's diplomats would have agreed, which was why they were such sticklers for protocol. Even in 1949, the vice marshal of the British Diplomatic Corps, advising new diplomats on coping with a 'world full of humbugs', instructed that if faced with two choices, they 'should always choose the one that is more pompous and old-fashioned'.[18] He might have been right then, though somehow I doubt it. He is certainly wrong now.

The international conference or summit has become an exercise in diplomatic and political vanity. Anyone hoping for the failure of the European Union project would be heartened to watch an average European Council. Leaders fix the timing, for example of a G20 or G8, to ensure they get a boost in advance of domestic elections. Yet in reality – as the experiences of Nicolas Sarkozy, Gordon Brown and many others show – that poll jump rarely materialises.

Ease of contact combined with increased media interest brought a new challenge for diplomats: the official gift.

Diplomatic gifts no longer have the importance of early diplomatic encounters. Except perhaps for the media, desperate for a bit of colour. As advisers to leaders, we would spend hours debating presents, especially for US presidents. The British media was beside itself with rage when President Obama removed Churchill's bust from the Oval Office and gave Gordon Brown a box set of the best American TV series – actually quite a good selection. We used to give Chancellor Angela Merkel of Germany DVDs of her favourite British TV series, *Midsomer Murders*. She once asked me for tickets to the Last Night of the Proms, a personal favourite of hers.

The best gifts now have either a personal touch, or – more often – can be used to project innovation and creativity. British prime ministers don't get to keep the eclectic presents they receive: all those worth more than £140 have to be given away or auctioned, a diplomatic minefield in itself. The 2013 White House gifts register includes a full-size zebra skin from President Kikwete of Tanzania. Former Secretary of State Colin Powell counsels that staffers should always check any gift of a portrait before it is unveiled – he received one from a Balkan leader that made him look like Count Dracula.

Gifts have always been an essential element of statecraft. But one of the more galling sights in modern diplomacy is the exchange of presents among diplomats at the start of any EU presidency. Huge amounts are spent on ties, pens and folders for fellow public servants, all at the public expense of course. The ties are invariably ghastly, polyester, and unwearable. They only intrude on the public consciousness if there is a gaffe. For one UK presidency, schoolchildren were asked to contribute images based on their perceptions of the member states. The Italians were understandably miffed that the history, antiquity and glories of Rome were passed over in favour of a picture of a pepperoni pizza.

The schedule of most modern conferences is heavily pre-cooked. Many diplomats see it as their role to minimise the actual debate among leaders as far as possible, smoothing down any disagreements and producing a lowest common denominator fudge of a public communiqué. The blander the better. What was the last summit conclusions text that anyone outside the drafting team can remember?

Normally, those preparing a summit will throw in a couple of set-piece themes or announcements on the issue of the day – climate change, say, or transparency. These are meant to define the event, and catch the attention of the media and public. Diplomats and leaders will make grandiose claims about the 'once in a generation' or 'historic' nature of what they have agreed. They want their career-defining Congress of Vienna moment.

Yet these announcements are often ignored by the media, and the population at large. They focus instead on the leader missing from the family photo – it was usually the Canadian former prime minister Stephen Harper for the conferences I helped organise. Or the awkward attempt to dress down at the informal supper – G8 leaders can compete to see who can make chinos and a blue shirt look most abnormal. Or the ridiculous traditional hats that the host makes his grimacing colleagues wear on arrival, normally to placate an indigenous rights lobby, while the visiting leader's entourage try frantically to prevent the media getting a photo. Former US vice president Al Gore, who must have sat through more dreary summits than most, skewers brilliantly the tedious habit of dressing up in the clothes of the host nation. This 'recalls the parable of the child who noticed that the emperor has no clothes. Except in this case, the clothes have no emperor.'[19]

The most important work at any summit is done away from the cameras, in what diplomats call 'the margins'. There you find a frantic form of diplomatic speed-dating. It can take place in a range of formats that are not as steamy as they sound: plenaries, bilaterals, brush-bys, pull-asides, one-to-ones. Some are carefully choreographed. At one UN General Assembly, I organised an ambush, literally, of the South African president Thabo Mbeki, who wanted to avoid a difficult meeting with the British prime minister over Zimbabwe. We worked out his route based on where South African security were stationed, and emerged from behind a curtain at the crucial moment.

In the summit itself, leaders barely tolerate each other's lengthy and tedious interventions, often rolling their eyes, working on their papers or playing Angry Birds while colleagues read from prepared scripts. The UN General Assembly, the diplomatic equivalent of the World Cup, is the ultimate form of this hot-air summit diplomacy. As with the football, there is usually some unruly behaviour, although with Hugo Chávez, Gaddafi and Ahmadinejad no longer on the pitch, this is now less likely, sadly. There is also a certain amount of tedium: the hall's acoustics and temperature, plus a tendency to reduce most crucial issues to platitudes, mean that some speeches can be the equivalent of a grinding nil–nil draw. Before such exchanges, diplomatic advisers will haggle over the length and size of the meeting as well as the substance of any press statement. Even translation can be a contested area, with some delegations adept at using up meeting time to avoid reaching the issues they find awkward.

The type of press conference is also heavily contested. The rough ranking is in descending order of importance and difficulty. A full press conference features podiums, flags, prepared statements and media questions, most agreed in advance. A 'pool spray' is more informal, with cameras at the start of the meeting and footage of the leaders discussing the weather. A 'grip and grin' is normally a handshake, a rictus smile or two, but no words. Press conferences are the hardest to get right. They present more practical challenges, such as finding a discreet hidden step for shorter leaders. And if the UK media are involved, you have to warn foreign leaders to expect much more personal and provocative questions than they get at home. I will never forget the look on President Sarkozy's face when I told him the questions on his private life that he was likely to get after a particularly grand UK–France summit at the height of the financial crisis. I tried to suggest that this was a by-product of 'freedom of the press'. His reply was short, Gallic, descriptive and unprintable.

All this prancing and declaratory diplomacy often gets in the way of the practical, direct and honest diplomacy that is needed to settle the big global questions. As Chris Patten, who must have had to sit through his fair share of summit waffle, points out, 'I am unconvinced that the right place to sort out all of our international problems is at some great international jamboree.'[20]

Already, the summit to prevent war seems to have faded into history. Take for example the challenges now facing the Middle

East, from Iran to Syria. Churchill, Stalin and Roosevelt might have camped on Cyprus for a week until they had found some sort of accommodation. Yet the last proper great-power summit was Yalta, 1945. It was fear of the atomic bomb that later prevented the Third World War rather than traditional international diplomacy. Ironically, leaders can now talk more easily to each other, but they lack opportunities for real discussion.

Increasingly, the public are confused and disengaged by summit diplomacy. Despite all the efforts to engage people outside the room, through campaigns in the media and by NGOs who try to drag the agenda towards issues of poverty or climate change, the actual discussion and decisions remain aloof and distant. Few people care to keep track of whether a meeting is G7, G8 (which actually has more than eight members at the table, as the European Union has snuck in two leaders) or G20. For a while during the 2008–9 financial crisis, world leaders debated establishing a G14. As security measures move protesters and campaigners further from the leaders themselves, much of the world feels excluded from these exchanges.

Diplomacy does need its pinch points, when a meeting or conference forces compromise, debate and agreement. But unless we find a way to debate the world's problems in a more transparent, meaningful and representative way, we will find that other forums make the average G8 or EU summit look like the Congress of Vienna.

So while the diplomats of the late twentieth century stumbled from conference centre to airport lounge, clutching hard-fought communiqués that no one would read or remember, wider leaps in communication technology were already – once again – about to challenge and transform their trade.

From E-mail to E-nvoys

Why do diplomats feel the need to let it all hang out?

Oliver Miles, former UK ambassador, *Guardian*, 12 July 2010

The first email between heads of government was sent on 4 February 1994, from the Swedish prime minister Carl Bildt to the US president Bill Clinton. Bildt congratulated Clinton on the lifting of the Vietnam embargo, and added that 'Sweden is one of the leading countries in technology, and it is only appropriate that we should be among the first to use the Internet for political contacts and communications around the globe.'

Clinton replied the following day, in hindsight perhaps with less panache than the moment required: 'I appreciate your enthusiasm for the potential of emerging technologies. This demonstration of electronic communication is an important step toward building the global information highway.'

The language was as clunky as the software, but e-diplomacy was under way.

Traditionally, the main means of communication between diplomats and capitals has been the telegram. In the British system these are always addressed to the foreign minister, and always in the name of the ambassador, although usually written by a political officer. Likewise, instructions from the Foreign Office to embassies always go out above the name of the Foreign Secretary, though it is exceedingly rare that he will actually see them, let alone write them, in advance.

In Paris in 2007 I recall seeing the trolleys of paper telegrams being rolled around the French foreign ministry on the Quai d'Orsay. They would arrive first with the director, and slowly work their way down the corridor. The desk officer, who more than anyone needed to see what was happening in the country he was working on, would normally receive his battered, coffee-stained, cigarette-singed version late at night, long after it had been overtaken by events.

To be fair, this is one area that has evolved rapidly in the last ten years, at least in the UK Foreign Office. We switched to electronic telegrams in the 1990s, and now send e-grams, or diplomatic telegrams – diptels for short. These have the same content, but arrive instantly on the screens of those who need to see them. An average diptel will have a short three- or four-line summary, and seven or eights paragraphs of analysis or advice. Given that whatever is being reported will have been on Sky News in the minister's office for several hours before the report arrives, the emphasis is increasingly on explaining and analysing the news rather than reporting it. As media cycles accelerate and concentration spans shorten, we cannot be far from a system of 'diptweets', quick and dirty analysis on breaking news, aimed to compete with what readers at the headquarters are getting from Twitter or news outlets.

Traditionally, diplomats have always tried to minimise and manage the amount of direct contact between leaders. We encased their exchanges in protocol, prepared lines and statements. I worked for one minister, Chris Mullin, who admirably made a point of not being connected by phone or pager, despite the strenuous efforts of his party's whips and managers. As I used to tell him, this is a civil servant's fantasy. But his technological detachment did not seem to stop the world from turning.

New ways of communicating are now breaking down the restrictions that officials put up. Leaders text, email and tweet each other direct. During negotiations, the text messages between them (and between their advisers) are often more important than the conversation at the table. It will become less necessary for them to meet as often, yet they will get to know each other better.

Neither Bildt nor Clinton could have anticipated the speed at which the 'global information highway' was being built around them. In terms of diplomacy, it is Twitter and Facebook that have built it.

@jack (aka Jack Dorsey, Twitter's founder) sent the first tweet at teatime on 21 March 2006. Within three years, a billion tweets had been sent. Eleven accounts are started every second, and 500m are sent every day. Facebook has 1.55 billion users, and this figure has grown by a third a year. Most of these users are on mobile devices.

Diplomats are among them. Bildt was the first minister to make it compulsory for ambassadors to have social media accounts. Over 80% of world leaders now have a Twitter handle.[1] Barack Obama was the first leader to join Twitter, in March 2007, and is the most followed (though he still comes in well behind Lady Gaga). Pope Francis has over 20 million followers on his nine different @Pontifex accounts. Maybe those behind his account are aiming at quality not quantity – he gets retweeted much more than Obama: 11,116 times per tweet, as opposed to Obama's 2,309.

More leaders are wresting control of their own social media accounts from their staff. They have recognised that if you're not tweeting yourself, you're not really on Twitter. In early 2014, John Kerry tweeted 'It only took a year but @StateDept finally let me have my own @Twitter account', and used the hashtag #JKTweetsAgain. Increasingly, such accounts – especially those of US National Security Adviser Susan Rice and US ambassador to the UN Samantha Power – are replacing carefully scripted formal statements. 'It won't be a substitute for a meeting or a substitute for a phone call,' explains Douglas Frantz, Assistant Secretary of State for Public Affairs. 'American foreign policy is probably too nuanced to explain in 140 characters. It will be used to deliver quick messages and amplify existing messages.'[2]

Diplomats need to pick arguments. Twitter and other social media tools allow them to do that in new ways. One of the pioneering digital diplomats, former US ambassador to Russia Michael McFaul, had online fights with the Russian ministry of foreign affairs over freedom of assembly and speech. He saw it as a way to avoid having his views censored or filtered through traditional Russian media. UN Security Council arguments between permanent representatives are now regularly played out in real-time on Twitter. The brilliant French ambassador to the US, Gérard Araud, regularly takes on US presidential candidates and others in public. This would all have appeared unseemly just a few years ago. But in some ways it is simply a return to the lively political debate of the Roman forum.

The US are the market leaders in this 'pivot to the people'.[3] President Obama was a community organiser long before being elected, and saw the power of connecting digital communities to policy. States need to build networks and alliances with non-state actors. As a result of the State Department's '21st Century Statecraft' initiative, US diplomats reach more than the number of subscribers to the top ten US newspapers put together.

Diplomats are putting these tools to increasingly creative use. In Iran, both the US and UK had virtual embassies – allowing them online engagement without the physical risks of locating diplomats. I remember how dangerous it felt to be organising a joint town hall meeting between the UK and Chinese premiers in 2009, the first of its kind in China. There are now virtual town halls everywhere online.

Some of the most innovative digital diplomats are from smaller countries. Perhaps they find it easier to embrace a more fleet-footed, start-up approach. Estonia leads the diplomatic market on use of blockchain technology, and online citizenship. Since its independence in 2008, Kosovo has been recognised by only half the world. So its deputy foreign minister, Petrit Selimi, persuaded Facebook to allow users to place their location in Kosovo, and not in neighbouring Serbia. The success of this effort means that Kosovo's existence is more widely recognised online than offline.[4] It is possible to imagine a similar process with other entities where some want to become sovereign states – Palestine, Catalonia, Scotland, Kurdistan.

Digital media are also increasingly important resources for those responding to humanitarian crises. The idea of consulting refugees on refugee issues sounds obvious, but only now are we able to try. Humanitarian agencies are aiming to get social media channels and devices to those hit by disasters, and use Google Earth to locate survivors. In Lebanon, we used smart cards to deliver cash to the neediest refugees, and sophisticated social media mapping tools to locate them.

Of course, all of this digital diplomacy brings risks. In September 2012, while under direct attack as the result of unrest caused by the rapid spread of a video critical of Islam, the US embassy in Cairo condemned the efforts of some to 'hurt the religious feelings of Muslims'. The backlash in the US led to the White

House disowning the tweet. Separately, the US ambassador in Egypt had to apologise to his sensitive hosts when the embassy Twitter feed retweeted a clip from *The Daily Show with Jon Stewart* that criticised the Egyptian government.

So digital diplomacy is not without its critics. Former British ambassador Oliver Miles wrote in 2010 (when William Hague was Foreign Secretary) that we need to 'Stop the blogging ambassadors. The immediacy of social media does not lend itself to the measured nature of international diplomacy ... The issues with which ambassadors have to deal are better dealt with *penseroso* rather than *allegro*.* Blogs by ambassadors were bound to end in tears. Let's hope William Hague will blow the whistle.'[5]

The number of blog posts written annually by UK ambassadors has since risen tenfold. If the whistle was blown, it was too *ponderosa* to hear. Of course there will always be a need for considered diplomacy, but diplomats will also have to be part of the conversations that everyone in the real world is having.

Sir Leslie Fielding, another former UK ambassador, has also lambasted the 'trivial chirpiness and dumbing down' of social media, saying that it 'cuts no mustard when applied to the sheer complexity of many world issues. The global waters are often opaque, even muddy.'[6] He is right, of course, about the fiendish complexities of foreign policy, and indeed the inane nature of much social media. But that is not an argument against trying to communicate in new ways, and to use the new tools to make the global waters a little less murky.

The examples of diplomatic digital disasters – inadvertent insults to former opponents, misguided attempts at humour in serious situations, disgruntled hosts – will not seem so dramatic

---

* A Milton reference. 'Il Penseroso' is his poem about sober contemplation, as opposed to the frenetic world of 'L'Allegro'. Personally, I think Milton would have tweeted.

in a few years. There is no other way to pursue digital diplomacy effectively except through loosening the reins of control.

For a trade that relies on communication, diplomacy has obviously had to adapt to successive waves of dramatic technological disruption. This canter through the history of diplomacy suggests that the most important innovations to shape statecraft throughout history were language, writing, ships, rules, the printing press, trains, telephones, and now the Internet.

So the tools of diplomacy are constantly evolving. Diplomats now compete over who has the most Twitter followers rather than where they are placed at a diplomatic dinner. Talleyrand would have been out of his depth in a twentieth-century summit, just as John Kerry would be in a twenty-second-century summit.

While the basics of diplomacy have changed little from Ug's time, diplomacy had surrounded itself by the late twentieth century with immense paraphernalia – titles, conferences, summits, rules and codes. But strip these away, and we can identify the diplomatic skills that made our ancestors more likely to survive the hostile 200,000 years of hunter-gathering, the eight millennia of the Agricultural Age and the two centuries of the Industrial Age. Maybe these can get us through the new uncertainties of the Digital Age.

The history of diplomacy suggests that diplomats have always been most effective when they have understood, channelled and represented real power. When emperors held power, diplomats were flunkies in their citadels. When monarchs held power, diplomats were courtiers in their palaces. When military leaders held power, diplomats hung around outside their tents. When states became the dominant power brokers, diplomats started ministries and tried to get as close as possible to their elected (or unelected) leaders. As democracy took hold in the West, diplomats rein-vented themselves as its most ardent supporters, while trying to ensure that their trade stayed out of its sight. We need to consider what this means for diplomacy in an age when power is once again shifting and diffusing. If diplomats are not where the power is, they are simply slow journalists with smaller audiences.

The history of diplomacy also shows us that, at key points in our collective story, and normally following shocks such as war, shifts in power required diplomats and politicians to work together strenuously to recalibrate systems and establish new rules of coexistence. Modern diplomats are standing on the shoulders of the curious, canny and sometimes courageous individuals behind Westphalia, Vienna, the League of Nations and Bretton Woods. Two centuries after the Congress of Vienna, are we again at such a moment of flux and uncertainty, and do diplomats have the legitimacy and credibility to help manage the next global reset?

Only if they have the foresight to understand diplomacy's future, and the hindsight to learn from the best of its past.

So what do more than 500 years of formal diplomatic history tell us about the qualities that make a good diplomat?

What Makes a Good Diplomat?

Diplomacy is to do and say the nastiest thing in the nicest way.

Isaac Goldberg, *The Reflex* (1930)

There is nothing dramatic in the success of a diplomatist. His victories are made up of a series of microscopic advantages: of a judicious suggestion here, of an opportune civility there, of a wise concession at one point and far-sighted persistence at another, of sleepless tact, immovable calmness, and patience that no folly, no provocation, no blunder can shake.

Lord Salisbury, 1862

Salisbury was right – diplomacy is about nuance, subtlety and the ability to make the best of a bad hand. It is rarely black and white. There is rarely a right answer and a wrong one. The history of diplomacy is studded with colourful and extravagant characters, plying their craft at key moments of global change, smoothing the rough edges of their leaders' positions and trying to hold the whole show together. It is also populated by countless greyer or more vanilla individuals, quietly suggesting the odd adjustment, or picking up the pieces after the leaders have left for the banquet or the press conference.

Before we look at how diplomacy can help us get through the twenty-first century, is it possible – after over 500 years of more formal statecraft – to pick out the characteristics of the kind of diplomat we need?

First, let's junk the ones that we don't. I suspect that there are four stereotypes of diplomats, particularly ambassadors, which are lodged in the public consciousness. All of them have some link to reality, but an increasingly tenuous one.

① Firstly, the 'Ferrero Rocher ambassador'. A chocolate-covered hazelnut in a gold wrapper has dogged a generation of diplomats. In an incredible piece of 1980s marketing, an Italian chocolate manufacturer managed to associate their brand with a pastiche version of ours. 'Why Ambassador, with these Ferrero Rocher you are really spoiling us.' Most ambassadors, I suspect, have a secret wish to be the suave hosts of the cocktail party captured in the famous advert. Waiters in tailcoats and white gloves glide between attractive guests, a string quartet shimmers in the background, the champagne flows, and the ambassador himself is at the centre of an alluring scene of wealth, privilege, intrigue and glamour. Smooth and mysterious diplomats sip cocktails at the bar.

Just occasionally in real life, a diplomatic reception might come close. But it is very rare indeed. With most diplomatic services under intense pressure to reduce costs, the champagne no longer flows, and receptions tend to be more cheap fizz and finger food than champers and canapés.

There is not a single British diplomat in the world that has not been faced with a gag based on Ferrero Rocher, normally accompanied by something on the lines of 'I bet you hear that all the time.' 'Yes. We do,' we respond through gritted teeth, wondering about the aggressive potential of a small nut-crusted chocolate.

The danger for modern diplomats, competing for resources and relevance, is that the image has stuck fast. It makes us look out of touch, overfed and overpaid. It plays to a sense that many have that we are 'swanning around' the world. Again through gritted teeth, we are not.

(2)   A second stereotype is the aristocratic amateur. Think of the diplomats in television series such as *Yes, Prime Minister*. Here, the Foreign Office and its ambassadors are presented as a set of decent chaps, almost exclusively male and pale, smug and smooth. They glide between diplomatic encounters, never without a withering put-down, utterly independent of political control and occasionally in the national dress of whichever country they are serving in. Lawrence of Arabia with fewer principles. Most are seen as insufferably pompous, patronising and grand, infused with an unshakeable sense of self-importance. In a recent lecture, retired diplomat Sir Leslie Fielding described the modern British diplomat as 'a civil servant, albeit of a superior kind'.[1] Or as Harold Nicolson wrote in 1961 in reference to the 'amateurism' charge, 'If ambassadors were required to become experts, then surely great confusion would arise.'[2]

According to this stereotype, the elite foreigners with whom the aristocratic amateur interacts are far more interesting and in all ways more worthy than his own countrymen, especially politicians. Most are assumed to have 'gone native' early in their careers, caring more about the country to which they are posted than their own. The story goes that a Whitehall policeman was asked in 1939 for directions to the Foreign Office. 'Which side is the Foreign Office on?' He responded, 'I don't know sir, but they claim to have been on our side in the last war.' A number of world leaders, including Margaret Thatcher and Ronald Reagan, believed that the trouble with their diplomats was that they thought that their role was to represent foreigners. Finance ministries tend to agree, bemoaning diplomatic negotiations or international conferences where diplomats ensure that everyone leaves with something. Veteran US diplomat William Burns recalls Secretary of State George Shultz asking ambassadors to point to 'your country' on the globe. They would invariably indicate the country to which they were posted, allowing Shultz to spin the globe back to the United States and remind them that this was in fact 'their country'. The message would stick.

In reality, diplomats tend to be far more in need of endorsement and love from their political masters than this suggests. There is no doubt that they risk understanding more about the elevated circles of the countries in which they are serving than real life in their own. But they are becoming more representative of the populations from which they are drawn. The British Foreign Office now sends ambassadors who have been away too long on recalibration tours of the UK, where they are encouraged to study populations of the regions that they might not know, so as to represent them more credibly. Most diplomats would bristle at the suggestion that they spend more time representing the countries in which they are serving than the ones they formally represent.

(3) A third stereotype, perhaps even more ingrained in diplomatic folklore, is that of Perfidious Machiavel. It used to be said that to get on in the British foreign service, you had to be an assassin, boffin or boy scout. After all, doesn't the British national anthem talk of the need to 'confound their politics, frustrate their knavish tricks'?

There are plenty of folklorish examples of assassins who made it to the top, sometimes pretending to be boy scouts, and who manipulated the careers of others along the way. The legend suggests that they would tend to be as fiendishly cunning in international negotiations. Think of the smooth but untrustworthy British ambassador Lord John, who pops up occasionally in US political drama *The West Wing*, or any number of louche but despicable diplomats in John Le Carré's novels. There is a famous story of Sir John Kerr, then British ambassador to the European Union, hiding under the table during one leaders-only discussion during the Maastricht negotiations, in order to pass notes to Prime Minister John Major.

This is a stereotype of British diplomats that persists in parts of the Middle East, most notably Iran. I find that those who see a dastardly British hand behind every twist and turn are disappointed when I explain that we are really not that clever. After all, if we were that cunning, we would still be running the world.

In reality, I suspect that most foreign services are now more boy scout than assassin. Many have introduced assessment centres that, with a strong focus on delivering through others and interpersonal skills, tend to work against the assassin's less inclusive qualities. Indeed, some would say that we have too few assassins in circulation. To misquote Reagan, diplomacy is the second oldest profession, but should still borrow much from the first.

At the other end of the scale, a fourth stereotype is the hopeless but well-meaning chump who tends to arrive after the key decision has been taken, and invariably lets down any fellow countryman needing consular help. He is frequently drunk, usually inept and sometimes inappropriate. Terry-Thomas played just such an inept diplomat in the Boulting brothers' 1959 film *Carlton-Browne of the FO*, with the main protagonist devising a plan to partition an island by painting a white line across it. P. G. Wodehouse also captured this character very effectively. More recently, he was portrayed by David Mitchell in the BBC series *Ambassadors* – dishevelled, tired, only just about holding it together, trying to do his best but overwhelmed by his job, and indeed by the modern world.

There is no doubt that Hapless Henry exists, and the world is a more amusing place for it. But he is increasingly weeded out by poor-performance procedures and by the much greater oversight that capitals can now exercise over embassies. The gin-soaked amateur is fading from history with a hiccup.

Of course, there is much further to go in most foreign services before diplomats can claim to be as diverse as the populations they represent – there has never been a woman in the plum British ambassadorial postings of Paris, Washington, New York or the EU. But the reality is that, while some increasingly endangered and sulky examples exist of all these stereotypes, they have been replaced by very different types of diplomats. Of the British diplomats in my team in Beirut, there were periods when I was the only white man. The weekly Whitehall meetings of the Foreign Office leadership convened by the Permanent Secretary, which used to be called 'morning prayers', have long since ceased to resemble a meeting of public school prefects. There remains work to be done on equality in foreign services, but you are far more likely to meet a Foreign Office director dashing to reach the nursery before it closes than sipping a sherry in his elegant club.

So what really makes a good diplomat?

The poet Robert Frost suggested that 'A diplomat is a man who always remembers a woman's birthday but never remembers her age.' Maybe that helps. But the diplomatic archives give us plenty of other clues as to the attributes that a diplomat really needs. The consistent themes are courage, curiosity, tact and the ability to eat anything.

The Venetians had no doubt what they wanted in their envoys. In 1566, Ottaviano Maggi, a humanist and diplomat, wrote a treatise on 'the perfect ambassador'. He described the ideal qualities of a diplomat in the era of the Italian city states as 'trained theologian, familiar with Greek philosophers, expert in mathematical sciences, competent in law, music and poetry, proficient in Greek, Latin, French, German, Spanish and Turkish, of aristocratic birth, rich and handsome'. A daunting skill set that would make a modern diplomat blanch.

The presentation has always mattered. The seventeenth-century analyst of diplomacy Rousseau de Chamoy judged that ambassadors could be assessed by the magnificence of their table, the nobility of their birth and the quality of their physical appearance. He would not have met the diversity or austerity criteria for modern diplomacy.

Harold Nicolson – an extraordinary character who went from handing the declaration of war to the German ambassador as a junior diplomat in 1914 to politics to writing, and had an 'open marriage' to Vita Sackville-West – wrote after the Second World War that the 'key qualities of the diplomat are truthfulness, precision, calmness and modesty'.[3] Most of the best diplomats I've encountered master three of those four attributes, but not always the same three. Lord Gore-Booth, head of the British Diplomatic Service in the late 1960s, concluded that the ideal ambassador 'must be able to contrive anything, eat or drink anything and appear to like it, and to be surprised by nothing. And all this must be done without loss of sensitivity or courage.'[4] Anthony Acland, another head of the Foreign Office, used to tell new diplomats to be 'humane sceptics'.

Sir Christopher Meyer, British ambassador in Washington from 1997 to 2003 and renowned for always wearing bright red socks, lists a more modern set of necessary qualities: insatiable curiosity about other countries, an abiding interest in foreign policy, a willingness to spend half your working life outside the UK, and a profound knowledge and understanding of some foreign countries. He suggests that the diplomat must be able to negotiate, to win the confidence of the powerful and influence them, to understand what makes a foreign society tick, and to analyse information and report it accurately and quickly, including news your own government does not want to hear.* Most of all, a diplomat needs 'a quick mind, a hard head, a strong stomach, a warm smile and a cold eye'.[5]

The ledger of qualities gets longer. As another former British ambassador, Oliver Miles, observed: 'some have listed other qualities such as good horsemanship, good looks and a good head for alcohol. The more qualities you add, the less it looks like the specification of a good diplomat and the more like a combination of King Solomon and Jeeves.'[6] We should put that on the recruitment adverts.

Long studies were written in the past about the art of diplomacy, and the skills required of its practitioners. A kind of cult has emerged among diplomats, including between those of different nations. So the Congress of Vienna, that high point of conference diplomacy, is often depicted – rightly – as European elites making the compromises necessary to keep themselves and their class in office and power. As we have seen, the diplomats had more in common with each other than most of their compatriots. They very clearly saw their roles as to represent their monarch, not their citizens.

There have always been lots of diplomats who are not good at diplomacy. Harold Nicolson saw great danger in the professional detachment – 'functional defects' – developed by diplomats. He generously blamed this not on them but on exposure to the

---

* The workload of a modern diplomat is often as heavy and as serious as this list suggests; but diplomacy doesn't all need to be hard work. Part of my role in Downing Street included building in moments to watch the football, beat me at tennis or let off steam in other ways. President Sarkozy gave David Cameron a pair of excellent tennis racquets at their first meeting in Paris, which we put to good use after dinner, slipping and sliding barefoot in the dark on the embassy's grass court.

'human folly or egotism' they tended to witness from politicians, and the ignorance of the general public they claimed to represent. He judged that as a result, diplomats 'underestimate the profound emotion by which whole nations may be swayed'. A diplomat could become 'denationalized, internationalized, and therefore dehydrated, an elegant, empty husk'.[7] There are plenty of those empty husks working in international organisations today, and in some cases running them.

Ernest Satow, writing in the early twentieth century at the high point of the British empire, was less generous about politicians, describing most diplomats as ground down from being too often 'compelled to contend for a bad cause'. Many diplomats had as a result concluded that the best they could manage through 'prudence and love of peace is the postponement of the evil day'.[8] A pretty sobering mission statement.

But in his massive guide to diplomacy, Satow also notes that although 'telegraphic communication now enables a negotiator to remain in constant touch with his government', the basic ingredients of statecraft – 'national character and human nature' – do not change. He identifies as the essential diplomatic attributes an open and serious spirit, small ego, sangfroid and equal humour, and the ability to remain calm under pressure. A diplomat must be 'an honourable spy', discreet and patient, neither too timid nor too '*plein de feu*'. He should know the customs and the history of his hosts inside out. He should be able to put himself in the place of his interlocutor. Satow deflates the egos of his contemporaries, and plenty of mine, by reminding us that 'a diplomatist must be on his guard against the notion that his own post is the centre of international politics, and against an exaggerated estimate of the part assigned to him in the general scheme'.[9]

There is no doubt that detachment and tact matter. As Isaac Newton put it, 'Tact is the knack of making a point without making an enemy.' It was always said that a diplomat should always think twice before saying nothing. But I'm increasingly sceptical about the idea of diplomats only as observers rather than picking the right arguments. As ever, Winston Churchill, whose negotiations with President Franklin Roosevelt to bring the US into the Second World War were a masterclass in the use of all the instruments of persuasion available, was tweetable: 'Diplomacy is the art of telling people to go to hell in such a way that they ask for directions.'[10]

So are the best diplomats actually also the best liars?

Machiavelli, who wrote the handbook on how to take, maintain and use power, would have said that they were. Metternich also saw deviousness as part of the diplomatic DNA, especially in his enemies. On hearing of the death of his diplomatic rival Talleyrand, he reportedly muttered, 'Now I wonder what he meant by that.' Palmerston seems to have agreed about diplomats being (in the Conservative minister and diarist Alan Clark's infamous phrase) 'economical with the *actualité*', claiming that 'I tell ambassadors the truth, because I know they won't believe it.'[11] Another nineteenth-century statesman, the Italian Count Cavour, also saw a lack of morality as essential to the process of statecraft, concluding that 'if we did for ourselves what we do for our country, what rogues we should be'.[12] In his case, it did no harm, allowing him to create Italy and become its first prime minister.

For US academic Charles Hill, who has looked at how literature influenced statesmanship, the most successful diplomats are indeed those prepared to break the rules, to dissemble in the service of their higher cause.[13] Cavour, Cardinal Richelieu, Talleyrand and Oliver Cromwell were all amoral but effective. Legendary king of Ithaca Odysseus got his way by changing the messages he carried between Agamemnon (the king of Mycenae) and the warrior Achilles. Bohemian politician Albrecht von Wallenstein got the Treaty of Westphalia agreed by manipulating the facts against his own side. Maybe this is justified in pursuit of the greater good? As Tony Blair wrote of the Northern Ireland peace process, 'it was sometimes necessary to bend the truth further than it should strictly have gone'.[14] He may not have been popular for it, but he was right.

Sometimes I had to tell white lies for my country, as when one elderly Middle Eastern monarch asked what was written on the 'nice placards' being waved at him in London by the 'friendly crowds'.

So was Sir Henry Wotton, a late-sixteenth-century English diplomat, right in his joking description of an ambassador as 'an honest man sent to lie abroad for the good of his country'? Only in part. Perhaps the best diplomats understand when to say nothing, or when not to say everything. No decent negotiator starts a negotiation by laying all his cards on the table. But honesty is in fact central to the work. Sir Leslie Fielding rightly says that 'plain dealing is best. Deviousness always backfires. Charm not coercion; good manners, not ill; persuasion not deception.'[15] Oliver Miles goes further in suggesting that 'scrupulous regard for truth, not a quality always associated with diplomats' is the key quality.[16]

The reality is that honesty has been and remains one of the most important qualities of a diplomat. In negotiations, you live or die on your reputation. The best negotiators recognise that trust is essential. Edward Murrow, the CBS journalist turned diplomat, counselled diplomats that 'The really critical link in the international communications chain is the last three feet, best bridged by personal contact – one person talking to another.'[17] Harold Nicolson agrees. 'Good diplomacy is akin to sound banking, and depends on credit. Even if your opponent gains a trick or two by sharp practice, you should yourself abide by the rules of the game.'[18]

Greater transparency and oversight mean that you are now more likely than ever to be caught out if you are lying, or trying to have it both ways. In an ideal world a diplomat is actually an honest man or woman sent abroad to tell the truth about his or her country. As a former French ambassador in Washington, Hervé Alphand, put it: 'a diplomat is a person who can tell the truth to anyone in the government to which he is accredited without offending him, and to anyone in his own government at the risk of offending him'.[19]

Diplomats also need to lead. I represented the British prime minister at Senator Edward Kennedy's funeral. I gave Sinn Fein leaders Gerry Adams and Martin McGuinness a lift in my car. One of the speakers told us that John Kennedy had inspired America, Bobby Kennedy had challenged America, but it was Teddy Kennedy who had changed America. The best leaders must be able to do all three – set a compelling vision, engage people to deliver it, and then establish the structures and plans that help them to do so. Getting this right is not straightforward – most leaders with whom I have worked master two of the three. The best diplomats have to do better than that if they are to lead their teams effectively.

It is also striking the extent to which many modern autobiographies – most recently those by former UN Secretary General Kofi Annan and former US president George W. Bush – stress judgement, and the ability to take the big decisions, as the key to foreign policy. If we include leaders rather than purely diplomats, perhaps Nelson Mandela was therefore the greatest statesman of the twentieth century. He knew when to use strength and when to make concessions. His deployment of measured language was often supreme diplomacy. He knew when to lead from the front and when to lead from the back. He even knew when to put on his opponent's jersey, literally in the case of his personal backing for the South African rugby team, previously seen by many black South Africans as the epitome of white dominance. In his book on Mandela's leadership, Richard Stengel also said that Mandela recognised the importance of looking the part, knowing your opponent and playing the long game.[20] Good diplomats recognise that there is an element of theatre to what they do.

As well as needing to be accessible, flexible, culturally aware and able to improvise, diplomats also have to eat and drink for their countries. Diplomatic dinners and receptions remain an art form. At many official dinners, the *placement* determines who sits where, with feathers ruffled and snubs nurtured for years where necessary. Sir Christopher Meyer calls the effort to get this right 'one of the most sublime arts of diplomacy'. Lord Carrington, when British High Commissioner in Australia, observed one diplomatic counterpart refuse to eat his food because of his irritation at his position at the table – 'but only his first course, for he was extremely greedy'.[21]

Discussion at such dinners can be lively and meaningful, but it can at times also be more than usually stultifying. Diplomats are expected to soak this up, wearily. In R. G. Feltham's guide to diplomacy given to my intake of Foreign Office diplomats, we were encouraged to 'engage the lady on either side of you equally, regardless of their relative charm or vivacity'.[22] I still think of this whenever there is an obvious gulf in vivacity between my dinner companions and the next course looms.

There is no doubt that food, and especially drink, makes it much easier to do business, as it does in the private sector. As the Marquis de Sade observed (though his objectives were rarely strictly diplomatic), 'conversation, like certain portions of the anatomy, always runs more smoothly when lubricated'.[23] The normally teetotal President Sarkozy gave a notoriously squiffy press conference after being repeatedly toasted with vodka by Putin. Stalin reportedly substituted his vodka for water in order to stay sober long enough to outwit his opponents. Churchill's ability to work during and after imbibing enormous quantities of alcohol helped to forge the diplomatic alliances necessary to win the Second World War and create a new world order. No diplomatic handbook suggests that mild alcoholism is a prerequisite to effective statecraft, but perhaps a little of Churchill lives on in the *Sun*'s August 2014 claim that British diplomats spent a 'scandalous' £16,137 on cigars in the previous year – 'Are you Havana laugh?', the newspaper wondered.

Every diplomat has stories of eating weird and wonderful dishes at such dinners. According to Foreign Office folklore, the Queen gamely tucked into a bat in South America, and a variation of rat in the Pacific. Many of us in the Middle East have been given the dubious honour of eating the sheep's eye when its head is served. I once confused a chef at a function in Africa by asking for a cappuccino. After great debate in the kitchen, and several anxious returns to the table, I was gingerly offered a much less satisfying cup of tuna, while the entire hotel staff gathered to watch. When governor of Hong Kong, Chris Patten was at a banquet for the World Wildlife Fund mission to promote conservation at which he was perplexed to see bears' paws served. I once persuaded Gordon Brown to try a Japanese meal, but the culinary experiment was aborted after he ate an entire bowl of wasabi in one go. Fondue with President Sarkozy and Carla Bruni was an adventure. Prime Minister Berlusconi would only serve dishes coloured in the red, white and green of the Italian flag. The ice cream and pasta were more palatable than the bread.

Once the *placement* is navigated, cutlery creates plenty of potential for awkwardness. Stalin used to think that Churchill had the place settings made especially complicated in order to gain a tactical advantage over him, a feeling probably shared by many guests at state banquets. We used to judge the Chinese reaction to our meetings not by the number of courses served at the subsequent dinner but by how easy or hard they made it for us to eat them all. After a particularly tough discussion on climate change, few of the British diplomats present succeeded in getting past the second course.

There is no reason to let all of that go. We all still need to eat. But this is a global race, and we can't spend our time indulging in pointless triviality or seeing the dinner as more important than the dialogue it allows. As Chris Patten observes on diplomatic dinners, 'I think there is a certain amount of tosh talked about this, principally by those who confuse foreign policy with being nice to foreigners.'[24] Rightly, we do now need to show that every truffle has a tangible effect on national interests. Most do. But we also need to avoid getting trapped in functions that no longer generate influence or information.

Harold Nicolson in 1961 captured, deliciously, the traditional national day event – 'these parties tend to degenerate into stagnant pools in which the same old carp circle round and round gazing at each other with lacklustre eyes'.[25] I have been at plenty of those. Diplomatic receptions are of course not as glittering as the popular stereotype suggests. Some well-placed observers even characterise them as 'cheap wine, plastic cups and sponsorship by easyJet'.[26]

Perhaps the best advice for diplomats in any era is in a letter written in 1813 by James Harris, the first Earl of Malmesbury – a former ambassador to Russia, Prussia and France – to Lord Camden, with advice for a nephew shortly to start a diplomatic career. The earl captures a long history of diplomatic apprenticeship in suggesting that 'the best school will be the advantage he will derive from his own observations'. But he offers some sage words nonetheless:

> The first and best advice I can give a young man on entering this career, is to listen, not to talk at least, not more than is necessary to induce others to talk. I have in the course of my life, by endeavouring to follow this method, drawn from my opponents much information, and concealed from them my own views, much more than by the employment of spies or money ...
>
> To be very cautious in any country, or at any court, of such as, on your first arrival, appear the most eager to make your acquaintance and communicate their ideas to you. I have ever found their professions insincere, and their intelligence false. They have been the first I have wished to shake off, whenever I have been so imprudent as to give them credit for sincerity. They are either persons who are not considered or respected in their own country, or are put about you to entrap and circumvent you as newly arrived ...
>
> Never to attempt to export English habits and manners, but to conform as far as possible to those of the country where you reside, to do this even in the most trivial things, to learn to speak their language, and never to sneer at what may strike you as singular and absurd. Nothing goes to conciliate so much, or to amalgamate you more cordially with its inhabitants, as this very easy sacrifice of your national prejudices to theirs ...
>
> Not to be carried away by any real or supposed distinctions from the sovereign at whose Court you reside, or to imagine,

because he may say a few more commonplace sentences to you than to your colleagues, that he entertains a special personal predilection for you, or is more disposed to favour the views and interests of your Court than if he did not notice you at all. This is a species of royal stage-trick, often practised, and for which it is right to be prepared ...

In ministerial conferences, to exert every effort of memory to carry away faithfully and correctly what you hear (what you say in them yourself you will not forget); and, in drawing your report, to be most careful it should be faithful and correct. I dwell the more on this (seemingly a useless hint) because it is a most seducing temptation, and one to which we often give way almost unconsciously, in order to give a better turn to a phrase, or to enhance our skill in negotiation; but we must remember we mislead and deceive our Government by it.[27]

These are points that should resonate with any modern diplomat too captivated by the sound of his or her voice, too beguiled by the flattery of diplomatic groupies, too condescending about the customs of their host country, too seduced by a few kind words from a leader, or too ready to sex up his or her reports.

From Malmesbury to Mandela, the most important diplomatic skills can be distilled to tact, curiosity, courage and the ability to get on with anyone and eat anything. The rest is detail. Stripped of the diplomatic baggage, *naked diplomacy* must hold fast to those qualities. Yet it cannot be static, nor a rarefied and impenetrable cult. Instead it must constantly evolve, and draw from the best of the trades with which it increasingly finds itself in competition.

The history of diplomacy helps us understand what makes it such a vital profession, and the essentials of the craft. But this is not an academic exercise. Can diplomacy cope with the Digital

Age, with disruption on an unprecedented scale, and with the opportunities and challenges that come with a hyper-connected world?

PART TWO

Statecraft and Streetcraft: Power and Diplomacy in a Connected World

iDiplomacy:
Devices, Disruption and Data

All cultural change is essentially technologically driven.

William Gibson

Writing in 1961, against a backdrop of social change and the spectre of nuclear war, Harold Nicolson saw that the fundamentals on which the international politics that he knew had been built were shaky. The rules of the game – an elite talking to fellow elites in Europe about how to carve up the rest of the world – were changing. 'The old diplomacy was based on the creation of confidence, the acquisition of credit ... the old currency has been withdrawn ... we are now dealing in a new coinage.'[1]

Let's be in no doubt. The coinage of global politics is now digital.

Human progress is not about IQ but how we collaborate and exchange ideas. Innovation thrives on the ability of smart people to create and compete together. So the faster that we can communicate with people all over the world, the more amazing products and ideas we will be able to invent. The breakthroughs in the Industrial Revolution were the result of a combination of tiny tweaks by a series of inventors.[2] The Internet now allows cutting-edge innovators in Mumbai or Mombasa to connect the light

bulbs like never before, accelerating a process of stunning inter-
continental and intergenerational creativity. We are, in former
UK Foreign Secretary William Hague's words, in the networked
century. Our ability to succeed, compete and prosper will depend
more than ever before on the quality and quantity of our networks, and our ability to work them.

It is going to be a ride. By 2020, more than 50 billion
gadgets will be exchanging information on a continuous basis.
Al Gore predicts that 'there is no prior period of change that
remotely resembles what mankind is about to experience. We
have never gone through revolutionary change so pregnant with
peril and opportunity, nor experienced so many simultaneous
revolutions.'[3]

In an internal Microsoft memo in 1995, Bill Gates wrote that
'the Internet is a tidal wave. It changes the rules. It is an incredible opportunity as well as incredible challenge.' But it has proved
to be much bigger than that. As Google's Eric Schmidt now
describes it, 'The Internet is the first thing that humanity has
built that humanity doesn't understand, the largest experiment
in anarchy that we have ever had.'[4]

Already, the digital revolution has changed the world faster
than any previous technology. Weapons such as spears and axes
led to 200,000 years of hunter-gathering. Farming tools led to
8,000 years of agriculture. The Industrial Revolution set off 150
years of rapid technological and social change. It is seventy years
since mainframes arrived in academic and military institutions.
Fifty years since the arrival of the microprocessor. Twenty years
since personal computing started a mass migration of human
effort and attention towards digital. Twenty years since Sergei
Brin and Larry Page decided to name a search engine after the
googol, a 1 followed by 100 zeros. Twenty years since that Bill
Gates memo.

Today, more than 3 billion people are connected to the Internet. The number of Internet users has doubled in the last decade (in Britain, 36 million people use the Internet every day, double the figure in 2006).[5] The web is no longer for our downtime, but for all our time. These changes are astonishing. We have access not just to more information than we can process, but more than we can imagine.[6]

Respectable academic research from just ten years ago predicted that cars could never self-drive. Fifty years ago, a committee organised by the US National Academy of Sciences concluded that 'there is no immediate or predictable prospect of useful machine translation'. Now, Google Translate provides more translations in a day than all human translators do in a year. It is easy to scoff at the futurologists and soothsayers who have so often in history been wrong. But as Nobel Prize-winning geneticist Richard Smalley says, 'When a scientist says something is possible, they're probably underestimating how long it will take. If they say it is impossible, they're probably wrong.'[7]

And we're only just getting going. We have got used to the idea of that change as linear. The patterns show us – whether in regard to data, computer-chip advancement, global temperatures, portable telephone size – that change is now speeding up at a staggering and bewildering rate. Every area of life and work will now be opened up to disruption and automation. Digital technology has already transformed just about every industry – ask anyone who used to work in travel agencies, or a video rental, photography or record store. Historian Ian Morris has shown that in just a century we will go through the equivalent in technological transformation of the shift from cave paintings to nuclear weapons. We will feel overwhelmed and unable to keep up.

These trends will rip apart established states, ideas and professions. This creates two major challenges for diplomacy: managing the fallout; while retaining the trust needed to do so from an increasingly empowered and sceptical public. Furthermore, diplomacy is going to be disrupted at a time when it lacks resources, will and energy. We have seen that what it represents – states, hierarchies, the status quo – is becoming weaker. And meanwhile the challenges it needs to confront are becoming greater. Diplomats risk finding themselves in that most awkward of positions: thinking that they are in power long after the rest of the world has realised that they are not.

So in this part of the book, I want to look at what this means for the way power can be built and channelled in the Digital Age. What are the implications of our desire for connectivity and networks, and how can those in power become more responsive to those they serve? What are the challenges presented by the end of deference and the decline of trust? What are the essential and hard-won skills of negotiation and peacekeeping that mankind is going to need to get through the tumultuous period ahead.

But first I want to look at the specifics of how diplomacy itself will change in the next phase.

Let's not kid ourselves. Diplomats will never be the world's greatest technological innovators. But they must harvest and adapt the best ideas. The next wave of diplomatic innovation will be driven by big data. It will reshape how diplomats find and use information; how they deliver a service; and how they network and influence.

First, how will diplomats collect information? For the next decade, when asked the question 'where were you when you first heard x', the answer will probably be Twitter. More than 90% of data was created in the last two years. The Large Hadron Collider's computers could store an amount of music that would take me about 150,000 years to listen to. Being the recipient of enormous amounts of information is already a challenge for all of us.

Twenty years ago, telegrams from embassies would arrive in paper form, and pass slowly from hand to hand. Now many foreign ministries have enabled instantaneous communication, with multiple recipients receiving reports as soon as the author presses Send. The average UK diplomat now receives forty diplomatic telegrams a day, as opposed to five twenty years ago. Add to this an average of 200 internal emails and he or she is struggling to get away from the desk – even before going online where most of the rest of the world is.

So knowledge management is ripe for innovation. Few senior diplomats have handovers, and – thanks to WikiLeaks and time pressures – less and less of what we learn is written down in a way that our successors can use. When I meet contacts who have been around for several decades, they assume that I have in my suitcase their back catalogue or greatest hits – a distilled version of all their interactions with British diplomats over the years. This is very rarely the case. But new tools such as blockchain technology will allow the creation of databases that store and filter masses of data.

They will also allow news and public-opinion monitoring on a dramatically different scale. The idea is not new – governments, businesses and media have always tried to track and understand public opinion – but traditionally a diplomatic report would make grand claims about popular trends on the basis of two cocktail conversations and an editorial. Now we have the means to look for patterns about how people think in huge amounts of data. The task may seem overwhelming, but the tools, including sentiment analysis, are becoming more efficient.[8] The app 'Ushahidi' shows the potential. It originally used volunteers to map post-election violence in Kenya in 2008 through monitoring open-source material. Now it can process Twitter content in real time to help humanitarian organisations and NGOs respond to crises – locating those with greatest needs. Of course, big data does not have all the answers. Internet users are not yet representative of the overall population, especially in Asia and Africa. But as more people get online, it will become more representative of society and those answers will be easier to identify.

All that information is of course worthless unless you know what questions to ask the machine, and how to interpret the responses you get. Those who can curate, interpret, analyse and present it will wield disproportionate influence. To every compli-cated and entangled international issue there is always one answer which is simple, lucid and logical – but which is invariably wrong. Big data will not put diplomats out of business, if they can show that they have the imagination to identify insights, nuance and responses. We will need diplomats to stop us from drowning.

Even more exciting than accessing all this data will be the potential to use it to predict the future. Notoriously, US store Target knew that a woman was pregnant before she did based on her consumer choices. This can be applied to international rela-tions. The American academic Kalev Leetaru has used a new quantitative analytical method called 'culturomics' to retroac-tively predict the Arab Spring and pinpoint Bin Laden, using big-data analysis of media reporting.[9] We will be able to predict where conflict is likeliest, to measure trends in human society, and even to show the likely consequences of policy decisions. Effectively, this crowd-sources foreign policy trends. So, for exam-ple, when we talk of 'rising sectarianism' or other changes, we can now do so with genuine authority.

We can't predict the future yet, of course. Human agency, flukes and cock-ups will all continue to play their parts. But there are more powerful historical forces at work than human agency alone. The ability to mine data in much greater detail gives us for the first time the power to better understand those forces. War rooms in ministries will be staffed with people able to track comment and sentiment that influences national interests. In what ways do people's views of our national brand change, why, and what impact does this have on our core business of security and prosperity?

To some, this may seem sinister. In the wrong hands, it is. We should not open the door to industrial-scale spookery. It is important that we focus on the data that people produce for wider consumption – Facebook, Twitter, etc. – rather than their private information. As I will argue, governments will need to do more to win the argument that they are to be trusted to use all this data wisely. But the reality is that they will have no choice but to do so. Our new opponents aren't constrained by conventions and silos. If we want to seriously compete, nor should we be.

Vitally, the telescope won't be pointing in only one direction. The public will be able to use new technology to keep a closer eye on those in power who are using it. And the content that diplomats themselves produce will help define and recruit them. Companies are already using big-data curators to screen applicants based on their digital footprint. There will still be a need to see if a personality and skill set is right, but this can be supplemented by a more accurate picture of ambassadorial suitability than a one-hour interview and a subjective CV. Does the candidate understand how technology influences the world around them, and what is their contribution to that debate? I would think twice about hiring anyone who was on Twitter, and check their posts carefully. But I would not hire anyone who wasn't on it at all.

Digital technology, and the masses of data it generates, should also make government better at discovering and delivering what people want from it. McKinsey assess that better use of big data by the US health-care sector alone could save $300 billion a year.[10] In 2009, Google claimed to have developed a system to track – by crunching search terms – the spread of influenza through the US without a single medical check-up and faster than the Center for Disease Control and Prevention.

Government monopolies over services such as passports and visas mean that most countries and embassies have not innovated in these areas as fast as we would have done had we been fighting for the space. Yet failures in these areas have a cost. Businesses take their investment elsewhere if they are unable to secure a visa with speed, dignity and efficiency. The countries that are able to innovate fastest to respond to evolving customer expectations will give their businesses and tourist trade a distinct market advantage.

So any serious foreign ministry is going to have to understand the revolution in consumer power, and rising expectations. Social media allows people unprecedented opportunities to share, compare and rate their experiences. They want faster and more personal service. A business used to instant and personalised online responses is not going to wait four weeks and complete multiple forms to secure a government service. An individual visiting a government website is not going to stay on it for long if it is clunky or standardised. We need to design public services in a way that serves the public. This means cutting out the layers, and directly connecting people with the service that they need.

Technological change can also make contingency planning for crises less opaque and amateurish. For example, we could have the ability to know – if they agree – how many people are in Tunisia at any one time, and (through location technology) where they are. This would make an evacuation much easier to plan and execute.

Some non-digital natives will feel left behind by these changes. But we would be mad not to take maximum advantage of these new tools where the benefits are so clear. Diplomats will need to take their services to people, not wait for them to come to them. When a businesswoman arrives in Ghana, she should receive information about how to get help, an offer of what the high commission does, an invitation to get in touch. When a tourist arrives, he should receive a package on how to get help if needed, and advice on where to go. If he is moving into sensitive areas, he should receive a message on his phone telling him that.

Can diplomacy even be automated? Some critics would argue that many diplomats are already robots. Everything that diplomats do will have to pass the test on whether it can be done by new tools. Can a computer generate a fairer deal on climate change or energy, say, than diplomats? Can a machine write a better press summary, or issue a visa faster and more fairly? Like every profession, diplomats will need to be honest as to what can be done better by computers, and focus all their energies on retaining a market lead on what can't. As Jarvis Cocker sang in the Pulp song 'Mis-shapes', 'We'll use the one thing we've got more of, that's our minds.'

Just as we shouldn't need detailed plans to tell us how to speak or write, it will become unnecessary in a decade to have plans to tell us how to digitise. Foreign ministries will need to establish staff placements at technology companies rather than businesses or NGOs. They should have a recruitment blitz of Bletchley Park proportions, before the disruptive competition hires all the brain-power. Governments will need to think of technology as an arms race with their opponents.

Greater digitisation also changes the nature of government, dramatically. It should make it smaller, more accessible, responsive and fleet-footed. That is good for government. It is excellent for diplomacy. Bring it on.

But all this technology and transparency is going to have massive implications for the public's trust in authority, and in particular for one craft that has always been central to diplomacy – secrecy. No area of foreign policy will be hit as hard as that beguiling, seductive and normally misunderstood aspect of state-craft: espionage.

The End of Secrecy?
Assange, Snowden and the Death of Bond

Jim: Are you telling me the Foreign Office is keeping
something from me.
Bernard: Yes.
Jim: Well, what?
Bernard: Well I don't know, they're keeping it from me too.
Jim: How do you know?
Bernard: I don't know.
Jim: You just said that the Foreign Office is keeping something
from me. How do you know if you don't know?
Bernard: I don't know specifically what, Prime Minister, but I
do know that the Foreign Office keeps everything from
everybody. It's normal practice.

Yes, Prime Minister, 'A Victory for Democracy',
Antony Jay and Jonathan Lynn

In one of the later scenes of *Skyfall*, James Bond pounds through
the Whitehall traffic to reach a committee room in which his
boss, M, is being grilled by parliamentarians. Unknown to her
and the MPs, their lives are in severe danger. Pressed for greater
transparency, M tells the committee that, 'Our enemies are no
longer known to us. They do not exist on a map. They're not

nations, they're individuals ... Our world is not more transparent now, it's more opaque. It's in the shadows.'

Our enemies no longer identify themselves with a helpful monologue or an underwater hideout. Of course, Bond gets there just in time to save M from the killer, and – indirectly – from the committee's suggestion that the spies are obsolete Cold War relics, unfit for the modern age. Point made.

Secrecy has always been an essential element of diplomacy. Diplomats have always pretended to be spies and spies pretended to be diplomats. Indeed, as a recently serving diplomat, there are – rightly – very clear limits on what I can discuss in this book. Experts have checked it carefully to ensure that there is no information that breaches the Official Secrets Act, nor that reveals confidential advice to ministers. Ironically, this is a process I used to help carry out.

Diplomats have also always spied on each other. Envoys like ploys and toys. They have throughout history sought to gain competitive advantage, to understand what their opponents are thinking, and to spot emerging threats. Many of the original embassies were often just buildings in which spies could base themselves undetected.

Innovation in espionage has often been driven by military necessity. Greek historian Herodotus thought the Greek victory at Thermopylae was because the Greeks had developed a form of 'secret writing': a Greek in Persia, Demaratus, had discovered that Xerxes was preparing a surprise attack and had warned Sparta. Ancient Egypt also had a sophisticated spying system. Espionage features in the *Iliad* – Odysseus somehow fooling the Trojans with his horse, condemning them to be remembered for immense naivety. In the Old Testament, King Joshua sends spies to case Jericho before he attacks it. The prophet Moses could even claim that God had instructed him to spy on his opponents in

Canaan (some serious political cover). The Chinese diplomat sliced up in my preface would have read Sun Tzu's treatise on deception and intelligence.

In many cases, spying networks, such as the one run by Sir Francis Walsingham under Queen Elizabeth I, preceded foreign services. In his 1716 handbook for statesmen, French diplomat François de Callières called secrecy 'the indispensable weapon of negotiation'. Renaissance diplomats recognised that their role involved a public element of representing their monarch, and a private element relying on discretion and confidentiality. There was no doubt which element they spent most energy on.

This remained very much the case during the seventeenth century – Abraham de Wicquefort noted that an ambassador is on the one hand 'a messenger of peace' while on the other 'an honourable spy'. In his massive guide to diplomacy he lists countless secret missions and meetings between the royal courts of Europe, including in the preparation of the key treaties of Münster, the Pyrenees and Ryswick. Every great European power would try to intercept and read correspondence between ambassadors and their hosts, with the Secret Office being created in 1653 in England to break the seals on diplomatic mail. Ambassadors would use secret inks or codes to try to evade oversight, and royal courts began to be accompanied by families of cryptographers.

The twentieth century's great wars moved spying from the individual derring-do or subterfuge of the likes of Mata Hari to the more sophisticated effort to control what might now be called big data, for example through the Enigma code-breaking machine at Bletchley Park. In an age of more clearly demarcated state/state conflict, civil libertarians do not appear to have been as worried then as now about how that information was collected, secured and used.

The two biggest recent challenges to trust in statecraft and espionage have come from Julian Assange and Edward Snowden. Assange and his WikiLeaks insurgents have tracked down and released masses of mainly US government confidential information. They do this without discrimination, believing that everything should be out there for examination. Meanwhile, whistle-blowing US intelligence analyst Snowden lifted the lid on what he claimed were systematic efforts by Western governments to monitor the communications of other governments, and even their own populations.

Has Assange made it harder to counter the threats we face as a global community? Many involved in diplomacy naturally believe so, arguing that the greatest threats to national security now come from modern-day Kim Philbys,[1] information anarchists motivated not by creed or crusade but by a desire to get back at the system. Fight the power. American science-fiction writer Bruce Sterling judges this to be seismic – 'Julian Assange hacked a superpower.'

The superpower agreed. In condemning WikiLeaks, US Secretary of State Hillary Clinton pulled no punches. 'It puts people's lives in danger, threatens our national security and undermines our efforts to work with other countries to solve shared problems ... disclosures like these tear at the fabric of the proper function of responsible government.'[2]

WikiLeaks also creates dangerous implications for the ability of diplomats and governments to protect confidential information and exchanges. Former British Foreign Secretary David Miliband argues that

the best diplomats, outside of formal negotiations, make a difference by being a transmission belt for valuable insights, born of real knowledge and good contacts in their host country. It is judgements, preferably expressed in memorable prose, that you most want from people on the ground. WikiLeaks makes that task tougher. It is one thing for people in politics or business to be wary of writing anything down, but quite another if they fear to say anything to foreign diplomats. And if ambassadors fear to tell it straight and loud to head office then we are all poorer.

In reality, though, WikiLeaks was less of a shock for diplomats than many observers have suggested. Everyone in diplomacy knows that detailed records are kept by their interlocutors. For those involved, the more honest, colourful and bold that these reports are, the more useful. There is a danger that fear of disclosure makes them vanilla or substance-free. But, as Miliband also recognises, 'WikiLeaks is not the end of diplomacy, or of secrets. It will inject caution and care, but everyone wants to influence the Americans, and many people want to impress them, so they will go on talking to them.'[3] Indeed, some in the Middle East have said to me that WikiLeaks revealed the Americans to be more straightforward and honourable than they had expected or hoped.

WikiLeaks has indeed made diplomats more cautious. They are writing less down, especially online. Historians will have less to work with as a result. But maybe the way in which we give advice to leaders will change, and so future generations analysing our decisions will have different data sets. Those seeking greater transparency will press to see emails between officials, maybe even text (gulp) or WhatsApp messages. Maybe the thirty-year rule – under which public documents are disclosed in the UK – will disappear. Maybe someone will have hacked it all by then anyway.

WikiLeaks has given the public a greater insight into the workings of government. It has accelerated the process through which governments acknowledge the need for greater openness and transparency. It has embarrassed plenty of people, mainly American diplomats whose private views have been exposed, and their interlocutors who thought that they were sharing theirs in safety. But it has not fundamentally hacked diplomacy and government.

In fact, Edward Snowden's revelations were more damaging than those of WikiLeaks. Critics of Western governments claimed that the leaks of classified documents from the US National Security Agency revealed that American spies – and their British counterparts at GCHQ – now use the Internet to sweep up vast amounts of data from the digital trail people leave every day.

Snowden has therefore displaced Assange as the poster boy of the transparency movement. *Foreign Policy* magazine even put him top of the list of 2013 global thinkers. Michael Hayden, a former director of both the NSA and the CIA, suggests that 'Snowden has compromised an entire generation of investments in US tactics, techniques, and procedures. He represents the single greatest hemorrhaging of legitimate American secrets in the history of the Republic.'[4] He didn't mean it as a compliment.

The revelations of telephone surveillance certainly triggered public and media curiosity. Plus anger – some genuine, much synthetic – from leaders who believed that their privacy had been disturbed. But it did not change the fundamentals. Every leader knows that his or her phone is vulnerable to attack from foreign powers. In government I worked on the basis that mine was regularly targeted by at least six countries. It would often halt calls and play them back to me. Diplomats and leaders speaking on an open line are careful to discuss sensitive issues cryptically or not at all. Snowden's revelations therefore created a sense of public awkwardness for leaders in explaining this, especially to close allies. But they did not move the dial.

So maybe Snowden has not hacked diplomacy either? Perhaps he will get just a brief mention in the history books. What did we think intelligence agencies were doing? Spies spy, get over it.

I am evangelical about the need to shine a light into some of the darker corners of government, and to increase public awareness and oversight. But I don't want to live in WikiWorld, as a diplomat or a citizen. The ability to do some of our policymaking and diplomacy in secret will remain essential.

However, what Snowden and Assange have indisputably done is accelerate the loss of trust in traditional authority. Many in the media and public are more sceptical as to whether they can trust governments with the information those governments claim that they need. In fact, trust in all institutions is falling. An October 2015 YouGov survey catalogued declining British public confidence not just in journalists (down 29% in twelve years) and politicians, but also doctors (down 6%), police (down 18%) and teachers (down 9%). This is a dramatic shift in our relationship with authority.

Increased transparency changes the relationship between the governed and the governing. Will countries with less transparency gain or lose advantage? Who curates all this data, and how do we keep them honest? Benjamin Franklin said that 'Three may keep a secret, if two of them are dead.' Who do we now trust to keep our secrets, if anyone, and who should hold them to account?

Looking back on his life, Gabriel García Márquez concluded that 'all human beings have three lives: public, private, and secret. Secrecy is what is known, but not to everyone. Privacy is what allows us to keep what we know to ourselves.'[5] But the modern reality is that the boundaries between his definitions of secrecy and privacy are now being rapidly eroded. We are not far away from a context in which we have to ask the people with whom we are having dinner whether they are filming us on their wearable technology. We'll be in an age when nothing we say, even in what we used to call private, is off the record. That's a problem for diplomats – most of their work has tended to be off the record, protected by codes and laws, hidden from public sight.

It is positive, however, that Edward Snowden's revelations have accelerated a justified debate about surveillance and the Internet. Security agencies argue that they have to mine an ocean of data to identify the new threats from legitimate intelligence targets. This means sifting through information from those who aren't targets, in the way that a Bond-era spy looking for a SMERSH villain would cast his eyes over a crowd. As the former GCHQ director Sir Iain Lobban has put it, 'We're looking for the needle, not at the hay.'[6] Robert Hannigan, his successor, argues that US technology giants are becoming more reluctant – following Edward Snowden's whistle-blowing revelations – to cooperate with GCHQ, yet 'privacy has never been an absolute right', and US tech giants are 'the command-and-control networks of choice for terrorists and criminals'.[7] He is right that ISIL and other organised terror groups are using digital media in a more savvy and intelligent way than their predecessors, including al-Qaeda. Monitoring them is getting harder. But we have to be careful not to focus on the mechanism rather than the message. We did not ban the telephone when terrorists communicated by phone.

Many observers, and probably many practitioners of diplomacy, wish that we remained in the Age of Bond, a time when the trade was more glamorous and when it was clearer who was the enemy – he either spoke with an Eastern European accent or had a striking quirk. Ideally both, and an improbable lair. But we are no longer facing a comprehensible, if shifting, set of alliances that would have made sense to the crafters of the Congress of Vienna. Or indeed to Genghis Khan or Ug. Instead, diplomatic alliances are more fluid, issue-based, and flexible. And so are diplomatic enemies. Those we pay to protect our security argue that they can no longer do so simply by spying on states. They need to spy on individuals.

Meanwhile, public and media expectations of oversight of policymaking are increasing. Officials are more paranoid about leaks and inquiries than ever before – a generation of policymakers are scarred by the various Iraq inquiries, which seem to have been a constant feature of the last decade. The carefully drafted minute that looks brilliant and witty in the prime minister's red box will seem reckless to a parliamentary committee armed with hindsight and media outrage. There is quite rightly an intense interest in what advice goes to leaders, especially on issues relating to war and peace. Recent inquiries have shown that no one comes out with much credit when their real-time communications are put under an intense spotlight. In the past, a Private Secretary might put some additional personal advice in a Post-it note on top of a submission if they wanted to avoid becoming part of the public record. That's increasingly likely now. Advice also becomes less candid, and more cautious.

So, faced with this context in which there is legitimate public interest in greater transparency, but also a continued and evolving security threat, it will be necessary to establish clearer international guidelines that govern twenty-first-century espionage in democratic states. What might they be?

Firstly, clearer rules. Most of those involved in legitimate espionage genuinely want to know where the lines are. US intelligence chief Michael Hayden says, 'Just give me that political and legal guidance, and we'll go play hardball. We'll stay inside the box.'[8] This applies to new means of collecting intelligence too. As another former head of GCHQ, Sir David Omand, says: 'Democratic legitimacy demands that where new methods of intelligence-gathering and use are to be introduced they should be on a firm legal basis and rest on parliamentary and public understanding of what is involved.'⁹

Secondly, decent oversight. The need for secrecy cannot be a protection from scrutiny, or used to conceal mistakes. Trust cannot be taken for granted. Again, a senior civil servant in *Yes, Prime Minister* captures this well: 'Politicians are dependent on us to publicise their little triumphs, the Official Secrets Acts to conceal their daily disasters.' Liberal democracies do better when there are checks and balances, decent accountability and over-sight. The perception that those with access to secret information are manipulating it or misleading their own people is deeply corrosive. We need to find a system that allows the spies to do their jobs, while reassuring the public that they are pursuing the right people.

Thirdly, an understanding that we still need our intelligence services and those who negotiate in secret on our behalf, within a transparent set of objectives. Foreign policy should never be wholly secret, but negotiations must often be confidential. Those in the front line of protecting their countries from increas-ingly sophisticated terrorism need the tools and support to do their jobs. The new technological giants must be part of this discussion. They have to help set the guidelines for where freedom ends.

As trust erodes further, we also need greater willingness of those who lead intelligence and foreign policy work to defend it. This has long been the case in the US, where intelligence chiefs account for themselves in front of public sessions of oversight committees. The appearance of the three British intelligence chiefs – John Sawers of MI6, Iain Lobban of GCHQ and Andrew Parker of MI5 – in front of a parliamentary committee in November 2013 was rightly seen as a seismic moment, creating a frisson of excitement through the parliamentary and security correspondents. Up to this point, MI6 chiefs such as Richard Dearlove had appeared in front of parliamentary inquiries, such as Lord Hutton's into the intelligence preparations for the Iraq War, but behind a screen or hazily pixellated. For the first time, there in front of the public, three men with such responsibility for their safety could be seen. And they were – shock horror – pretty normal. Probably a bit more male and pale than the average citizen, but otherwise decent, serious officials with decent, serious jobs. They used phrases like 'lapping it up' in describing al-Qaeda's reactions to the Snowden revelations. They spoke with pride about their people. This was all positive and powerful. But the business still has its idiosyncrasies. Two days after this very public appearance, I mentioned John Sawers' name in an internal email, rather than referring to him as 'C' (as MI6 chiefs have always been called), and was reprimanded for undermining national security.*

How far are we from the first Twitter account for an intelligence chief? I suspect that it will come within the first six months of the first monarch joining Twitter (in person, rather than through a communications adviser). The CIA already has an official Twitter account, which it opened in June 2014 with uncharacteristic but impressive panache by tweeting that 'we can neither confirm nor deny that this is our first tweet'.

As intelligence chiefs and diplomatic mandarins fight for resources and relevance, like all of us they will also have to battle for public support and credibility. That will mean greater openness, not about their specific operations but about their objectives and oversight mechanisms. That allows the professionals to do their jobs – the shadows will still be there, and we will still need

---

* In 1932 Compton Mackenzie was fined under the Official Secrets Act for using 'C' in one of his books.

people to fight in them. It is not yet farewell, Mr Bond. But you'll need to earn our trust.

Those of us representing countries that claim to stand for freedoms also need to use these new tools to promote those freedoms much more aggressively online. Even without the pressures of such technological change, there is a strong case to be made for greater openness and transparency. President Obama set it out in Shanghai in 2009: 'The more freely information flows, the stronger the society becomes, because then citizens of countries around the world can hold their own governments accountable. They can begin to think for themselves. That generates new ideas. It encourages creativity.' The US, more than any other nation, has sought to use this new instrument to promote democratic values in other countries, whether through presidential YouTube messages to the Iranian people or energetic defence of the rights of free speech of bloggers facing greater restrictions. That must continue.

In the short term, this information free-for-all acts as a brake on the diplomatic flexibility of democratic leaders compared to their more dictatorial rivals. Every move by the US is heavily scrutinised, debated and exposed. The Freedom of Information Act in the UK has meant that advice becomes more cautious, and that officials spend a disproportionate amount of time managing information and responding to inquiries about what they are doing. Our opponents must chuckle. They no longer need armies of spies to expose our thinking – we do it for them. But we must hold our nerve. The response has to be to throw our openness back at them, building up coalitions for media and public freedoms in their own countries.

Any enlightened government should therefore be getting more people online. But the reality is that, of the 5 billion people who will become connected in the next decade, most will be in more repressive societies. Some states, such as Turkey, have already taken on Twitter directly. In Russia, pro-Putin oligarchs have forced more independent operators such as Pavel Durov out of control of large sections of the Internet. Dissident sites are blocked in an increasing number of countries, as are even sites such as Wikipedia and YouTube.

This repression is increasingly sophisticated and well resourced. Censors have always been ingenious and well funded. But for everyone trying to build a wall around the Internet, there are smart people building the Internet around their wall. Governments should support the effort to end Internet censorship in a decade.

Of course, this effort will be driven by activists and the Internet companies themselves, who have most to gain. The idealistic technology pioneers who designed the Internet saw it as a way to share information freely and without restraint. Sir Tim Berners-Lee famously declared after founding the World Wide Web that 'this is for everyone'. He must surely be right. We will have to fight hard to defend a single Internet that can benefit humanity as a whole, rather than one broken down by repressive states and censors.

The networked world has undermined traditional authority and hierarchy, destroying the claims of leaders and governments that they can control information. Everyone is now watching everyone, and the digital tools available to an increasing proportion of humanity will increasingly enable them to hold those watching them to account. These questions are bigger than the intelligence agencies involved.

So who runs the Internet?

Every three months a number of the Internet's fourteen keyholders meet in the US. Each has a key to a safety deposit box and a smartcard, which together contain the code that the Internet Corporation for Assigned Names and Numbers (ICANN) uses to maintain Internet security. Journalist James Ball describes the ceremony as 'one part *The Matrix* (the tech and security stuff) to two parts *The Office* (pretty much everything else)'.[10] No one can say who put ICANN in charge. In governance terms it is the Internet's equivalent of FIFA, though without the brown envelopes. It is an imperfect system, but no one has come up with a better one.

Meanwhile, an Internet Governance Forum (IGF) is meant to set the ground rules. But I suspect most Internet users have never heard of it, and do not see it as in any way representing them. The acronym-rich, process-dominated and jargon-heavy attempt to structure the Internet looks like trying to shut the door long after the horse has bolted. It is hard to see how either governments or the big technology firms will feel obliged to cooperate, let alone citizens.

Big data is going to be one of the most contested areas. With the right guidelines, we can use it to evaluate better how we live as a society, for example in assessing our levels of happiness. But science is already running into ethical dilemmas over big data. With the ability to search all tweets – which are after all public documents – they can ask more sophisticated questions. But what about the rights of those who have generated the tweets? Do they need to be consulted, as they might if they were photographed in a public place? Or have they forfeited that right by putting their material in the public domain?

On these huge questions, many activists have long dismissed 'the government' as some sort of monolithic, conservative block on freedom, captured by big business and traditional elites. Fight the system. But it should be increasingly obvious to anyone that, as power diffuses rapidly and digital-information transfer accelerates, governments have long lost anything vaguely resembling a monopoly on information and influence. We have seen that secrets are becoming harder to justify and harder to keep.

There will always of course be reactionary pockets of governments, and many are dominated by them. But increasingly in freer societies, those pockets simply do not call the shots. Policymaking is much more fluid, flat and free. Just as governments need to get past an elitist 'us and them' or 'we know best' view of society, so activists need to look again at which parts of government to work with and, yes, trust.

This can provide the basis for a serious debate about how society adapts to the Internet in a way that maximises liberty and transparency. Governments will need to show that they have sufficient safeguards in place for the data that they can and will need to collect. Individuals will need to lead the debate about how we shape the digital services we use.

These are fundamental questions. We can't just mooch through them. The Estonian president Toomas Hendrik Ilves has called for a 'John Locke of the Digital Age' to set the balance on the role of the state in defending freedoms and rights of citizens online. Sir Tim Berners-Lee has said that we need a 'Magna Carta for the Internet'. American poet (and retired cattle rancher) John Perry Barlow has produced a 'Declaration of Independence of Cyberspace', an attempt to establish an Internet nation, with its own community and identity.

Some countries are already trying. The Brazilian 'Statute of Liberty', a bill drafted with full public participation, sets out a 'Bill of Rights' or Internet constitution, safeguarding freedom of expression, limiting government collection of data and setting out the parameters of 'net neutrality'. But we are still some way off a set of global standards.

Technological bling and must-have gadgets aside, the answers to these questions on the balance between digital freedoms and oversight pre-date the digital era. We still need to understand where authority begins and ends; what issues fall under the rule of law; and how to balance the rights of individuals and communities. The Internet won't solve all our problems, but we can't win without it.

We behind the wall cannot dismiss or play down the views of those outside the wall. Hoarding information can be even more dangerous than sharing it. Government depends on the consent of the governed, and that demands trust. Security and rights must be two sides of the same coin.

We are living in the age of distrust. People are losing confidence in those in traditional positions of authority. So those who wish to exercise power will need to be more open, authentic, humble and responsive. To do that, they will need to get smarter about using the power they have. Or continue to watch it slipping through their fingers.

Building New Power:
Bombs, Books and Beckham

Diplomacy is the art of letting other people have your way.

Daniele Varè (1880–1956), Italian diplomat and author

As the Second World War raged across Europe, a diplomatic adviser approached Josef Stalin tentatively, as most people did.

Stalin despised diplomats, and indeed most people. He had no wish to understand diplomacy, which he saw as characterised by compromise and capitulation. Instead, Stalin wanted to understand power, so that he could have more of it.

Nevertheless, his nervous adviser wanted to make the case that the Soviet leader should stop repressing Catholics in order to reduce hostility to Russia in Europe. This would in turn help curry favour with the Vatican, aiding Russia's diplomatic strategy.

But Stalin was underwhelmed by the idea he need consider such a feeble compromise with the Vatican. The adviser was put back in his place as Uncle Joe exploded with rage: 'The pope? How many military divisions does he have?'

Throughout history, many leaders have seen power in this way: as the pure martial strength to conquer, intimidate and subdue. Across the contemporary Middle East, those such as the Assads in Syria, several Israeli prime ministers, Yasser Arafat, or the warlords of Lebanon, have viewed politics as the art of survival. They live by what journalist Tom Friedman calls 'Hama rules', after the Syrian town that President Hafez al-Assad levelled in 1982. When you have power, you use it. When you're strong and winning, why compromise? When you're weak and losing, why compromise?

The Vatican had no tanks. But, unlike Stalin's system and Stalin's statues, it is still standing. History is not always won by those with the biggest armies and economies. This century is the first where power is not founded on how many people your army can kill.

Of course, military might still matters. Wars are not going away anytime soon. A country unwilling or unable ever to use force gets pushed around. As nineteenth-century British jingoists sang of those they colonised, 'Whatever happens, we have got the Maxim gun and they have not.' As we have moved from hunter-gathering to the European Union – not a positive thing in the eyes of all Europeans, of course – conflicts along the way have often helped humanity increase our life expectancy and raised our collective living standards. (The Second World War accelerated the creation of the United Nations, the National Health Service and the liberation of women, for example.)

But this is easier for a statistician or historian to argue than anyone actually experiencing conflict and times of momentous change. There is limited patience from those who experienced the Arab Spring for the idea that the violent backlash against them was vindication that they were on the right side of history. Increasingly we also find that populations retain great affection for those serving in the military, but don't necessarily want them to fight. Sir Jeremy Greenstock, a former UK ambassador to the United Nations, sees this as due to the moral force of the concept of self-determination, the growing power of the people's voice, and increasing distaste for humanitarian consequences of warfare. It is also due to the evident limits of military power, as insurgencies in Afghanistan and Iraq have demonstrated. People tend not to want to be at war for long, and the willingness of Western populations to tolerate the deaths of soldiers is rapidly decreasing. Defence spending by non-NATO countries will be greater than that by NATO countries by 2021.

However, well-meaning diplomacy without the threat of war tends to fail. As President Theodore Roosevelt thundered, 'nothing could more promote iniquity for free and enlightened peoples than to render themselves powerless while leaving every despotism and barbarism armed ... righteousness unbacked by force is as wicked and more mischievous than force diverted from righteousness'.[1] Without the threat of hard power, diplomacy quickly becomes 'Speak loudly and carry a small stick.' 'We will not stand idly by' quickly becomes 'watch us standing idly by'. As the 2014 Russia/Ukraine crisis demonstrated, 'you must not invade your neighbour' becomes 'you should not invade your neighbour', and then becomes 'let's discuss how we can ensure that you don't invade another neighbour'. Traditional diplomacy often fell into the trap of assuming that silver-tongued ambassadors alone could prevent conflict – 'when dictatorship is harsh, beware our démarche' as the motto on many foreign ministries could have read. Former UK Foreign Secretary Jack Straw says the European Union often gets bullied because it lacks real hard power.

However, military power alone does not generate the results we want. We discovered in the first decade of the third millennium that you can't deliver democracy on the tip of a missile. Between 2009 and 2012, as US drone attacks increased, public support in Pakistan for US aid to militant areas dropped from 72% to 50%, while those regarding the US as an enemy rose from 64% to 74%.[2] Many people globally know as much about Guantanamo as the

Statue of Liberty. Even modern dictators who pose with muscles flexed on horseback have recognised that hard power alone is not enough.

We are not the first generation to make this discovery. Even the most brutal empires got it. Genghis Khan would have been unlikely to describe anything he did as soft, nor appoint a soft-power guru, but he realised that it was easier to maximise his own influence if people felt that they were better off with him than without him. The Romans were also weak when they forgot the importance of bread and circuses, relying on subjugation alone. Instead, Rome was at its strongest when it offered people a sense of magnetism (the early version of John F. Kennedy's and Ronald Reagan's references to American exceptionalism symbolised as a 'shining city on a hill', watched by the world). The Jewish rebels in Monty Python's *Life of Brian* debate 'What have the Romans ever done for us?', before cataloguing a long list of popular Roman innovations.

So modern power depends on offering something more sophisticated than force alone. It now requires a savvier combination of cultural and economic tools.

It should be a rule of modern diplomacy that a British embassy can never have too many pictures of David Beckham on the wall. Ditto Argentina and Messi, Portugal and Ronaldo. When you have individuals whose faces are known the world over, it is insane not to deploy them.

While I was in Beirut, we never missed the chance to fly the largest flag we could find over a Bond car, premiership footballer, or visiting celeb. This wasn't because we were star-struck (though perhaps we were a bit) – it gave us the best possible platform for our message about Britain's global role.

Our largest soft-power experiment in Lebanon was a massive 'Britweek' to mark the Queen's Diamond Jubilee in 2012. Over six days, with over sixty events, hundreds of thousands of participants and a £1 million budget – all raised from sponsors – we showcased a Britain that was modern, outward-looking and attractive. We threw a party for over 2,000 people, the first event at Beirut's iconic new marina. I gave my speech from the bow of a British super-yacht. Elsewhere in the city, we held a fashion show inspired by the Queen's style; a film festival; live cooking shows with chefs from the Dorchester; an art exhibition of Union Jacks; a concert of British music 'from Elgar to Adele' hosted by the Lebanese prime minister; Manchester City FC training sessions for kids; and exhibitions of touch-screen technology, British inventions and classic and modern British cars. A Lebanese brewer concocted a Jubilee beer, local design companies repackaged everything from ice creams to bags to taxis, and *Time Out* ran a special supplement. British Airways returned to Beirut. Wedgwood and Lush cosmetics opened branches.

We could not have hoped for better coverage across Lebanese and regional TV and newspapers. Our favourite piece was a generous editorial in *An-Nahar*, one of the top Arabic dailies, exhorting other embassies to follow the UK lead. I presented a Radio 1 show of the best British music. Online, our website saw a 43% increase in visits. A #Britweek hashtag was second only to the football throughout the week in Lebanon. I had a tweetup (sadly, virtual only) with Lebanese diva Haifa Wehbe ('the Middle East's Madonna') on British music.

Britweek was exhausting and exhilarating. It wasn't treaties, Ferrero Rocher or protocol. But it was diplomacy. And, in a less obvious way, it was modern power.

Of course, soft power – the Beckhams and the Beatles – is also insufficient on its own. Like hard power, it has its limits, as photos of jihadists drinking Pepsi in Levi's jeans remind us. On visits to universities in the Middle East, I am often harangued about Western cultural imperialism by students in Premiership football kits.

Instead, the most effective approach combines hard and soft power. The American political scientist Joseph Nye calls this smart power: 'a powerful blend of defense, diplomacy and development ... which underscores the necessity of a strong military, but also invests heavily in alliances, partnerships, and institutions of all levels to expand influence'.[3] Any government now needs to think far more strategically about how to harness that smart power. David Cameron describes Britain as 'the smart-power superpower'. The UK topped the table, put together using statistics and panel scores, in 2012, on the back of the London Olympics, and came second to Germany in 2013.[4] The US won in 2014. This is a competition that should matter, and not just to diplomats.

Like soft power, the concept is a new phrase rather than a new idea: the modern version of Roosevelt's 'Speak softly and carry a big stick.' Smart power is basically common-sense diplomacy, albeit using new ways of working. Nye's idea got as much attention as it did because of its place and time – a rejection of the neocon approach of the George W. Bush administration and its cheerleaders.

So how do nation states harness their magnetic power in the Digital Age? In my experience, it comes down to three ideas: having a strong national story; knowing how to tell it; and knowing how and when to mix the tools at your disposal.[5]

Firstly, know thyself. A nation needs to tell a good story.

That story is most effective when it is aspirational, inclusive, and doesn't rely only on killing people from other nations. It makes it easier to persuade others to support our agenda, on the basis that it is theirs too. It makes it simpler to persuade others to share our values, because those values work for them too. And it makes it more likely that they buy our goods, because they want them too.

Defining the story is easier said than done. But as Professor Simon Anholt is right to ask, 'If the hand of God should accidentally slip on the celestial keyboard tomorrow and hit delete and Britain went, who would notice and why?' Scottish film director Danny Boyle's brilliant telling of Britain's island story during the 2012 Olympics opening ceremony was an attempt to answer that question. As a result, it moved many of us to tears, and a small number of the usual suspects to rage. History is rightly contested, and any attempt to define a nation even more so. The national message does not need to be sophisticated or detailed, but it does have to be something that people can buy in to, and that other countries can take as an authentic and attractive vision. Sometimes others will define it for us, for better or worse.

In 2005, the UK tried to build a narrative around creativity, innovation and quality. In the 1990s, the 'Cool Britannia' campaign was much derided and parodied, but captured a sense of why Britain was climbing the soft-power league. More recently, the 'GREAT Britain' campaign developed both these ideas to highlight the key national features we want to project: green, technology, business, creativity, sport. The government estimates that it has added £500 million to the tourism economy. Other countries have their own narratives. China's 'peaceful growth' attempts to place its recent rapid development in a broader context. France has a hard-fought national brand of liberty, equality and fraternity.

Successful country branding uses stereotypes and national symbols rather than fights them, recognising that people want some familiarity. The British royal family understand the importance of their brand (though they would be horrified to hear it described in that way): 'The Firm' has put powerful symbols in place, established a clear story about itself and its place in society, and works relentlessly to reinforce that, and neutralise challenges to it.

In some of my blog posts and speeches in Beirut, I argued that Lebanon lacked such a binding narrative. I tried to write about what a future Lebanon could look like, arguing that to get through the tunnel we had to see the light at the end of it. The danger is that without such a national story, however aspirational or vague, it is harder to keep its fragments glued together.

The second stage in harnessing magnetic power is understanding *how* to tell that story.

Promotion of the national brand will be more credible when carried by sportsmen, artists, royals or businesses, most importantly by people. It is often easier to promote modern British music rather than traditional British values, or the power of Premiership football rather than our position on human rights. Diplomats have to draw on the power of those who can best promote the national brand, while avoiding looking like an awkward uncle dancing at a wedding. Building soft power has to be, in the words of Martin Davidson, the former British Council head, a 'slow-burn activity'.

Conchita Wurst, Austria's transvestite winner of the Eurovision song contest in 2014, a glorious cross between Shirley Bassey and Russell Brand, did more for its reputation as an open and liberal country than years of government speeches and press releases. The Nobel Peace Prize will keep Norway near the top of the soft power league table as long as leaders aspire to win it. The 2014 World Cup in Brazil had a huge impact on Brazil's reputation, for better or worse.

To survive in the digital jungle, organisations need a strong 'big picture' message, underpinning the entire effort and providing a framework for individual announcements, themes and campaigns. So, for example, British foreign policy is about making our country safer, and creating jobs and growth. American foreign policy is about projecting global power in a way that makes Americans more secure.

This then creates space for more tactical core messages. In Britain's case – what do we do to promote national security and prosperity? How do we protect our people? In America's case, how is US policy in Cuba or Congo helping to make someone in Connecticut more secure? Tools such as Twitter or Facebook are important, but the message matters more than the medium.

Nations must build trust. Thus Peter Horrocks, former director of the World Service, says that the BBC is 'no longer people in London saying "This is how the world is" to people around the world. It is a dialogue; it is a debate.'[6] It deliberately sets out to be a global institution rather than a British one. The British Museum calls itself 'a museum of the world, for the world'. The English Premier League is the most international in the world, and there-fore the most followed and the richest. Some managers even see themselves as more powerful than politicians. I remember some-one asking Arsenal manager Arsène Wenger if he was pleased to be meeting Gordon Brown and Nicolas Sarkozy when we held a summit at the club's Emirates Stadium. His response, only partly tongue-in-cheek, was: 'They are meeting me.'

So countries have to promote the national brand in a coherent and punchy way. Yet most still devote too little promoting their influence and attraction. Former US Defense Secretary Robert Gates, who called himself a dove in uniform, recognises that 'The United States had to change from exporting fear to inspiring opti-mism and hope.'[7] But the United States spends less than the annual advertising budget of some multinational companies to communicate America's vision to the rest of the world.[8]

Many emerging economies – Brazil, Russia, China – are not making the same mistake, and are now investing massively in media, cultural institutes and scholarships. TV station Russia Today's annual budget is over $700 million, and China spends over $2 billion a year on China Central Television and the Xinhua News Agency. In the last decade China has set up over 400 Confucius Centres (promoting Chinese language and culture) around the world, over 100 of which are in America. June Liu Yunshan, the official in charge of the network, describes them as 'spiritual high-speed rail'.

Governments can and should do more to focus the instruments directly under their control. This starts with greater coherence between development, defence and foreign affairs ministries. Overseas aid should not be tied to foreign policy outcomes, but should amplify a country's smart power. The fact that Britain funded all the schoolbooks in Lebanon gave me much more political credibility and access. When navies help deliver humanitarian aid following natural disasters, it increases the attraction of their government. Likewise, when diplomats secure and use influence, it is easier to deliver policy changes that help deliver development. There will naturally be tensions between these three arms of overseas work, but they must be creative tensions.

Any power strategy must also acknowledge that those it is trying to influence are shaped by a different set of narratives, values and beliefs. I frequently bounced into classrooms in the Middle East to talk about British creativity, openness and innovation. Yet what the class saw was the great-grandson of Arthur Balfour, whose declaration is seen as having laid the basis for the Arab world's humiliation. Or the grandson of Mark Sykes, whose redrawing, with Picot, of the Middle East's twentieth-century borders is often seen in the region as having created every subsequent problem.[9] They see serious imperial baggage.

Of course, we all have baggage. We can't wish it away. If we do not acknowledge it, we come across as arrogant, or cultural imperialists. After all, in the Middle East, I engage constructively, you meddle persistently, he is an arrogant neo-imperialist aggressor. Arabic has the same word for intervention and interference. We have to try to see ourselves as others see us, but not be defined, or knocked off balance by that.

So new power is more likely to work when we can show people that we are genuinely on their side. In the Middle East, the majority of those who joined the Arab revolutions in 2011 did so not just because they wanted democratic institutions, but because they sought their *own* version of freedom, justice and opportunity. When we made our support just about their right to live exactly like we did, we lost their attention.

A large part of our media effort in Beirut was to put these historical episodes in a wider context, for example explaining the role of other Brits, such as my wartime predecessor Edward Spears, who did so much for Lebanese independence, albeit with a certain amount of perfidy. There is no point in simply ignoring or dismissing the baggage, given that many who we need to engage cannot see past it. The same applies to other former colonial powers, and to newer global actors. US soft power, from McDonald's to music, has immense strength. But throughout the Middle East it is still accompanied by great suspicion of US foreign policy.

Unshakeable myths can also now be created in hours rather than over decades – and diplomats will need to be even more fleet-footed in confronting them. As Mark Twain said, 'A lie can travel halfway around the world while the truth is putting on its shoes.' Modern governments and their diplomats have to be agile in preventing it from doing so.

As nations weigh up their comparative advantages in the global power race, any negotiator, business or diplomatic, can confirm the advantage that they are given when discussions are conducted in their language.

For the next hundred years, at least, English-speaking nations have that advantage. For anyone who wants to succeed in the twenty-first century, English is the language of information, education, opportunity, of the Internet and of globalisation. For traders and travellers, the language of Shakespeare, Facebook and the London and New York stock exchanges is not just useful – it is indispensable. The days when London sought to impose our language on the world are over – now the world is demanding our language, as I find when teaching at the campuses of Shanghai and Abu Dhabi.

In 2015, 2 billion people spoke English. There are already more conversations in English between people whose second language is English than there are between native speakers of English. Every year, 400,000 international students study in the UK. From 2006–14, the number of pupils in Lebanon learning English grew by 25%. The Lebanese have always been quick to react to changing circumstances. These statistics say that they have seen that English is the future. (And the Lebanese should know, of course – the Phoenicians helped give us our alphabet in the first place.)

A love of English-language teaching is in my DNA. My first job was as an English teacher, to Palestinian schoolchildren. My grandfather spent fifty years in Nigeria, promoting access to English education. And my father has devoted his life to making it easier and more fun for people to learn English. We must maintain our support to the English language profession. We must ensure that our immigration procedures do not push students to study elsewhere. And we must continue to back institutions such as the BBC World Service.

We can also do more to make English texts available to all. It is easier to find the seminal works in our literary canon translated into Catalan than Arabic. If we want to help reformers in the Middle East and elsewhere win the argument against the sword, we should do more to share with them the pen. Not through some sort of paternalistic or orientalist hangover, but to help others better understand the foundations on which we chose to construct our societies. It is then their choice what to choose for themselves.

I once brainstormed with Indian politician Rahul Gandhi about how best we could support India's need for English. I suggested a scheme through which we would send 1,000 young British graduates every year to train teachers and pupils in India. Rahul liked the concept, but derided the ambition – 'Send us 100,000 a year,' he said.

When it comes to projecting global power, the language skills also still matter too. Prussian master diplomat Otto van Bismarck understood this, warning colleagues to 'beware of Englishmen who speak French too well'. But not every ambassador has sought perfection in foreign languages. Asked why he spoke otherwise perfect French with such a strong English accent, Lord Bertie, the British ambassador to Paris during the First World War, replied: 'To remind them that I have the fleet behind me.'[10]

Each year the World Economic Forum compiles a list of essential skills. For 2015, creativity was ranked tenth. As artificial-intelligence technology becomes more sophisticated, WEF judge that creativity will become more important, so that by 2020 they predict it will rank third.

New power will also demand that creativity is prioritised. No ministry of foreign affairs has a Department for Creativity. Indeed the very idea is probably a contradiction in terms. Ronald Reagan joked that the nine most terrifying words in the English language were 'I'm from the government, and I'm here to help'; likewise, no one needs a civil servant to tell them how to be creative. Yet the countries that will succeed in the Digital Century will develop for themselves an outlook of restless pioneers, an ability to innovate, explore and engage the world around them. Historically, that is when they have always been strongest.

Marshalled effectively, the technology tsunami that I have described creates more space for that creativity and innovation. This is what makes the Internet so much more influential in social and developmental terms than, for example, television or the telephone. It is our creativity that sets us apart from computers, and what will give us a competitive edge in the global marketplace.

We also have to protect intellectual property rights if we are to preserve ingenuity and creativity. The counterfeiters have always been a fact of life (although they cannot replace the creators). In a world where anything can be copied, we need a digital Pantheon, a way of branding or kite-marking the genuinely innovative. Quality has to matter. The first attempt to define intellectual property was made in the UK, under Queen Elizabeth I. Globalisation and the Digital Age have made the issues more fiendishly complex and contested in the second Elizabethan Age than the first. Emerging economies such as China's are going to have to play fairer, and to be part of a rules-based system.

For the global economy to work, and for our national economies to compete, governments and diplomats need to agree those rules, create the conditions where the best thinkers and ideas can speed-date across national boundaries, and then stand back and let it happen.

Governments will need to send their diplomats where the innovation and ideas are, and ensure that our best innovators have constant access to the most creative ideas out there, and the tools and networks to benefit from them. They should be constantly scanning the horizon to see where the next innovation is. They should be much more creative in how they bring people together, and in how they use their convening power to drive growth. They need to chart the ways in which people are making connections within and between societies, and be present there, supporting and nurturing exchanges that contribute to the common good, that further genuine diplomacy in its purest form. In the Digital Age, diplomats will need to be able to capture and hold attention, interest, relevance and influence. As veteran diplomat Richard Holbrooke used to put it, 'attack the problem from every angle, and bring in unusual people'.

To help rediscover the pioneering mindset that we need in order to thrive in the coming period, embassies should also seek out and offer passports to top innovators and business people from overseas, and make the case for greater openness to those who can build our economy. I asked the Nigerian guard at the Jefferson Memorial in Washington why he had come to America. Without missing a beat, he said he was there to 'make money, think freely and work hard'. The points at which cultures are interacting and fusing are often the points of greatest potential and energy.

In the Digital Age, power is fluid, unpredictable and diverse. Those who wish to exercise it need to recognise that there are different muscles to flex and sometimes to use. Military power must be deployed sparingly, but never neglected – as President Theodore Roosevelt said, don't punch unless you have to, but when you do, never punch soft. But hard power alone is insufficient – effective modern power also requires that a nation's talent, creativity and cultural magnetism is put into battle. Governments need to marshal all the tools at their disposal.

Military power without soft power fails, and vice versa. You can't have one without the other. You need boots on the ground and books in the hand.

As power changes, there will be many snake-oil salesmen catching our attention with new ways of describing it. But it matters less whether you call it soft, smart, new or whatever the next catchy moniker is. What matters is that you call it power. And that you get out there and use it.

In the Digital Age, you will only be able to do that if you are able to connect.

Using New Power:
Only Connect

Only Connect the prose and the passion, and both will be
exalted, and human love will be seen at its highest. Live in
fragments no longer.

E. M. Forster, *Howards End* (1910)

The most effective and influential leaders have always mastered
the medium of their age to establish a meaningful connection
with the people on whom they relied to keep them in power:
Abraham Lincoln's speeches, Lenin's pamphlets, Churchill's
radio broadcasts.

But powerful communication in the Digital Age is different. It
will take more than a certain flair with a Twitter handle or a natty
blog. We crave authenticity. We are more sceptical, less trusting
of authority. So leaders, politicians and diplomats need to respond
with greater honesty about what they are trying to do, and how
that impacts people's lives. We want connection, not just connectivity.

One of the reasons for diplomacy's slow decline is that it has
failed to understand this. It is typified by French diplomat Jules
Cambon, who in 1931 lamented the dangers of media and popular interest in diplomacy: 'The activities of the press, and igno-

rance of a public that insists on being told everything, do not create an atmosphere favourable to prosecution of political designs.'[1]

He was right that the power of the media was set to sweep away many of the comfortable and previously impenetrable levels of secrecy surrounding politics and diplomacy. This transparency would be uncomfortable for many who had plied their trade, their 'political designs', behind the curtain. But he was wrong that it was bad for diplomacy.

Those in public life should now be anti-Cambons – should see the media as contributing to their wider purpose, not as an awkward distraction. They need to be in the arguments, to have a personal media profile, and to be thinking constantly about how to reach and influence the widest possible audience. Transparency now safeguards relevance more than it threatens it. This is not about narcissism or self-promotion. People have a right to expect authentic communication from the people they pay to represent them.

Yet too much diplomatic communication is patchy. There are moments of excellence, such as during the Kosovo campaign in the 1990s, when the public were given unprecedented insights into the conflict. But too often the effort to explain international relations is confused, patronising or amateurish. Many diplomatic channels have embraced the shift to digital but are sharing too much – hourly updates on what the ambassador is doing, and retweets of every mundane statement made by the ministry. Jonah Peretti, founder of BuzzFeed, cautions that brands are harmed when they give their audience content they don't want. As my grandmother would have said, if you've nothing good to say, say nothing.

The Digital Age presents other big challenges to powerful, authentic communication. The 24/7 news cycle destroys the ability to be strategic, exposes areas of weakness to opponents, and makes it harder to compete for attention for the business that actually matters. The London G20 summit in April 2009 – at the height of the world financial crisis – was one of the few international conferences in recent history that actually made a difference to people's lives. Yet it lasted a media cycle at most, and was rapidly overtaken – ironically by the resignation of a spin doctor, Damian McBride.

This reality makes it harder for leaders to set out a longer-term perspective, or to step out from the crush of events – we are all looking at our smartphones after the first thirty seconds. The public complains about sound bites, but that is increasingly all that we have time to absorb.

The reduced flash-to-bang time – from an event to coverage of it – for a major media story creates the sense of time speeding up. The pace can feel destabilising for policymakers just as it can feel empowering for everyone else. We reel from issue to issue, swamped by social media reactions, the addiction of the immediate, that don't wait for analysis or fact. We are heading towards 'One Big Now'.[2] Any journalist will now reflect the popular reaction, often through social media, as part of their initial report on a story. Communicators have to shape the argument before Google or Twitter shapes it for them.

I have a confession. I spent more of my time in Downing Street working on communications than diplomacy. I became a spin diplomat. It is striking how often we got it wrong, across administrations, thereby contributing to the decline of trust and confidence in the political class.

One origin of this problem was that much of our foreign policy effort was overshadowed by our underestimating a breaking media story, because we were too swept up in what we believed to be a more important global issue. Maybe we were right in policy terms in setting these priorities – we thought that avoiding conflict between India and Pakistan mattered more than the prime minister's view of the latest *Strictly Come Dancing* result – but the media, desperate to catch us off guard, rarely saw it that way.

So officials became more media savvy than our predecessors, always with a good story in the back pocket. We tried to sate the beast, to create or share stories that our press team could use to keep the travelling media happy. Often this would be small titbits about exchanges with leaders, the menu plans, and colour on the encounters to complement the more serious messages we wanted to get across. We would often set up an argument – normally at an EU summit – because the media liked a sense of a clash or confrontation. Several delegations did the same, most notably the French. My job in Downing Street often included deciding with foreign counterparts who needed to be seen to win each battle. This got harder as more international and domestic journalists started watching rival press conferences, quickly working out that we and the French had frequently set up completely separate arguments for our leaders to win.

As a result, the policy debate often became sidetracked by the need to focus on 'deliverables' – announcements designed, more in hope than expectation, to prevent the media from writing negative alternatives. We had to think more about the visuals of any meeting with foreign leaders, as demonstrated by our often grim experiences over meetings with successive US presidents. I would often spend as much time negotiating the type of press event as on the content of the meeting. The UK media focused on the former. The White House even took to calling senior UK journalists to tell them that they had not snubbed the UK. Undeterred, this tended then to be written up by the hacks as a 'non-denial denial'.

This pantomime rarely ensures the public get good information about what their representatives are doing. Often it created an unhealthy complicity between the media and leaders and their advisers. More often it stimulated hostile elements of the press to develop competing narratives. Our efforts to dictate the story were often patronising, and created an extra incentive for journalists to ignore our narrative and seek out their own. It means that officials learn that their value to ministers, and therefore their promotion, depends on delivering good headlines, not on executing policy effectively. It also means that government is paralysed by aversion to risk – the fear of failing the test of whether a policy will look good in the *Daily Mail*.

One man's propaganda is another man's spin is another man's public diplomacy strategy. But the sad reality is that this approach was not just bad communication; it was bad politics, bad government, and bad diplomacy. Understandably, it left people feeling disconnected.

If we are to reach for a more honest and authentic connection with the public, all that needs to change fast.

To start with, this means junking the jargon.

Diplomats are often a bit too good at making simple issues more complicated, more fudged, less transparent. In his book on Renaissance diplomacy, historian Garrett Mattingly notes with approval the 'platitudinous character' of the advice-to-ambassadors literature of the sixteenth and seventeenth centuries because 'the simple and difficult rules of any enduring art' always sound like platitudes.[3]

Sometimes fudge is necessary – Talleyrand was a master of the 'short and ideally unclear' agreement, drafted to ensure that everyone could explain it to their own constituencies in different ways. Diplomats in Brussels or New York remain brilliant at this, hence the way in which leaders can often all claim victory at the press conference after a European summit. This approach might work with thirsty journalists keen to write their copy and tuck into their *moules frites*, but it does not work for long.

So diplomats can too often talk about 'being unable to remain indifferent' to, for example, an execution or imprisonment of a human rights defender – a phrase that drips with indifference. I still hear ambassadors say things like, 'My country views, without satisfaction, the violation of our borders.' What? Diplomats can spend hours in international conferences debating whether to be 'concerned' or 'gravely concerned' about a massacre, while the militia involved continues the slaughter and the rest of the world carries on oblivious to the difference. They pump out bland statements saying that a situation is 'unacceptable' or 'intolerable', only to carry on accepting and tolerating it. Too many diplomatic declarations follow the tired formula 'Minister Jack and Ministre Jacques discussed a wide range of issues of mutual concern.' These are meaningless and fluffy platitudes – did anyone think they were meeting to discuss issues that weren't of mutual concern?

By reducing everything to such froth, those in power patronise and underestimate the public, who simply turn elsewhere for their information. So I love it when a diplomatic meeting is described more honestly, when a leader or ambassador says, 'Actually, it was a very tough meeting. I respect Russia's position but I profoundly disagree with it.'[4] In David Cameron's early days as prime minister, we were criticised for his candid comments on Pakistan/India and Gaza/Israel, and worried that we had got it wrong. But his more direct language has been proved right in both cases.

In 1951, the British contingent fighting in Korea found themselves under serious aerial attack. On the radio to the nearby US reinforcements, a wireless operator described this as 'a spot of trouble', a classic British understatement. The reinforcements did not come in force, because US commanders took the British description at face value. The British were routed. Never had Churchill's dictum about 'two nations divided by a common language' been more apt. Precision matters.

Sometimes a bit of diplomacy, in the sense of smoothing off the harder edges, can reduce tensions and avoid confrontation. But it can also often leave the observer or interlocutor confused, irritated or, worse, emboldened. Better to tell it how it is. Well-informed members of the public and media will become increasingly able to see the way in which different leaders use weasel words or tricks of translation. Likewise, deliberate diplomatic obfuscation, while it has its place, will become harder and harder as negotiators face intensified pressure to explain what they have agreed with greater clarity. Those in power need to remain relevant by presenting their work in a more accessible way.

When *Yes, Prime Minister*'s title character complains to his Civil Service aide that a draft statement says nothing, his Private Secretary thanks him. The public won't. By hiding behind platitudes, we are not put on the spot to explain what we're actually trying to do. By spending time debating whether we 'condemn' or 'are gravely concerned' we waste valuable hours that should be spent doing something about the issue that we condemn.

Of course, as language evolves, there is a risk of replacing the wrong language with the wrong language. Former UK ambassador in Rome, Sir Ivor Roberts, wrote caustically in his 2006 valedictory telegram of 'bullshit bingo' in the FCO: 'Wall Street management-speak ... discredited by the time it is introduced. Synergies, best practice, benchmarking ... roll out, stakeholder ... fit for purpose, are all prime candidates for a game of bullshit bingo, a substitute for clarity and succinctness.'

It did not used to matter as much if leaders were not carrying people with them. But as power continues to move towards the individual, those 'in power' will have to ensure that their message is connecting with the public. They have to remember for whom they are working.

And to what purpose. Winston Churchill knew this, of course. The wartime ambassador to Spain, Samuel Hoare, once made the mistake of protesting to Churchill that pressing Franco to release captured British pilots would jeopardise Hoare's warm bilateral relations with the Spanish government. Churchill blasted back, 'Stuff your diplomatic relations, what do you think they're for?'[5] These words should hang at the entrance of every foreign ministry. The objective of a diplomatic meeting should not be to leave everyone feeling warm, but to pursue the national interest. Finance ministries often understand this better than foreign ministries.

So for me the most infuriating phrase in diplomatic jargon is 'warm bilateral relations'. There is a sliding scale for measuring the warmth of a relationship that is only really understood by diplomats. Heaven forbid that relations become just 'cordial', 'businesslike', or that a meeting be 'candid' or 'full and frank'. The rough running order for descriptions of a diplomatic encounter is: excellent, productive, constructive, practical, warm, good, businesslike, cordial, full and frank, candid and difficult. In a separate category is a 'summons'. Given the diplomatic tendency to massive understatement, anything below 'cordial' implies a serious dust-up. 'Full and frank' probably means that punches were thrown. This is the kind of language that leads some to judge the quality of a meeting not by its content but by the length of the press conference or the official gifts exchanged.

'Warm relations' between countries are too often defined in terms of the number of visits, or feedback from courtiers. There is no league table of the warmth of our partnerships with other countries. There is no public opinion survey against which to rank changes in temperature. There is no way of saying whether our relations with Portugal are warmer than a year ago, although if you believe the telegrams most ambassadors send, relations everywhere are getting warmer and warmer. Ambassadors are not always the people best placed to judge the ebb and flow of the relationship, and certainly shouldn't mark their own homework.

Diplomacy of course depends on the quality of relationships you can build, particularly at the top. But these relationships must be for a purpose. Do they make the countries we represent more secure and more prosperous? How do they change the lives of those we represent? Are you making a meaningful connection?

So I always said in Beirut that it was not 'concern' I felt about the human cost of the war in Syria. It was outrage, frustration and a determination that we must stop it getting worse. It was not warmth I felt about what we can do to promote modern Britain in the Middle East, but passion and pride to wear the shirt. I was not in Lebanon to promote 'warm relations'. We were there to double trade, double the number of students learning English, and maximise tangible support for Lebanon's stability. Sometimes we succeeded, sometimes we failed. But we tried not to describe the effort in tired clichés.

This is not just a question of taste. My concern is that empty rhetoric and purposeless platitudes make politics even less connected to those it needs to engage. Leave that vacuum and it is filled with demagogues and extremists. Powerful political communication requires a change of mindset by those in authority.

*

New technology is an extraordinary opportunity to jump-start the connection between the public and public servants.

Increasingly, those in political life will have to use people's desire for connectivity rather than push against it – I now encourage people to fiddle with their phones when I am giving a speech rather than ask them to put them away. People want to play their part in finding solutions to problems, and technology makes that easier.

Content is now king. And good diplomats have never shied away from producing quality content themselves. Normally in the form of a diplomatic telegram, this was traditionally read by a handful of fellow diplomats. A recent UK Foreign Office innovation measured how many – or as it turned out to our disappointment, how few – colleagues read our internal reports. Now social media gives a means to amplify decent content at a much more influential scale. There should be no set rules on how we do this – individuals need to find their own tempo and their own voice. Governments have to recruit and empower digital natives to whom it comes naturally; and train and equip the rest of us.

New technology can even help us to crowdsource diplomacy, the ultimate in connectivity. Crowdfunding generated over $2.6 billion in 2012,[6] more than the budget of most foreign ministries. But the finance matters less than the possibility of making policy decisions more democratic and accountable. To at last empower the mob. Now that is a game changer – chaotic maybe, but as I'll argue later, the more that policymaking, including foreign policy, has been democratised, the better it has become.

Anyone seeking to connect with people and build influence using new digital tools needs to be authentic, engaging and purposeful. All three. Because authenticity and engagement without purpose equals eye-catching but meaningless stunts and slogans. You can get people's attention, but they won't necessarily listen to what you have to say afterwards. Much cute-cat social media does not need to be purposeful (and it would be a killjoy who suggests that it does), but a government's social media presence needs to add up to something more than follower numbers or Facebook likes.

I worry that an increasing amount of hashtag diplomacy falls into that category. It is a great way to get attention for an issue or campaign, but social media has to be a way of marshalling action, not a replacement for it. I've become increasingly frustrated by online campaigns showing solidarity for countries in conflict. They are wonderful in many ways, and the cause could not be more important, but I don't want people just to like a site or watch a YouTube video. I want them to be moved by their anger to actually do something, to contribute financially to a charity on the front line of the humanitarian response, or to lobby their government. We must avoid an era of armchair activism. As Chloe Dalton, a former special adviser to William Hague, puts it, 'No one has ever been saved by a hashtag.'

Authenticity and purpose without engagement equals Sending Out Stuff, transmitting without listening. Much political and business communication still falls into this trap. Digital diplomacy will also fail where all it means is putting hashtags in front of what you were already going to say. The trend in marketing is away from direct advertising towards telling brand stories in a more engaging way. It has to be a two-way street, and people want to talk to a person not an institution.

Engagement and purpose without authenticity equals insincerity. Sometimes I think it is worse for leaders to be on social media but faking, than not to be on it. Being too risk-averse is a risk. If you don't really care about football, your online avatar should not pretend to as a means of seeming more approachable – you will get caught out.

Governments, diplomats and others exploring social media should not get too hung up on which tools they use. In reality, it depends on the country they are working in, and personal preferences. Better to use the wrong tool authentically and effectively than the right tool insincerely and ineffectively. Again, the message matters more than the mode of communication. Let's not forget of course that many of today's shiniest and newest ideas and tools will quickly seem dated. Future books will sneer at the 'innovative' ideas here in the same way I have at diplomats who did not see the potential of the telephone or stirrup.

Public humiliation aside, there are growing threats from more online engagement: the smartphone through which I connect with people can also be the means by which terrorists track my movements. But the biggest risk is not to engage. The smartest businesses aren't debating this. They are just doing it.

So governments and diplomats need to go where people are, finding new ways to create online spaces, or public squares where we can engage and communicate. Political movements are doing this already. The Greek Pirate Party used Loomio to create almost 500 groups from municipal to national debating policy, breaking down the physical barriers to getting large groups of people in one place at a time. Those involved argue that such systems will replace representative democracy. People are much more likely to be influenced positively by direct, people-to-people connections than by anything that smells of government. Governments need to create space for those opportunities – for example by connecting school classrooms – and then stand back.

Communication that genuinely connects with people now also requires a campaigning approach. It is a journey not an event.

The best campaigns pick the right fights; create moments of jeopardy; and retain the flexibility to respond to events.

Big data and the democratisation of power will mean we need more people in government who are argumentative and challenging. Diplomats too often toil for hours, days, weeks or even months to seek consensus and agreement, crafting language that ensures people rub along. They see it as their role to be the lubricant in the machine, to ease tension and deliver compromise. They shy away from controversy. As Harold Macmillan, then Foreign Secretary, told Parliament in 1955, the diplomat is 'forever poised between the cliché and the indiscretion'.

Yet politicians set up dividing lines and arguments. They recognise the danger of vanilla communications where everyone says the same thing. I spent many hours writing speeches with prime ministers. Gordon Brown would hold long conference calls with key advisers to identify the crux of the argument. Emails would fly through the night as he honed in his own mind where the dividing lines lay. David Cameron would ask his speechwriters to identify the argument or constituency that they wanted him to take on. Both sought out the points of contention and divergence. By doing so, politicians are able to make their discourse not just more edgy and interesting, but more relevant. As any married couple will tell you, sometimes you need to have the argument. Diplomacy should not be about avoiding those arguments, just picking the right ones.

I tried to do this in Lebanon by redefining political divisions. While most think the country is divided on sectarian lines or by political party, I argued that the real dividing line in the twenty-first century was between those with the courage to coexist and those promoting division. The idea was to create 'are you with me or against me?' moments, which challenge listeners to engage, and to define themselves. A bit of controversy can often be the grit in the oyster.

The best campaigners also stimulate interest through creating moments of jeopardy. So in the run up to the G8 Gleneagles Summit of 2005, the public was encouraged to set tests for the leaders and to engage with them to press for delivery. At the G20 financial summit in London in 2009, the communications plan deliberately set out a sense that the world was at 'a minute to midnight', on the verge of a historic deal or failure. Crunch moments are more likely to get the attention of those who can put meaningful pressure on their leaders.

But this strategy carries risks if it is not authentic. There is only so often that the public can be told that a conference on agriculture or a trade mission to Uzbekistan is 'make or break'. Sometimes you need what Bono calls 'unusual coalitions' to deliver change. In developing the 'Make Poverty History' campaign, he pounded the corridors of Congress and the Senate, promoting the case for tackling inequality to the religious right. The shock value mobilised groups who would otherwise be neutral or acquiescent.

As part of such campaigns, authentic symbols can be more powerful than any politician. By celebrating Malala, whom the Taliban tried but failed to kill, campaigners did far more to promote women's rights than any leader could have done. We need to create heroes, not just victims.

I wanted to do this in Lebanon as part of our effort to counter inequality, in particular the mistreatment of migrant workers. So I swapped places for a day with an Ethiopian housekeeper, Kalkedan Nigusie. She joined me for a call to the interior minister and a press conference. I spent time cooking and cleaning. The photos went viral in Lebanon, allowing us to use the platform to raise awareness about new guidelines on treatment of foreign workers. But the key was that Kalkedan was front and centre. She could speak far more powerfully than me about the nature of the challenge. We put a face to the campaign and triggered dinner-table debates across the country.

Diplomats have huge convening power, which makes them well placed to galvanise campaigns but then step back and let others carry the message more effectively. An example was our work towards a 'One Lebanon' concert. At a moment of real vulnerability in Lebanon, as old divisions re-emerged due to the Syrian crisis, we put together a coalition of celebrities and activists to perform together for the first time, on a theme of youth 'United for Tomorrow'. Several divas, pin-ups, boy bands and comedians took the stage to reject sectarianism and divisive politics. Sunnis from the most violent part of Tripoli rapped about coexistence with Allawite neighbours. The largest cheer of the evening was for a hybrid of 'Ave Maria' and the Muslim call to prayer, sung by Sunni, Shia and Christian choirs.

This was broadcast live on prime-time Saturday night TV. Thousands of 'One Lebanon' wristbands were sold. Over a hundred youth activism organisations took part on the night, and the event was staffed by volunteers from throughout Lebanon. Our social media highlighted the contrast between the concert and failure of Lebanese politicians to agree a Cabinet; the resilience/talent on show; and the message sent to those taking Lebanon back towards violence and division, not least through a car bomb in Hermel that same day.

The concert tapped into a particularly Lebanese stream of sentimentality, schmaltz and national pride. A combination of Last Night of the Proms, _Les Misérables_ and Live Aid would not work everywhere or be to everyone's taste. Lebanese divas make Lebanese politicians seem straightforward. But the egos landed, and the messages on diversity, tolerance and unity were much more powerful coming from them.

Another example of the way that campaigners and diplomats can interact was the 2010 Cluster Munitions Convention. In No. 10 at the time, we spent as much time discussing tactics with relevant NGOs as we did with other governments. The team built a strategy around public pressure, aggressive lobbying by embassies, and carefully timed interventions. We exposed campaigners outside the negotiations, our main allies, to the nitty-gritty of debates inside the room, so that they could focus their interventions and lobbying of other countries.

Perhaps the best recent example of this more modern campaigning diplomacy was the 2014 conference on Preventing Sexual Violence in Conflict, hosted by British Foreign Secretary William Hague alongside Angelina Jolie. This was open to the public, and modelled at Hague's suggestion on the interactive aspects of a political party conference. It worked because there was a compelling campaign message, it engaged a much wider selection of the public than the average summit, and it had practical objectives. It was, as Hague's special adviser Arminka Helic explained to me, 'built from the ground up, starting out small, making sure each intervention had substance and purpose'. Plus a sprinkling of Jolie's stardust.

It is possible to imagine a future conference, say on climate change, where a world leader will be tweeting from inside the meeting in a way that builds pressure on his counterparts from their own public, all amplified by the more trusted voices, the Malalas and the Bonos, outside the room. This will break a few taboos, and ruffle some diplomatic feathers, but it is inevitable. Leaders will compete to get their interpretation of events across in real time. Fluid, interactive and exciting diplomacy.

The ability to ride waves is also increasingly important to authentic communication in the Digital Age. This requires flexibility. Campaigns were traditionally like super tankers – heading inexorably in one direction. Now they are more like sailing boats, needing to change tack when the wind changes, retaining the ability to be supple and agile. Good communication requires the courage to leave the campaign half planned for when the Internet suddenly throws up an issue that challenges preconceptions and assumptions. The most striking examples in international affairs have been the Kony campaign against child abduction by the Lord's Resistance Army in Uganda, the way that footage during the Arab Spring spread dissent from capital to capital like a fireball, and the shift in Western public attitudes to refugees as a result of a photo of the Syrian three-year-old boy Aylan Kurdi washed up on a Turkish beach. In all three cases, policymakers, commentators and campaigners were caught off guard by the surge in public engagement. They were running to catch up.

In each of those three examples, visuals were also important. There aren't many films about diplomats (*Lawrence of Arabia* being a notable exception), but mass communication is increasingly shaped by pictures – look at the way ISIL make horror films. The YouTube video of my farewell walk through Lebanon got over a hundred times the attention of the more formal goodbyes. Diplomats will never win any Oscars, but they need to understand how film and pictures, like other art, can drive change. And that the smartphone makes everyone a film-maker.

So the visuals matter. Does the backdrop match the message? Don't stand in front of a beach when talking about a crisis. Don't stand in front of a clapped-out car when talking about investment opportunities. When I had something a bit edgy to say, I wore a more conservative suit. If I was wearing a bright tie, it normally meant that I had a particularly underwhelming speech to offer. My team learnt to find an excuse to slip out quietly when I put on my snappiest neckwear.

*

Those representing the people have to get better at communicating with them. This requires them to entertain and engage, create genuine emotional connections, and take risks. It will draw from the best examples of the use of new technology by charities, businesses and politicians. It will rely on a better knowledge of the data underpinning people's decisions, and offer citizens a more personal, interactive experience.

The old division of labour, where politicians tended to be the face of a policy, with diplomats and officials writing them their lines, is breaking down. Good. Time differences and communication speeds take away the luxury of the carefully crafted press release.

While the proportion of time those in politics and public life spend on communicating will increase, it will be vital to ensure that the spin does not replace the substance. Any serious diplomatic effort should generate stories and angles that interest the media and public. But this must be the tip of the iceberg, underpinned by detailed work. The policy has to drive the announcement, not the other way round. We no longer have the luxury of allowing a gap between hyperbole and reality.

For most foreign ministries, all this fluidity is a shock to the system. Message control is over. As Hillary Clinton's former innovation adviser Alec Ross says, the twenty-first century is a terrible time to be a control freak. There will be moments of panic, especially after the first ambassador is fired over a Twitter slip. The answer will be further upstream, to recruit, train and then trust the right people to deliver the message in the right way. The slippage of control will be uncomfortable, but it is inevitable. Stanley McChrystal, one of the most successful US generals of the twenty-first century, recognises that 'information is only of value if you can get it to people who can do something with it. Sharing is power.'[7] Like everyone else, diplomats will need to embrace their inner anarchist.

Diplomacy has always been about helping our countries compete. To do that most effectively, diplomats must connect relentlessly.

We should be excited, energised and inspired by the pace of technological change around us. But let's not throw the diplomatic baby out with the digital bathwater. And nowhere is this ability to connect more important than in that most ancient aspect of statecraft – the ability to make peace.

Selling Ladders for Other People to Climb Down

It is never wise to gain by battle what may be gained through bloodless negotiations.

Attila the Hun

Since Ug, the ability to negotiate and make peace has been the most important weapon in the diplomatic armoury. It is an art, not a science.

Nations and peoples will still need diplomats to mediate the tricky issues that divide them, and to help them avoid conflict. While the 2015 Iran nuclear deal, for example, was accelerated by digital interaction, it would not have happened without immensely difficult negotiations, mainly in private. Most agreements come down to a small group of people in a dark room, late at night, thrashing out the detail and taking risks with their own political constituencies. (Negotiations are not just over war and peace – my toughest were with the French government over the arrangements for the seventieth anniversary of D-Day in Normandy.*) Much of this vital work will still be done in secret, though this will be increasingly challenging.

---

* I'm afraid that the detail of these negotiations falls into the category of 'best not written down'.

Throughout history, power has depended on the ability to negotiate the peace, not just win the war. So how do diplomatic negotiations succeed or fail?

My great-grandfather was a strict Orangeman, a Protestant minister in Belfast who was infuriated at what he saw as the loss of Protestant jobs to Catholics after the Great War. My great-uncle was the chief constable of the Royal Ulster Constabulary, one of the toughest and most thankless tasks in policing, then as now. I married a Catholic from the Republican south of Ireland, whose ancestors had fought on the other side of the conflict. I later worked as the Northern Ireland adviser to two prime ministers. I was with Gordon Brown through weeks of painstaking, exhausting and often infuriating negotiations between Republicans and Unionists, who united only when they saw a collective opportunity to get one over on the UK government. And I was with David Cameron as he put together his extraordinary, and very personal, response to the Saville Inquiry's report on Bloody Sunday.[1]

Diplomacy has transformed, and is transforming, Northern Ireland. The ongoing peace process also reminds us of many of the essentials of diplomatic negotiation.[2]

Firstly, decent peacemakers need to know their interests.

This sounds obvious, but it is striking how often diplomats arrive at negotiations without a clear sense of the outcome they want. Sometimes they come with unrealistic negotiating positions, or none at all. Often they are unable to rank their demands or expectations. Many of the best negotiators I have seen talk of a negotiating box that captures their upper- and lower-end expectations. They see their role as identifying which parts of that box overlap with their interlocutor's box. The sweet spot.

For the toughest peacemaking, you have to identify both a common vision and the leaders who have the courage to work towards it. In Northern Ireland, public opinion shifted gradually towards a rejection of violence. As Tony Blair has explained, this was a journey not an event. I think the Lebanese, since the civil war, have made a similar journey, which is one reason why Lebanon has held together, defying logic and those who have sought division for narrow political or sectarian gain.

When this vision exists, those who try to use terror to break it will find life harder. The Omagh bombings, the most deadly terrorist attack in Northern Ireland, took place after the Good Friday Agreement. They shook confidence in the process, but did not break it, because people knew there was something bigger at stake than a vicious cycle of revenge and retribution. Recent terrorist attacks in Lebanon, including the assassination of my friend Mohamad Chatah, have had the same effect. They have forced competing players to ally against a common threat, and appalled the silent majority. Sometimes, though, the assassin or terrorist wins. The killer of the Israeli prime minister Yitzhak Rabin in 1995 buried the peace process with Palestine for two decades and counting.

A decent negotiator also needs to know their opponents. Part of the diplomatic art is to identify solutions that are based on mutual interest. So we now try to arm the prime minister at European Councils not just with a sense of what his opponents will be fighting for, but why it matters to them. Most leaders turn up at summits armed with the latest polls on their colleagues – it helps to know who is feeling more confident or crestfallen. Attila the Hun, whom I would dearly love to see negotiating at a European Council, told his followers to never trust negotiation to luck. Knowing what your enemy wants makes you stronger.

One reason for the failure of the 2009 Copenhagen climate change summit – a miserable event which scarred a generation of negotiators – was that while we had done enormous amounts of preparation on the views of China, India and other emerging countries, we made the mistake of assuming that they negotiated like us. We anticipated that a greater part of their initial position consisted of elements that could more easily be given up ('negotiating fat') than was actually the case. We thought that they would want a deal as much as we did. That's how we had all got used to negotiating in Europe. As a result, we ended up with the unedifying spectacle of several Western leaders sat around the table late at night with junior Chinese and Indian officials, desperately making concessions to interlocutors who had no mandate to negotiate. I remember several European leaders being adamant that they would not accept a deal hammered out without them, but struck by President Obama and the leaders of Brazil, Russia, India and China (the 'BRICs'). We did.

I've been evangelical about how digital technology can help us exercise power in new ways. But any decent negotiator should also know when to turn off their smartphone. This is partly for security – most modern embassies will no longer allow guests to bring in their portable telephones. Sometimes it is because etiquette still matters. When British Cabinet minister Clare Short was attending the Queen in the Privy Council, her mobile phone went off loudly in her handbag. While she fumbled for it, the Queen reportedly paused before asking, 'Someone important?'

But the main reason for periods without the smartphone is that no one can conduct a negotiation with the world watching and commenting on every twist and turn. The 2015 Iran deal was a case in point, with negotiations mainly taking place behind closed doors, and with rare updates for the media. This helped insulate participants from public pressure from hardliners in

Iran, Israel and the US. Sometimes we simply have to turn off the devices, shut out the noise and lock ourselves in a room with the protagonists.

Contrary to the argument that confidential diplomacy is becoming harder, we are seeing a steady increase in informal negotiations done privately through academics, activists or retired officials. This approach can identify more creative ways of resolving or preventing conflict, or build confidence in periods when direct talks would not be possible. It is harder to control, but many of the most important peace processes have begun in this way.

Creative and audacious diplomacy also means talking to people you wouldn't want to invite into your home. The best diplomatic negotiators have also always known when to go dark – to act in secret, and to talk to the bad guys. Too often, engagement with opponents is wrongly presented by its critics as some kind of reward for them. Sometimes, when the moment is right, we should instead take Nelson's advice: 'Never mind manoeuvres, go straight at 'em.'

The Northern Irish peace process took immense courage from those involved. It showed that you have to be prepared to sit down with your enemy. I remember many such excruciating and painful late night meetings with Unionists and Republicans. They demanded great political risks, and uncomfortable compromises. It took time for bitter rivals to see the common humanity in those they had fought. We had to avoid unrealistic expectations or conditions – if the British government had demanded disarmament of the IRA before talks could start, we would still be at war with them today. The process took creativity, patience and thick skins.

It also takes extraordinary and inspirational individuals. I recently met an Englishwoman who was working on sharing the lessons of reconciliation. I asked her how she had become involved. She said that her father had been killed in the IRA terrorist attack on the Grand Hotel in Brighton in 1984. I turned to the man next to her, with whom she had travelled and would shortly share a platform, and asked him what his story was. He paused briefly before replying, 'I was the bomber.'

Jonathan Powell, Tony Blair's chief of staff and the principal architect of the Northern Irish peace process, tells a story about sitting down with Martin McGuinness and Gerry Adams in Downing Street in 1997. McGuinness tried to break the ice by saying 'So this is where all the damage was done, then.' Blair's team thought this was a reference to the IRA mortar attack on the building in 1991. In fact, McGuinness meant that it was the room in which the Republicans had negotiated with the British government in 1921. Our shared histories are open to different interpretations.

Powell scoffs at the idea that governments should not negotiate with terrorists. They almost always end up doing so. Menachem Begin's paramilitary group Irgun blew up the King David Hotel in Jerusalem in 1946, killing ninety-one, but he was later lauded as a statesmanlike prime minister of Israel. When Jomo Kenyatta, then president of Kenya, arrived for talks with the British government, he reminded them that he had been kept at Her Majesty's pleasure for many years.[3]

As William Sieghart, who is involved with many painstaking peacemaking initiatives, told me, 'Diplomatic conversations in Northern Ireland and South Africa were preceded by twenty years or so of secret conversations, mediated by a priest in both cases. The digital world makes it even harder to disguise contact between officials who aren't supposed to be meeting and raises the role and importance of unofficial intermediaries. Enemies ultimately have to engage in order to end conflicts. It's astonishing how many people once demonised can have their horns and tail removed at a later date.'

Unless there is a complete imbalance of force, any negotiator will also need to make concessions. Even in complete victory – the Versailles Treaty being the classic example – the winner may have an interest in doing so. The effective negotiator will have real red lines, and artificial ones. There will be cards that can be conceded. Before any serious negotiation, it is therefore worth building in 'negotiating fat'.

Good negotiators sometimes let their opponents win. British ex-diplomat Sir John Ure suggests that 'the best diplomatic victories are those when everyone goes away thinking they have won. Diplomacy is the art of building ladders for other people to climb down.'[4] Or as the American writer Sue Monk Kidd puts it, 'If you need something from somebody, always give that person a way to hand it to you.'[5]

Compromise has become a dirty word, associated with spinelessness. Heaven forbid that a leader should be presented in the media as like Neville Chamberlain. Yet short of conquering other countries, which we're less keen on now, compromise is often the only way to make progress. The trick is to ensure that you hold the lines on the issues that matter most, and give way on the ones that do not.

This does not mean weakness. In over two years of watching Gordon Brown negotiate with foreign leaders, I never once saw him offer a concession without establishing in his mind what it would buy him elsewhere. He was constantly in the business of establishing leverage. Even when the concession was in his interests, he would make his counterpart feel that he owed him something, in the manner of a mafia don creating a future obligation from the person he was helping. I once thought I had persuaded him to be gentle with the new and rather timid EU president,

Herman van Rompuy, in their one-to-one before a European Council. He came out and told me he had been 'as charming as any Foreign Office diplomat'. Van Rompuy was spotted leaving by a back door shortly after, pale and trembling.

Gareth Evans, former Australian foreign minister, argues that as international negotiators we also need to say 'sorry' more often. And to do it properly. In our private lives, diplomats rarely say to an angry partner that 'it is a matter of regret that you feel I have offended you'. Yet in international affairs, the way they describe touchstone issues of national sentiment can often be cold and seem insincere. Evans says that 'it is difficult to believe that when a wrong has been done, a sincere apology will not have some restorative impact. In public, as in private life, honest apologies are a powerful tool, and should be used less nervously and more often.'[6]

I agree. In 2010 I worked with David Cameron on his response to the Saville Inquiry into Bloody Sunday, and his apology was so powerful because it was authentic and sincere – a defining moment early in his administration, when he moved from being the leader of the largest party to being the prime minister. It recognised the context in which the situation had occurred, but did not blind itself to the hurt caused. He dictated most of it himself, and thought hard about how it would be received not just among the UK military and his own constituencies, but how those on the streets of Derry would react. Sorry seems to be the hardest word, but it is sometimes the best one.

The best diplomatic negotiators also understand the rhythm of negotiations. Not all negotiating contexts are the same. Each dance has its rules. Diplomats who do best at the United Nations in New York are those who don't put themselves at the centre of the story, who are able to craft the early drafts of written statements and then let others take the credit. They are often negotiating as much with their capital as with their counterparts. You have to build in incentives: there is a study to be done on whether more progress towards agreements is made just before or just after lunch. At the 2009 London G20 financial summit, we used football to get a better outcome. At that time, leaders did not have iPads or smartphones with them. Over dinner, several were desperate for updates on the World Cup qualifiers being played that evening. As the only official in the room, I would receive a piece of paper with the latest scores, and consult – as visibly as I could manage – the prime minister on whether I could update his colleagues. He would often fix those most needy with a fearsome stare, extract a concession, and then nod at me to give them what they wanted, once we had what we wanted.

Much diplomatic negotiation is now shaped before the summit or conference it leads up to. With a classic G8, for example, diplomats will begin working on the outcomes months before the event. Sherpas, supported by their yaks, meet regularly, testing where the real red lines are, and seeking new areas of common ground. But in reality, the sweet spot for the negotiation is at the moment leaders engage. Only then do the real interests emerge. If a negotiator does not leave a nugget that only their leader can deliver, they have not done their job. The worst summit outcomes, and the most boring and frustrating for leaders, are those where everything is agreed by officials beforehand. Most leaders want to feel that they have wrung every last bit of juice from the negotiation.

So, for example, at the London G20 summit in 2009, Gordon Brown secured a much more ambitious set of conclusions than expected because he exiled the sherpas to another building, and then hammered through the communiqué with leaders in person, many of them without the protection of their officials, or in some cases even their translators. As the only official in the room for long periods, my role was to soak up much of the resulting anger, most forcefully from President Kirchner of Argentina. I was fortunate that no translator was present for one of her longer and more dramatic tellings-off, but I got the gist of it. This is probably not an approach to summits that can be pulled off more than once.

The Foreign Office's current political director, Sir Simon Gass – who led most of the Iran negotiations for the UK in recent years – says that as part of any negotiating process, <u>effective negotiators conserve their energy when it is not needed, marking time or letting others fill the space until the context changes</u>. Much of the Iran nuclear negotiations felt like this, as does most Lebanese politics. As the Iranians have worked out, deadlines are normally more flexible than they appear. Red lines are often blurred. A good negotiator will assess whether the penalties for missing or crossing them really outweigh the error of a rash or hurried deal. Veteran peacemaker George Mitchell described one lengthy negotiation as '700 days of failure and one day of success'. So there are moments to stay silent. As the French put-down of those who have not mastered this art goes, *Il a manqué une belle occasion de se taire*.* This includes not picking a fight at the wrong time. I switched off one looming row with Argentina over the Falklands in February 2010, because it would have been escalated in unhelpful ways by the fact we had a UK election looming.

The negotiator can then engage with greater vigour at the moments that actually matter. Sir Jon Cunliffe, formerly the UK representative to the EU and now deputy governor of the Bank of England, was the most effective haggler I ever saw in action because he was prepared to be the last person in the room, putting his body on the line for the right outcome. This is not a recipe for

---

* He missed a good opportunity to shut up.

popularity with counterparts, but any leader would rather have the negotiator willing to fight longest, most tenaciously and harder for the right outcome. British prime ministers looked at Jon, exhausted from another night wrestling over fish subsidies or derivative swaps, and thought 'He may be a bastard, but I'm glad he's our bastard.'[7] No one said 'no' better than Jon.

Successful negotiations increasingly rely on understanding the interplay between private and public. Most leaders arrive at a negotiation with a clear sense of what is shaping the approach of their counterparts – their local media or polls, pressure groups, public opinion. In a rolling negotiation, they will often offer concessions when counterparts need some relief at home. It is no coincidence that an increasing amount of set-piece summits are hosted within a year of the host's election.

Increasingly, an EU negotiation or G20 summit will almost immediately be defined by the media and public as either a triumph or disaster. Leaders like Margaret Thatcher have helped to set up each encounter as a diplomatic joust, with clear winners and losers. In reality, any negotiation is much more complex than turning up and swinging a handbag. People win a bit and lose a bit.

To help deliver more victories, it is also worth moulding expectations of what victory looks like. Contrary to Michelangelo's view, it is better to aim low and reach your mark than aim high and miss it. It was often possible for all leaders to stride to their press conferences after a summit to claim 'game, set and match': they were talking about different matches.

The zero-sum approach to international summits is not always the most effective. In my experience, the leaders who used it most tended to be men. The European leader who has most consistently got what they wanted, over a longer period of time and with fewer claims of triumph, is Angela Merkel.

Diplomacy takes time. It is a process, not an event. It helps to build alliances, even if they subsequently shift. Ultimately, for the toughest of peace negotiations, the parties have to own that process. While external support can break the logjam at key points, it cannot alone sustain the process, as US negotiators have often found on Israel/Palestine. The UK would probably not have been able to sit down with Sinn Fein without pressure from the Americans, who could see that we all needed to change the paradigm. The Unionists and Republicans in Northern Ireland would not have been able to work together in the way they did without concerted pressure from the Irish and British governments. Where trust is lacking, there often needs to be a sense of an impartial referee, whether verifying that arms have been destroyed, thinking creatively around problems when both parties want talks to fail, or simply providing a neutral space and standing back. But ultimately we found that in Northern Ireland, the individuals involved – and the communities they represented – had to want it too. And had to own it.

As in business, diplomatic negotiations require protagonists to manage their emotions, and to use them. Many of the most successful diplomats have been good actors. Nikita Khrushchev famously banged his shoe on the table at the UN in 1960, enraged by a speech by Harold Macmillan. There are times when you have to show your fangs. The best negotiators I have seen can pick ferocious arguments, but they make sure that they pick the right ones.

In any diplomatic negotiation, there has to be an incentive for a political outcome. The Northern Ireland peace deal recognised that if you want people to put down their weapons, you have to show that they can better secure their legitimate aims through a political process. In this respect, while I understand the anxiety some feel, I have always said that it is welcome that Hezbollah are becoming more involved in state politics in Lebanon. They have a constituency, and a voice. They, and other parties in Lebanon, should secure their political objectives through legitimate processes rather than violence or threats of violence. As parties across the world have discovered, there is nothing like governing to realise the challenges of government, compared to the tidy comforts of opposition. I never encountered their leader, Hassan Nasrallah. That made me the only British ambassador in the world not to have met the most powerful person in the country in which they served.

Sometimes, though, the deal is simply not worth it. In the heat of a negotiation, diplomats – often inclined by nature to seek consensus – will settle for an agreement that won't even survive the press conference afterwards. At times it is better to walk away. The American diplomat Philip Habib, talking in the 1980s, saw a number of 'horrendous and heart-rending' negotiations where diplomats had put in years of work and yet failed. He cites Vietnam: 'the length of negotiation and the intensity of negotiation – is no assurance either that it will succeed or that its results will be as they were expected to be'.[8]

Finally, diplomatic negotiations take resilience. David Lloyd George told Sir Ronald Storrs, his envoy in Palestine, that 'If either side stops complaining to me, you'll be dismissed.' I have often felt the same any time I have tweeted about Israel and Palestine, and most subsequent envoys to the Middle East will have had cause to draw on Lloyd George's advice. Diplomacy requires a thick skin, especially when you're the focus for anger from every direction. As a seasoned intelligence officer once told me about working on the Libya nuclear agreement with Gaddafi, 'Sometimes you have to get between the dog and the lamp post.' It is unsurprising therefore that the unofficial motto of the United Nations is 'Blessed are the peacemakers, for they shall take flak from both sides.'

Negotiating and peacemaking will remain as important to our collective future as to our past. We are going to need the people to provide the lubricant as states, armies and individuals grind against each other.

When it works, though, it is worth it. I took Lebanese leader Walid Joumblatt, one of the Middle East's most colourful characters, to Northern Ireland. Reverend Harold Good, the Methodist minister who had overseen the controversial disarmament of the IRA, told him about the visit to the last weapons cache. At his side throughout had been his silent but intimidating IRA minder. As the final weapons were put beyond use, Good said, 'At last, the gun has gone out of Irish politics.'

His minder quietly stepped forward, broke his rifle over his knee, and said, 'No, now the last gun has gone out of Irish politics.'

12

A Naked Diplomat

During my time in Lebanon, many of the themes I've described so far came together – the need for diplomats to work for peace, the Arab Spring and the online battle against extremism, the changing relationship between the public and figures of traditional authority, and the opportunity to use digital technology to reach and connect with people in new ways.

I begged for the job, despite the obvious dangers. At my leaving party from No. 10, David Cameron reminded me that I had sometimes argued against trying to rescue Brits kidnapped overseas, if the risks to our servicemen and women were too great. I need not worry, he assured me with what I hoped was black humour, the government would leave me chained to the radiator.

The gun has not gone out of Lebanese politics. The country is at the apex of many of the region's power struggles, a vector for the instability and change that is sweeping the Middle East. The most religiously diverse country in the world, it remains the best place to take the pulse of the Middle East. It is also a relatively free society that could in time help to provide the intellectual underpinning to the Arab Spring. Yet a fearful society that cannot absorb all its Palestinian and Syrian refugees and survive. A fractured society that is on the frontline of the regional power struggle between Saudi Arabia and Iran. And a bruised society that could do with a period of benign neglect from its region.

The contrasts of Lebanon are a well-worn cliché, but still hit the new arrival. The brash new market alongside the pockmarked Holiday Inn, a ghoulish remnant of the civil war. Hijabs and hotpants. A broke government, but Ferraris on every corner. It is where we have our most tested maritime evacuation plan, in preparation for the next crisis; and yet it remains a top destination for UK luxury yacht sales. Excess and abstinence. Huge flat-screen TVs and power cuts. Too much political rhetoric, and too little political dialogue. A country famous for its welcome suppers, but feared for its capacity to devour and spit out its guests.

Lebanon is a prisoner of history and geography. The losers, splitters and persecuted of the twentieth century sought refuge in its mountains, not anticipating the need to coexist with at least eighteen cults even more niche than their own. For many of them – Allawites, Druze, Maronites, Palestinians, Armenians, Orthodox, etc. – this is where they make their last stand, and success in the twenty-first century is survival.

The Lebanese are mountain people: resilient, tough survivors who put family and clan first. And sea people: adventurers, dreamers and traders.

Throw in the most difficult set of neighbours since 1940s Poland, and you have a cauldron of raw, often violent, politics; and a vector for regional instability. There are no permanent allies nor enemies. The veneer of the state is paper thin, with the Lebanese relying on it for no more than a passport, functioning cash machines and an airport. The Lebanese are fatalist about these problems. And they always have an outsider to blame, normally with good reason.

So by all normal standards of logic, Lebanon should not work. No one really understands how it does. My sense is that it is through a combination of money, fear and ingenuity. The Lebanese cash keeps on flowing – remittances from the 80% of Lebanese overseas that maintain economic growth against the odds; from the Gulf Arabs who take bling breaks in Beirut away from their normal obligations; and from Westerners keen to prop up a country – or at least bits of it – that we think looks and sounds like us.

Fear, because the brutality of civil war is etched on those who survived it, and the landscape. However much the factions hate and threaten each other, however itchy the trigger fingers get, no one judges it is in their interest to go back. Lebanon is a post-failed state that craves stability.

And ingenuity, because the Lebanese have always found a way to work through their problems. A fragile but somehow functional system of consent, patronage and compromise holds. Think UK coalition negotiations with militias outside the Cabinet Secretary's office, or a European Council with RPGs. This encourages brinkmanship and inertia.

External interventions in Lebanon – in recent memory Israeli, Syrian, American, French, British, Iranian, even Italian – tend to follow a set pattern: seduction, toxification, terror, and ignominious departure. Lebanon is easy to swallow, but hard to digest.

But Lebanon also has a highly engaged, political population. So I started to experiment. In 2011, we organised the first live Twitter Q and A between an ambassador and a head of government. Prime Minister Mikati and I spent an hour online simultaneously, to highlight a visit he was making to London and to seek ideas for new cooperation between our two countries. We answered hundreds of questions and engaged a set of interlocutors – honestly and directly – that we would never otherwise have reached.

Emboldened by this, I hosted the first ever <u>virtual diplomatic reception</u>, with participants encouraged to prepare the same meal as us, and those present in person live-streamed in order to interact in real time with those not physically in the room. We debated the steps Lebanon needs to take to skip a telecommunications generation and put in place the right infrastructure to be a twenty-first-century Singapore. Running the event was hard work: I had to be a combination of dinner-party host and television presenter, while tracking and responding to online questions and comments. But it stimulated a huge number of ideas. More importantly, it generated the connections to deliver them.

I started using Twitter walls during speeches in order to interact and take questions in real time. Again, this created challenges. It was disorientating to have what used to be called an audience commenting with each other on what you are saying, while you are saying it. But it delivers a much more useful and responsive discussion, and often means that I make rapid changes to the subjects we debate as we go along. Many of those who need to be part of the solution to Lebanon's challenges are members of Lebanon's massive diaspora. A digital element to public events created the opportunity to bring them more closely into the conversation.

We also decided that blogging would help us reach a completely new audience. One issue we were up against was short-termism, and a lack of any coherent national vision. So in 2012 I wrote an idealistic but controversial vision of what Lebanon could become.

Beirutopia

Diplomats hate making predictions. Churchill once said that you could ignore every other page of Foreign Office advice, because it tended to be in the form of 'on the one hand' and 'on the other hand'. The files are full of pre-election telegrams that hedge their bets.

There are good reasons for this. We don't like being wrong. And the more we study international politics, the more we realise how unpredictable it all is.

So this blogpost is no crystal ball. But – amid the pessimism – many people have been talking to me about the future of Lebanon. So I wondered what my successor would write in his report following the 100th anniversary celebrations in Lebanon in 2020.* Here is one of several possible versions:

Dear Foreign Secretary,

I represented you at today's centenary celebrations in Beirut.

There were many international leaders present. Lebanon's new wealth, the result of huge amounts of offshore gas, is attracting great interest. The eurozone president commented to me that Lebanon was now Singapore with more skiing, or Qatar with more culture.

The highlight of the celebration was the participation of so many talented poets, musicians and film-makers. Since the end of the Syrian occupation, Lebanon has re-emerged as the epicentre of the Arab Cultural Renaissance, as you know from the high numbers of film and music downloads in the UK.

The newly elected Syrian president was guest of honour. The Treaty of Recognition and Cooperation signed between Syria and Lebanon in 2014 established an equal relationship. The border was demarcated, and Lebanese businesses and community leaders of course played a key role in the reconstruction of Syria following the terrible 2011–13 civil war.

I spoke to many MPs attending. Most are now under the age of forty, the post-civil-war generation. Many returned from expat jobs overseas to help lead the country. Where once we spoke of a Brain Drain, we now see a Brain Gain. New technology has allowed the Lebanese diaspora to create one of the world's most

---

* The State of Greater Lebanon had been declared in 1920, as part of the division of the Ottoman empire after the First World War.

dynamic global business networks, with Beirut as the hub between Europe and Asia. In her speech, the president (one of the first citizens to have a civil marriage with a partner from another confession) said that as global power shifts south and east, we are on the cusp of a new Levantine age.

The 2014 Beirut Accord still seems to be working well. Of course, Lebanon wouldn't be Lebanon without some animated debate over political representation. But most parties feel their interests are safeguarded. For me, the key moment was the rebuttal by Lebanon's leaders of international offers to oversee the 'reset' of Lebanon's constitutional settlement. By insisting that this should be a Lebanese-led process, they ended the vicious cycle of external meddling and patronage. For the first time, the constitutional settlement is truly Lebanese.

There was little political debate at the ceremony itself, though politics is as lively as ever. The key dividing line is over what to do with the income from gas. The One Lebanon (centre left) party want to give each Lebanese citizen a dividend. The One Nation (centre right) party want to retain a sovereign wealth fund. The only party to retain a sectarian basis lost its last seat at the 2017 elections, though the Senate continues to act as the safeguard for cross-confessional interests.

Alphabetical protocol meant that the ambassadors of Israel and Iran were sat near to Great Britain, both in animated conversation. The 2015 peace agreement between Israel and Lebanon has of course been a key part of the regional gas boom. Borders were settled in the south, and both sides pledged no further aggression. The establishment of Palestine the same year, following intense US-led engagement, meant the return of many Palestinian refugees from Lebanon. Western tourists now visit Israel, Palestine, Syria and Lebanon on the same trip, and many Lebanese Christian and Muslim pilgrims from Lebanon visited Jerusalem last year.

Lebanon's kaleidoscope nation was out in force, a vivid reminder of the different groups who have made this land their home over the centuries. Having paid the price in the past for sectarian division, Lebanon is now a talisman for coexistence, and delegations regularly visit from countries in conflict to study the lessons. As in Northern Ireland, it is remarkable to see how far a number of former militias have come, committing to a genuinely national project. They have more political power as a result. The National Guard, including many former resistance fighters, marched proudly alongside the rest of the Lebanese army, many of whom have now returned from peacekeeping missions on several continents.

I arrived at the ceremony on the new citytrain, one of the flagship projects of Lebanon 2020, a private-sector-driven modernisation project. Beirut now has the world's first car-free city centre, and oil and gas revenues have funded the repair of the national grid, leaving generators a distant memory. The effort to discover and renovate ancient ruins remains at the heart of the remarkable tourist boom of recent years. Beirut is now the top citybreak destination for Brits, and many will I'm sure join me in Sky Bar tonight to continue the celebration.

Lebanon at 100 is an extraordinary, talented, resilient, hopeful, diverse, beautiful and enchanting place. I look forward to the next royal visit.

Yours,

HM Ambassador Beirut

PS: It was a pleasure to see my predecessor Tom Fletcher win the 100m and 200m at this year's Olympics.

A fantasy? Naive? It depends on you. Tell us what you think. #Leb2020

Much of the letter does indeed look naive. But it triggered a debate, and was widely shared. We realised that we had identified a way to cut through to dinner-table conversations, and to trigger new arguments, to break people out of comfortable but dangerous narratives.

So as part of our public diplomacy to mark the seventieth anniversary of Lebanon's independence in 2013, we decided to ratchet it up a level, and take a gamble by releasing a controversial open letter to the Lebanese people. Again, this aimed to tackle some of the fatalism about Lebanon's situation, to point out some hard truths, and to stimulate fresh thinking about the tough decisions needed if Lebanon was to make it to seventy-five. I pulled it together with help from colleagues and ran it by trusted Lebanese media contacts. I then pressed the button to 'finalise' and held my breath.

Tomorrow I'll hand a letter from Prime Minister Cameron to President Sleiman, with formal congratulations on Lebanon's seventieth anniversary.

The wonderful people at Rag Mag also asked me to write an open letter to mark the day. This is a tough and precarious assignment, and it will annoy or anger some people. But I've had a try, as I think this is an important moment for reflection.

I hope others will consider writing letters of their own.

Dear Lebanon,

I wanted to write to say Happy Seventieth Birthday.

I know that in reality you have been around thousands of years, and were trading and writing long before my ancestors. But that moment of your birth in November 1943 was special, different – you took your first steps as a new nation founded on uniting principles rather than lines of division.

I'm proud that my predecessor, Edward Spears, was there to support that, and that we believed as strongly then as now in the idea of Lebanon.

The thing is, Lebanon, do you still believe in that idea? This is a question only you can answer. Without doubt, it has been a bumpy seven decades, with troublesome teenage years and plenty of midlife crises, to put it mildly.

You now face another tough year, and rising anxiety that regional rifts can drive you apart once again. We have been reminded this week that there are plenty of people who want that to happen.

I hope that you'll forgive a bit of feedback, from one of your admirers.

You're so much better than you admit. Look back at those seventy years. Your writers, musicians, thinkers and business people have conquered the world again and again.

Your mountains, valleys and coasts are the envy of all of us. You have an extraordinary unquenchable spirit. You have found a way to move on from a devastating civil war, almost as though it never happened.

You are the world's best networkers, in a century that will be run by networks. You are also the most exceptional hosts, not just to ambassadors but also to the hundreds of thousands of Syrian refugees who have arrived in the last two years.

Whatever your religion, there are few more beautiful sounds than the intermingling of the call to prayer and church bells. Every day I meet extraordinary Lebanese people doing great things against the odds.

So, let's be clear, I'm a fan.

But I'm also frustrated, and I know that many of you are.

Your politics are dynamic on the surface. Yet broken and paralysed beneath it. You talk of unity. Yet often say things like

'Lebanon would be wonderful if it wasn't for the Lebanese', 'it will always be like this – this is Lebanon', or 'they [insert different group] are just too different'.

You have an impressive ability to absorb hardships such as power cuts. Yet you rarely confront the causes of them. You invest more than any country in the education of your youth. Yet they feel excluded from changing the country for the better. You have been a beacon for women's rights. Yet only elect a tiny handful to Parliament. You were the first country in the region to stand up against dictatorship and tyranny in the twenty-first-century Middle East. Yet your voice in calling for your own rights and those of others seems to have fallen silent, and in too many cases been silenced.

So here's some unsolicited advice.

First and most important, start ignoring advice from outsiders, including me: this is your country.

Second, celebrate the success that is all around you – yes, the talented and inspirational athletes, thinkers, explorers and activists. But also the grafters who tell me on the school run, in the street, shops, schools or hospitals – 'this is our country, we share it, and carrying on our lives is the best response to violence and division'.

Third, why not use this seventieth anniversary of independence to remember what independence meant and should still mean – that you'll prioritise national interests, Lebanese interests, over those of foreign patrons? And demand that your leaders do too?

Fourth, maybe it is time to renew those marriage vows, to spend a moment reflecting on what you admire rather than what infuriates you about each other. You're stuck together I'm afraid, for richer or poorer, for better or for worse.

Finally, don't forget your collective strengths. You may have difficult neighbours and a tendency to fatalism. But your location and diversity put you at the hub between continents and cultures. Your history gives you a resilience and free spirit that others in the region would die for. And are dying for.

Many of us are rooting for you. The UK is doubling trade, increasing tenfold our support to the army's stabilisation effort, and running our largest ever humanitarian effort to help you cope with the refugee influx. The Security Council, far from fighting their battles here, have come together repeatedly to prioritise your stability, and to provide peacekeepers, aid, political support.

For many of us you're too important, and too special, to let fail. If coexistence proves impossible in Lebanon, how can we be confident that it will work elsewhere?

I'm still buying shares in Lebanon 2020. All I encourage, humbly, is that you do too.

You're at a moment of jeopardy. Seventy is too young for a country to retire. You can't just Botox away the cracks. Whether you make it to seventy-five depends on whether you can find a way to regroup, to focus again on what unites rather than divides you.

That is not something that you can leave to outsiders. You have to decide whether you're on the side of those who are fighting *over* Lebanon. Or with those who are fighting *for* it.

Happy Birthday. Happy Independence Day. Happy One Lebanon Day. *Mabrouk, bon courage*, and solidarity.

Yours affectionately,

Tom

This was high-risk, and outside the usual rules of diplomacy. It set out to challenge and provoke. One journalist later called it a 'gadfly stunt'.

But it was a stunt with a purpose. And it cut through. In the first forty-eight hours, the letter received over 10,000 Facebook likes, was tweeted over 8,000 times, and was covered prominently by all major TV and radio outlets. It received over 1,000 online responses, and was debated on the Lebanese equivalents of *Newsnight* and *Question Time*. One blogger estimated that the letter had been read by a third of the Lebanese population.

Of those who responded online, roughly 50% were enthusiastic; 30% said that it showed the need for Lebanese people to debate stronger action to protect stability, and began discussing how; 10% passed it on as a bit of novelty; and 10% saw it as an act of condescending neocolonialism from the country of Sykes, Balfour and Blair. Television debates were 90% supportive of the letter and the UK, with several enthusing celebrities.

Lebanon's most brilliant satirist, Karl Sharro, then wrote a very effective parody reply from Lebanon to the UK, which triggered another twenty-four hours of debate. I responded with a YouTube video, encouraging satirists to poke fun at those in public positions and giving examples of British creativity and liberty. This led to a further round of interest, with over 4,000 views in the following twenty-four hours.

Over three days, we had stimulated an argument about Lebanon's challenges that would not otherwise have happened. And I hoped that we had positioned the UK, at least in the eyes of most who followed the exchanges, as an honest if critical friend. The campaign raised our local profile significantly, and helped to draw attention to our wider messages in support of Lebanon's stability, including the gift of seventy Land Rovers for Independence Day.

This is new terrain, and the direct approach would not work everywhere. But it showed that it helps to set up dividing lines, rather than seek the path of least resistance. It helps to create moments of jeopardy or cliffhangers, in this case around Lebanon's prospects for survival. We need to build unusual coalitions, such as with the divas and celebrities who promoted it.

Emboldened by the reaction to these experiments in authentic communication, we also experimented with the use of digital tools to increase trade between Britain and the UK. We wanted to use social media to connect our companies with the right Lebanese networks. So we launched a matchmaking service for businesses, using online dating technology. We doubled business in three years, and the UK/Lebanon Tech Hub is now flourishing. I hope that it will create the companies that invent the products we do not yet know we need, but will find we cannot live without.

More than blog posts, I tried to use Twitter to get across our support for Lebanon's stability, to present a more open and engaging image, and to promote the UK. Sometimes this meant unconventional approaches, such as trying to pick online fights with the Iranian and Syrian presidents, or individual regional politicians. For example, when the Russian presidency tweeted about an Olympic truce during the Sochi Winter Games, I tweeted back that they should therefore stop providing the Syrian regime with weapons for the duration.

Often it involved retweeting the views of others, or articles that reinforced our positions. At the moment the Lebanese presidency fell vacant, I started a Twitter campaign in which people set out what they would do for the country if made president. When the Parliament extended its mandate, we organised a flashmob of schoolchildren to showcase national unity. We ran an online campaign called #Leb2020, to try to get people to focus more on the future, and to create coalitions for change.

And not a Ferrero Rocher in sight.

In my last week in Beirut in 2015, as I careered between belt-busting dinners and emotional farewells, the BBC sent journalist Matthew Teller to Lebanon to look at this naked diplomacy in action. Over several days, he pressed me to explain why I was trying something different, and this exchange formed the basis of a World Service documentary, *The Naked Diplomat*. I wanted to show that this <u>social media effort was just part of our effort to focus on what diplomats actually do best: stopping people killing each other</u>. Just without all the paraphernalia that slows us down. We were scraping those barnacles off the bottom of the boat.

Below is an extract from our discussions. It forms what is in some ways a stream of consciousness, the product of exhaustion and exhilaration, and I hope that its unpolished state retains an immediacy that conveys what we were trying to do, and my raw excitement about the potential of connecting in new ways – the foundation of Naked Diplomacy that is the subject of this book.

One of the things we've had to get used to is a loss of control, it's a more anarchic environment we're working in, so you've got to trust your people to get stuck in. We're trying to use social media to get to people. If people are watching *EastEnders*, I'll get on *EastEnders*. I think social media is for everyone, even ambassadors. There are lots of risks from being on it. There are security risks for me, there are reputational risks – it's not to everyone's taste, it can become pretty self-indulgent. But the biggest risk is not to be out there engaging in those conversations, and I see the role as ambassador as not just representing a government to a government but representing a people to a people. You've got to connect.

There's still a need for confidential negotiations, for a certain level of secrecy, for old-fashioned message-passing. The digital is the tip of the iceberg, and you've still got to have an iceberg beneath the surface.

I'm also making some tough comments about the way politics works here and the way that a lot of these oligarchs are standing in the way of change – I'm saying some quite risky things about them. I'm trying not to be this arrogant, Western diplomat saying this is how it should all be, because they'd kill me for that. I want to start a debate, I want to start a conversation.

The Lebanese are terrific people and through social media I've found a connection with them that I would never have had otherwise. The response we've seen from them on social media is a reflection of the fact they know how passionate I am about this job, they can see it because it's come through over four years. So they're reflecting some of that and it's very humbling and it's very moving and I'm heartened, but that doesn't depend on me at all. There's a whole embassy machine that is up there on the border supporting the army, that is getting the textbooks to the kids, that is securing the embassy, promoting British interests, that is projecting soft power, and to be honest you can take the ambassador out, hopefully not literally, and that work goes on.

It's not to everyone's tastes, and lots of my colleagues look at some of the stuff and roll their eyes. We're all trying to do our jobs in different ways to suit the local context. What I'm not doing is saying 'here are the Rice Krispies I had for breakfast' and me in my underpants and so on. The *Sunday Times* wrote a couple of years ago saying 'isn't it crazy that the ambassador in Beirut is tweeting that Father Christmas came last night with a picture of an empty stocking by the fireplace at a time when the Middle East is in flames'. But if you're going to do it authentically then you're going to have to bring a bit of your own personality. The fact was I didn't spend Christmas morning running around refugee camps, I spent it opening stockings with my two boys. I think it's no harm to show an element of normality.

If at any point it's detrimental to national policy I shouldn't be doing it, because at the end of the day I have one job, and that's to be the ambassador of Her Majesty's Government in Lebanon. I think it's a difficult balance between public and private for all of us – we're building the plane as we fly it. I played in a football match with Lebanese celebrities in order to highlight the message of One Lebanon. But if you're running around scoring goals and that's going on YouTube, that can quickly tip into self-promotion, rather than just promoting your national brand.

If you stacked up my 10,000 tweets over four years, I hope you'd be able to say there's a narrative that runs through that and that it's all about Britain's interests, it's about making Britain more secure, making Britain more prosperous, and helping Lebanon get through this tough period. Now there'll be stuff around the margins of that, which is there to draw people in. Like doing a tweetup with one of the divas about her favourite British music. But that's trying to get people to join our conversation on issues where we need to win the argument. There are massive global challenges ahead of us. We've got to find a way to gain people's trust, gain legitimacy in order to influence those arguments in the right way, and a huge amount of what I've been trying to do on social media is basically saying to people: let us be in that argument.

I reckon I have more chance of getting the support that we need to get to the poorest here, of preventing instability here, of preventing ISIL crossing the border, of reducing the risk of radicalisation if I can enlist the largest possible coalition, and I can't do that just sat in an embassy writing press statements and giving interviews. I've got to do it by mobilising people through social media. And we don't know if that works or not – we're going to have to come back in ten years' time and judge it then. But I'd much rather be trying it than not trying it.

Digital changes every aspect of what diplomats do. Sadly it's been a fact of life that Lebanon has been hit by crisis in the past, and we have to anticipate that it will be hit by crisis again. Most days I read in the reports about different folk who would like to kill me, and not just in my own government. We did our last evacuation in 2006. We have between 4,000 and 6,000 Brits here at any one time and I have to be prepared to press the button on a big evacuation at very short notice. The media timelines are getting shorter and shorter. It wouldn't be very long after a big security situation here before I'd have people standing in front of the building saying 'what the hell is the embassy doing?' So we have to react very fast. We would be communicating with the Brits here by Twitter and over Facebook, using social media to tell them in real time where they should be, what they should be doing, areas to avoid. I think this is the area of greatest change in the way that diplomacy is done in my time in the Foreign Office. I've got a lot of military guys here who tell me that no plan survives contact with the enemy. It will never be perfect, but surely using digital technology is better than trying to send out a press release or a letter to every Brit. You're more likely to get the message through fast.

Digital has also transformed our work promoting British companies. We sell more whisky, salmon, luxury cars, yachts here per capita than anywhere in the world. Not many people would expect that. And we've used digital technology, like online matchmaking, the same tools that people have used to find a partner, find a date, find whatever else they're looking for, to connect British companies with Lebanese networks. That's the business model that's worked.

If you think about 2012 – the Jubilee, the London Olympics – there was a real pride about British soft power. For the first time in my experience we felt like we owned that whole British brand here. A massive part of that is Manchester United, a massive part is Daniel Craig, and the British artists who come out and perform. The last four years we've had all sorts, Tom Jones to Joss Stone, Keane, Snow Patrol, Ellie Goulding – and of course they're much better ambassadors for the UK than I could ever be. We give them a platform to go out there and project that sense of modern Britain.

They take persuasion. Part of our travel advice says 'please avoid large crowds', and the singer of Keane rightly pointed out that 'we tend to attract quite large crowds'. David Gray is coming this weekend, and I spent a long time explaining to him why it is worthwhile. You could argue that we should focus just relentlessly on the grim situation around us, and most of this embassy are doing that. But we also have a role in projecting a modern Britain in the midst of all that. If we stopped doing that every time there was a crisis here we would never do it. It can sound a bit trite, but actually people do want to carry on living. Particularly the Lebanese. They're notorious for bouncing back. Any time a conflict ends they're back in the clubs and the bars and the restaurants, in the mosques and the churches very quickly, and so I think we're tapping into that sense of resilience that the Lebanese have.

Yes, we have a mixed British reputation in the Middle East – we can argue about whether it's justified or not, and I spend a lot of my time having that argument with people here. But we're not just about the distant past. I'm a postcolonial ambassador, and I feel that using popular artists to project a different Britain to the one people are expecting, starts to correct misconceptions.

Digital diplomacy can be used for good and bad. Look at the way that Islamic extremists use these digital channels to recruit, to spread their message – they worked out before any of us the power of visuals in this medium and they've done that in a grim way but very effectively, to get attention for their cause. It makes us rivals in this space, we're going toe to toe, and if we're not out there trying to fill it, then someone else is going to fill it. So, yeah, I'm in that battle against ISIL in that space, and this is another form of warfare.

There will always be an element of secrecy and there will always be an element of a lack of transparency. I don't want to live in WikiWorld where we're just completely open about everything we do. Like reality TV but even more boring. Following me around with a camera 24/7 wouldn't be effective diplomacy or TV. And one thing I do say to ambassadors who are looking at coming onto social media is: don't fall into the trap of dancing naked on the Tube – you will get a lot of retweets, a lot of views and probably a lot of likes, but it doesn't mean that you're building up influence or respect. Quite the opposite: people are laughing at you, not laughing with you.

Look, power is moving from these hierarchies, and jobs like mine are in a hierarchy. In a structure, it's like a British banquet, everyone knows where to sit, there's a menu, it's very straightforward, very logical. Now it's much more like a Lebanese meal, it's a bit more anarchic, and chaotic, because power is moving out to those networks, and I can see that happening all the time. I can feel power draining through my fingers as an ambassador. I am working in a job where I represent governments, and governments are becoming weaker, compared to other sources of power, and within government diplomats are becoming weaker compared to other bits of government. People aren't waking up in the morning wondering what is Diplomat X thinking, so we have to work harder to get our message across, and that's why we do social media.

It's exhilarating and frightening when stuff does go viral, when it takes off, but what we're not trying to do here is muscle in or establish rules and structures around this space, we're competing in it with everyone else, on their terms. It's anarchy out there. You have to earn the credibility and the trust to keep it interesting. One of the things I find excruciating about lots of the replies is the ones that start 'Your Excellency'. Titles like that actually get in the way of what we're trying to do, because it creates an artificial barrier. When people are prancing around styling themselves as Excellencies, it gives them a sense of elitism and separation that is no longer justified or useful.

Not everyone is online. It's a narrow window compared to the world population. But it's an enormous window compared to the people we could reach ten years ago or twenty years ago, and so you'd be insane not to be out there using it. And a billion people are going to come online very quickly, so we need to be there too.

There's an unfollow button. People are very free not to follow me, not to follow the embassy account, I reckon you have a certain proportion of people who are interested in what you're saying, a certain proportion who are a little bit curious, a certain number who are following because they're actually quite hostile, and are waiting for you to screw up, a certain number of people who are annoyed by it but quite like being annoyed. I don't know, I can't read the minds of the people who've chosen to follow me, but mostly they're sticking around, so they're doing it for some reason.

In diplomacy you often have to speak to people you disagree with. In fact you normally speak to people you disagree with. If I insisted on only speaking to people with Swedish morals I'd have a very boring job. The militia leaders, the warlords who were in place at the end of the civil war do control a huge amount of power. If I want Lebanon to stay standing, if I want to promote British interests, then I do need to engage them vigorously. I suppose on social media I'm talking to everyone. I was talking to the Iranians on social media at a time when it was unfashionable to do so, I regularly have arguments with Syrian regime and with Hezbollah supporters on Twitter, so actually social media is allowing me to have conversations that I can't have in my more traditional role, where there are limits.

I know you're often told not to feed the trolls, I'll often go back and reply to people and quite often that works, you get into a debate and you find that their initial hostility ebbs away. They've got a perception of what the British ambassador is, they want to lob a brick at him, and when he actually picks up the brick and lobs it back they're quite interested and surprised and they want the discussion. There is a school of thought that says it is best not to draw attention to opposing views, but I have always preferred being on the front foot in rebutting them, as they otherwise tend to fester. This morning on my blog, I got tons of really fantastic and encouraging replies. But I got one saying 'basically all these Lebanese people are being fooled by this guy, he's Satan in disguise, and we all know the Brits are only here to assassinate us', so I replied 'sorry, you've caught me out, obviously I admit it: I am the Little Satan, and I am here to assassinate you all, job's up, game's up'. I would normally go back, engage a few times, but if I get someone who is tweeting in a racist, homophobic, anti-Semitic, a really abusive way at me, I'll block them. Life's too short.

Four years ago I'd get asked to remove tweets and so on, because I was probing the line, I was trying to find where the line should be. So we're learning all the time, we make mistakes all the time. I've only deleted two tweets. Early on I tweeted I was on a yacht. Every yacht we sell here creates ten jobs in Plymouth, so I tweeted something like 'I love my job, I'm on a yacht off the coast of Beirut, this is a win-win for jobs in Beirut and jobs in Plymouth'. I was trying to show accessibility but also demonstrate that being on a yacht was actually for a reason. But the sense was that the last thing the Foreign Office needs is ambassadors telling people they're prancing around on yachts. So I deleted that one. I wouldn't tweet a picture of me drinking a glass of champagne in the rare moments I get to drink one, no one needs to see that. It doesn't help us to get our message across about what we're really doing, which is not swanning around swigging champagne.

The other one I deleted, there were public sector strikes on pensions in Britain, and I tweeted that I was too busy that day to strike, but I had sympathy or solidarity with the people striking. And it was pointed out to me by the PM that this wasn't the right thing to tweet on a government handle. Now if I'd been tweeting on a @Tom Fletcher123 handle then fair enough, if I'd walked down Whitehall with a T-shirt saying 'back the strikes' then that would be fine. But I agree it was wrong to tweet from a government handle that I had sympathy and solidarity with the strikes, so that for me was quite a clear example of where the line rests.

... I have self doubt every time I press send on a tweet, or finalise a blog, because you think: am I going to screw this one up? Is this the one that causes some great outrage and ends up with British flags being burnt across the region or embassies being torched? You do feel that responsibility. I question myself every day about the decisions we take on security. Am I keeping the staff safe? It only takes one mistake there to overwhelm everything else we've done here in the last four years.

You need to know your followers. Of mine, 25% want to know more about the life of an ambassador (what's it like to have bodyguards? Do we really eat nothing but Ferrero Rocher?), 25% are UK political junkies, 25% are Lebanon political junkies, and the rest are a mixture of the informed, interested, eccentric, curious and hostile.

But you can't be defined by your followers. We need to reach out, without falling into the trap of courting popularity. We're not comedians, journalists or politicians, and we should not pretend to be. A high number of followers is a good sign you're getting through, but is not an end in itself.

If someone else is writing your tweets, you're not on Twitter. People need to see the human behind the handle. The best diplomacy is action not reportage, purpose not platitudes. So tweets should be about changing the world, not just describing how it looks.

Quality still matters. Just because there is huge amounts of rubbish out there, this does not mean we should compromise.

Just as diplomats fail when their report matters more to them than the action they're reporting, we should guard against caring more about the pithiness of the tweet than the subject we're tweeting.

It is a jungle out there, and we have to get our brogues dirty. Every time I tweet about Palestine or Israel, I get vicious abuse from supporters of both sides, in pretty equal measure. We should listen, try to understand, but we won't convince everyone.

Lebanon's going through a major struggle at the moment. Success here is not going backwards too fast. Success here is that Lebanon is still standing at the end of the Syria crisis, and I'd be delighted if that's the case.

What people love here is conspiracy. Over many years they've had this sense there's a conspiracy against Lebanon: the international powers, the Brits and the French, the Saudis, the Iranians, we're all arm-wrestling in Lebanon, dividing and ruling and so on, and the last two years that narrative has flipped, and they've now understood that actually there's an international conspiracy *for* Lebanon, there's a feeling that there's some kind of international decision that Lebanon won't collapse.

Lebanon now has 1.2 million refugees, one in four people here is a refugee, it's the equivalent of every Pole and every Romanian moving to Britain. With that comes an enormous humanitarian burden and the development guys have responded very fast to help Lebanon cope, working to get education to people, working to get shelter, food, medicine to people. We're now providing all the textbooks in all the schools and we're scaling up to get 200,000 kids into school next year. And imagine them in ten years' time, you either imagine an army of teachers and doctors, journalists; or imagine what they'll be like if they don't get education. So we have a real national interest in getting those kids into school and it is a daily struggle.

Lebanon has, for a very small country, an amazing number of TV stations and newspapers, so it's actually an easier place to do media. It's a relatively free media, and very vibrant, but it means that everywhere you go you have a lot of cameras and a lot of microphones. There's a danger, if you have a slightly narcissistic personality already, that it gets to you, so you have to have a number of people around you to stop that. I have two sons who, whenever I get home, chant 'boring ambassador', because they see me on TV being dull, so that tends to moderate the ego a fair bit. I think everyone should have someone like that following them around saying 'you're rubbish'.

I've learned a huge amount from this job. If I'm honest, I'm completely knackered. It's been a demanding posting. If Lebanon falls then you have a huge humanitarian crisis, even closer to our doorstep than the one in Syria. It's also a question of heart. If we can't find a way to coexist here in Lebanon, based on tolerance and diversity, then we will actually lose that battle closer to home, so I see it very much as a front line for what is going to be the massive battle of the twenty-first century.

That for me is the real reason why we have to engage here, why we have to get the books into the hands of the kids, get the right kit and training into the hands of the army, so they can win that battle. It's also why we have to be on the side of the positive people here, those who are looking to coexist, against those who are looking to divide the country, that for me is a battle worth being in. Those are enemy lines I want to get behind. And we're doing that.

I'm very proud to wear the shirt, to represent my country here, and to lead a team doing the work we're doing. I will leave with my head up, knowing that we were on the right side. When the rest of the region was in flames, when the barbarians were at the gates here, Lebanon held its corner, held the line. And we played a small part in that.

13

Envoy 2025

Let's imagine the British ambassador in Stockholm in 2025.

She is woken refreshed from a night in which her smartphone has measured her sleeping pattern to ensure maximum rest and assessed what nutrients she needs in her morning smoothie. As she has breakfast, her tablet projects onto the mirror, the wall, or her glasses a distilled stream of analysis and news, curated by experts to ensure that it focuses on her priorities. In the car on her way to work she has a video conference with her capital and neighbouring posts on the breaking news.

She enters her embassy through a series of non-intrusive but effective security checks. The embassy building is at the cutting edge of sustainable, innovative design. The ground floor is an engagement zone, a pavilion full of space and light, designed by Britain's best creative minds, not by civil servants. All services are online, with customers who want to access them in the building also able to explore virtual reality tours of the UK. Students are accessing language materials, online and in the library, and a class is meeting for its monthly discussion group.

Other customers are learning about cultural events or watching British films in the cinema space. People are making connections to British friends and strangers through hundreds of iPads with bespoke apps. Some are making business deals through a portal that uses online dating technology to link them to UK networks. Students are taking virtual tours of UK campuses, and sitting in on sample lectures.

A café serves organic British products, and some non-organic fish and chips. Interior walls feature a constantly changing virtual gallery of contemporary UK artwork. Kids are having photos taken with interactive models of British heroes, with Prince George the most popular.

This is not a space that people come to as a chore, but a place to which they choose to come. It projects the UK as fresh, innovative and creative. It channels the same spirit that lifted the London 2012 Olympics. This is an energising environment – there is a sense of possibility in the air.

Our envoy chairs a meeting with her key staff, most joining via their smartphones. All have tablets on which they can add to the meeting record, displayed on a virtual whiteboard.

She spends an hour online, engaging members of the public and helping visiting Brits understand where to get help. She joins a digital démarche on human rights, quickly backed by a million people, and picks a lively but respectful online argument with her Russian colleague, with thousands joining the debate on both sides of the argument.

She hosts a virtual coffee on climate change with civil-society activists from all over the globe, live-streamed. She uploads to the embassy website a digital clip of her response to the new Swedish energy policy, which is simultaneously translated. Having received intelligence on a possible terrorist attack, she checks the number of Brits in country, all registered through the embassy's visitor app, and where they are, just in case she needs to mobilise a rapid crisis response. She sends those in the capital a message reminding them to be vigilant.

At a public event on the UK's plans for reform of the UN, live-streamed and with a social media wall for interaction with what was once called an audience, she is pleased to see that most in the room are playing with their phones, a good sign that they are engaging and interacting. Struck by a comment from a participant in Texas, she downloads a paper written ten years earlier by a colleague in Finland and shares key elements with other participants as she speaks.

She hosts a video call between a local private sector group, a UK investor and one of her predecessors with particularly good business sense – in a networked world she needs to leverage every influence possible, and is not protective of her control of the UK brand.

She looks forward to a more traditional encounter, lunch with the Swedish foreign minister. As is now standard etiquette, there will be no smartphones on the table – not just because half the world could listen in, but because it is just rude.

It used to be said that the best diplomats are either boffin, boy scout or assassin. No longer. The 2020 envoy is a lobbyist, leader, communicator, pioneer, entrepreneur, activist, campaigner, advocate. She has learnt from the best in those fields, and has worked in several of them. She does crossover. She competes for space, attention, relevance and influence. She builds game-changing coalitions and alliances across business, civil society, borders.

She uses information rather than managing it. She understands that diplomacy is not some kind of secret art form, concealed by jargon and titles. She does not hide behind diplomatic platitudes. She bases herself less on structures and institutions than on networks. She unleashes the younger (and older) members of her team to reach the parts she cannot. She spends little time in international conferences. Instead, she finds out where people are, and goes there.

She doesn't see the embassy as a building, but as an idea. Hers is the hub for the national brand and UK companies she promotes unashamedly. Her appraisals include an assessment of her digital clout. She gives her Foreign Secretary added value through influence and analysis, not just reportage. She prioritises outcomes over relationships. She takes risks. She does not believe that diplomacy is a job for life.

I think she sounds authentic, flexible, connected, influential and above all purposeful.

And we need her to be, if we are going to survive what the Digital Century is about to throw at us.

PART THREE

What Next?

Who Runs the Digital Century?

International systems live precariously. Every 'world order' expresses an aspiration to permanence; the very term has a ring of eternity to it. Yet the elements which comprise it are in constant flux: indeed, with each century, the duration of international systems has been shrinking.

Henry Kissinger, *Diplomacy* (1994)

I met a traveller from an antique land
Who said: Two vast and trunkless legs of stone
Stand in the desert. Near them, on the sand,
Half sunk, a shattered visage lies, whose frown,
And wrinkled lip, and sneer of cold command,
Tell that its sculptor well those passions read,
Which yet survive, stamped on these lifeless things,
The hand that mocked them, and the heart that fed.
And on the pedestal these words appear:
'My name is Ozymandias, king of kings:
Look on my works, ye Mighty, and despair!'
No thing beside remains. Round the decay
Of that colossal wreck, boundless and bare,
The lone and level sands stretch far away.

Percy Bysshe Shelley, 'Ozymandias' (1818)

During my time in Lebanon, I sometimes needed to escape the tempo of Beirut, the intensity of the Syria crisis, the security bubble, and the constant connectivity of social life and social media. My hideaway was the magnificent fort of Byblos, one of the oldest continually inhabited towns in the world. Legend has it that the Phoenician Princess Europa was abducted by Zeus (disguised as a bull) from here – reminding us that Europeans were kidnapping and people-trafficking as well as the people of the Middle East.

From Byblos, people have watched the fleets come and go for centuries. You can stand among the debris of nineteen civilisations. Each of those empires thought themselves invincible or permanent. Each believed that they had something different, special, unique.

The castle was consistently reduced to rubble, like the civilisations.

Byblos is no place for hubris. I stood there whenever I thought I had the world worked out.

We know from history that the desire to gain and use power is hardwired into humanity. Empires, civilisations, families and individuals have risen up not just to run their own regions, but to conquer and rule those of others. We also know from history that they fall, normally when they become overstretched, lazy or corroded from within, when demagogues run amok, when they start to see the world as a source of anxiety not opportunity, or when hungrier power rivals emerge. A world where one country dominates cannot last long. Challengers always rise up to snap at the heels of the top dog of the age. Power ebbs and flows. Empires often collapse rapidly – look at the Mings in the seventeenth century, the Bourbons in the eighteenth century, or the British and Russian empires in the twentieth century.

The tectonics of global power are still in flux. 'Power', says former World Bank president Bob Zoellick, 'is easier to get, harder to use, and easier to lose.'[1] From Beirut to Bangalore, and from Birmingham UK to Birmingham, Alabama, we are feeling not only the tremors of changes in the geopolitical power balance, but also more fundamental power shifts, away from traditional authorities and hierarchies and towards greater empowerment of individuals.

Traditionally, power is measured by historians and diplomats in terms of territory, war and statecraft. This is usually a zero-sum game: power is a pie to be sliced up. China's rise, Europe's decline. Power can be won or lost by good or bad decisions or political systems, by military might or weakness. It is raw power by Machiavelli, Stalin's tanks, a never-ending struggle in which great states and great men – almost always men – compete constantly with blood and treasure for influence, land and markets.

It is naturally easier for diplomats to understand the world in terms of this great power narrative. We are used to it. The big questions in international affairs since the birth of modern diplomacy in the fifteenth century have been about how states relate to each other. Diplomats found and expanded a natural niche in that system. It also reinforces our roles – we send ambassadors to Paris and Beijing, not to Google and Apple (though a high number of former ambassadors seem to find their way onto the boards of defence companies). Perhaps most important, it is a comforting way of understanding the world – because for diplomats to accept a decline in states also means accepting a decline in statecraft.

Yet foreign ministries have long ceased to be able to monopolise their government's interface with the world, let alone their country's.

An alternative idea, often promoted by geographers and anthropologists, is that power is about maps not chaps.[2] As early as the fifth century BC, Greek historian Herodotus could show that 'soft countries breed soft men'. In this narrative, civilisations rise and fall not because of mighty battles and inspirational leaders, but because of the advantages and disadvantages of geography, and their proximity to the energy source of the era. So, for example, with the thaw at the end of the Ice Age, European soil became better suited to the domestication of plants and animals. And the Brits had the advantage from the seventeenth century, because they unlocked fossil-fuel energy. Great men might slow down or speed up these changes, but they are at the mercy of longer-term trends that they cannot comprehend at the time.

In either matrix for analysing power, we cannot be in any doubt that it is changing, fast.

We are living through four major trends: the erosion of US hegemony and a shift to a period without a lead nation; the collapse, perhaps rapid, of the twentieth-century world order; the increased influence of non-state actors and new elites; and the technological empowerment of individuals. I'll look in more detail at each of these.

Who is winning what David Cameron has characterised as 'the global race', the competition between states for economic and therefore military ascendancy? As the Chinese premier Zhou Enlai reportedly responded to Henry Kissinger when asked about the impact of the French Revolution, it is too soon to say.

The current American – and by extension Western – dominance is unlikely to be the exception to the ebb and flow of empires, but that is not to say that it will disappear as fast as many claim. US academic Francis Fukuyama famously asked in an essay in 1989 if we had reached 'The End of History?' He saw the great ideological battles between East and West as settled – Western liberal democracy had triumphed, and could not be bettered. Game over. It was not that events would stop happening, nor that there would be areas that held out against Pax Americana. But mankind would reach the end of our ideological evolution.

This seductive claim now looks harder to stack up. Many economists anticipate that the East will have the upper hand by the second half of this century. British academic Martin Jacques predicts with beguiling precision that the East will overtake the West in 2103.[3]

China and other dynamo emerging economies certainly have the wind in their sails. In the decade from 2003–13, China has gone from zero billionaires to over 300. It exports every eight hours what it used to in a single year (1978).[4] The Chinese economy was one-third the size of the US economy a decade ago, but will overtake the US by 2020. It has twice the number of Internet users as the US. The average American is earning ten times as much as the average Chinese, but China is lending the West money to buy its goods.

So what of the superpower? In 2013, the US had faster economic growth than the global average for the first time since the financial crisis. But it is becoming increasingly dependent on foreign capital; has had its military strength challenged and drained in Afghanistan and Iraq; and internally is increasingly politically polarised. Little wonder then that President Obama has sought to present a less expansionist military creed than his predecessor – 'just because we have the biggest hammer doesn't mean that every problem is a nail'.[5]

Europe meanwhile is in decline, if not free fall. Former UK Foreign Secretary Douglas Hurd suggests that 'in the penny-farthing relationship with the United States, the farthing is getting smaller'.[6] The European Union as an institution is unpopular with its citizens, and too often bossed about on the world stage. Europe is getting greyer – it is the only continent with a rising proportion of the population over sixty-five, and its birth rates are half of those in the Muslim world. President Obama is not just pivoting to Asia – he is pivoting away from Europe.

Meanwhile, nations with emerging economies such as Brazil and India are beginning to dominate economic growth. This is making them more politically assertive, and readier to challenge the post-1945 settlement that attempted to stall the decline of the former colonial powers. Some previously pioneer democracies such as Thailand, Sri Lanka, Turkey or Bangladesh are slipping backwards.[7]

So the balance between East and West is shifting, and the American unipolar moment, what Henry Kissinger called 'a triumph of faith over experience', looks to be passing.

But it is too early to say how long that will take, or what will replace it. The US is still spending almost as much on defence as the total spend of the next fourteen powers.[8] The Chinese model rests on sustaining improbably high growth rates, and China spends more on internal policing than external defence. So it would be rash to bet on the US resembling China in fifty years rather than China resembling the US. Much depends on whether successful Chinese Internet companies – Alibaba is bigger than eBay and Amazon combined – can win the argument for openness, and outward-looking confidence. Economies that don't base themselves on property rights, innovation and the rule of law will not win in the long run. China is the West's greatest challenge. And its greatest opportunity. There is all to play for.

Instead of a balance of power, we perhaps look set to be heading, faster than we realise, towards a period characterised by the absence of any hegemonic power. States, even the biggest and strongest, are discovering the limits of their influence. Syria has been a grim example of the limits of global reach, stomach and compassion. Assad has been a fortunate man – his brutality coincided with a period of global economic weakness, inwardness and war-weariness, and a moment when Russia was looking for painless – for Russia at least – ways to bite at the heels of the US. A leaderless world might sound attractive in theory, but it will not be pretty in practice.

Meanwhile, the international architecture is weakening fast, corroded from outside and rotting from within. The post-Second World War institutions such as the United Nations, World Trade Organisation, International Monetary Fund and World Bank are seen by most of the world as increasingly unrepresentative, irrelevant and powerless. Aspirations by many Western policymakers for the collective use of limited force to protect the most vulnerable – enshrined in what the UN at a more optimistic moment called Responsibility to Protect (R2P) – have been buried by austerity and Iraq. Once again, the Syrian people have been the main victims of this trend.

Emerging powers such as India, Singapore or Brazil that feel under-represented in these international institutions are likely to continue to mount an increasingly effective guerrilla war against them. Most want many of the same things as the powers who locked down control of the global structures after the Second World War – free-ish trade, economic growth, avoidance of terrorism or nuclear proliferation. But they also want a louder voice at the top table, and they will be disruptive until they get it.

This will threaten the entrenched powers. The privileged position in international structures of countries such as the UK and France will come under further attack. The states that dominated the nineteenth century need to lead reform before it is too late for them to influence it. Former prime minister John Major warns that the UN Security Council is 'grotesquely out of date', having been created 'in a world that bears no relationship to today'.[9]

The nation state has been the main arbitrator of global power since the Treaty of Westphalia in 1648. The Europeans exported the model, drawing lines – often randomly[10] – in the sand across the Middle East and Africa to create new nations. A century later, across the region, but most potently in Iraq and Syria, we can now see the rivets popping. But this is also part of a broader drive for decentralisation of authority, captured closer to home in the independence debates of Catalonia and Scotland.

At previous points of such power transition, protracted war or violent revolution reset the global structures. The 1815–1914 system, based on the concert of powers agreed in Vienna, was destroyed in the mud and blood of the two world wars. The post-1945 system then sought, with great idealism, to establish clearer rules to manage power, reduce the risk of military confrontation, and create space for economic cooperation.

That scaffolding looks pretty shaky now. The resources that China needs to fuel its continued growth (iron, copper, cobalt, timber, natural gas, oil) are located in the unstable crescent from North Africa to Afghanistan. The Ukraine crisis has shown that Putin's Russia is more robustly nibbling away at the edges of US authority, picking its moments to strike when it believes the US is distracted or turning inwards. The powers with most to gain from retaining the status quo are struggling to resource that aspiration. Those with most to gain from its destruction are not offering an alternative vision.

Meanwhile, post-1989 globalisation has meant that the major threats on the international agenda are now more cross-border and transnational – terrorism, climate change, weapons of mass destruction, disease. Most of the twenty-first century's wars so far have been fought on those issues rather than to secure territory or resources. Conflict is predominantly inside rather than between states.

This demands global action and global leadership. Yet, faced with these global challenges, more countries look set to prioritise unilateral interests over multilateral cooperation. As we have seen with the debate on migration from the Middle East and North Africa, the reflex is all too often defensive and nationalist.

The international architecture may be collapsing. But the answer to the twenty-first century is not another brick in the wall.

So if states are on the wane, and the US is ceding ground, who is really in charge? In the absence of an agreed methodology, the 2015 Forbes list of the world's most powerful leaders, business-men and other players is not a bad place to start.

Of those in the top seventy-two of the list, only twelve can be said to have gone through some form of democratic election (three of them are in the top ten), though we can argue as to whether that really includes the leaders of China, the Vatican and Russia. Nine of the top seventy-two (with two in the top ten) are international functionaries, central bankers or heads of United Nations agencies. One is a drug lord. (Sepp Blatter, who continues to fight corruption charges, appeared in previous lists – FIFA is now having a long overdue spring clean, and how Blatter will fare remains to be seen.)

Only two of the top seventy-two had parents in the list – the king of Saudi Arabia and Kim Jong-un. There are now nine women, still too low, but up from three in 2009. There are twelve entrepreneurs, and their average age is dropping. But those seeing US decline will be disappointed – though Forbes caught headlines by replacing Barack Obama with Vladimir Putin at the top of the league table, thirty-two of the slots are still held by Americans.

The list also shows the continued hold of business over power.
The twenty-seven CEOs in the list turn over $3 trillion annually.
Fortune magazine says that the three largest companies in the
world have assets worth $550 billion and employ more than 1.8
million people. It is much too soon to write off big business.

What will the Forbes list look like in 2025?

It will surely be more geographically diverse – more than the
one African, two Indians, three South Americans and six Chinese
in the 2015 list. The US will still dominate. On this trajectory, the
Europeans probably can't increase their pitiful contribution from
five (three of them heads of government).

The list will also surely be more gender diverse, though still
some way from parity. The business quota (roughly half) will
probably remain about the same, but with a higher proportion
of entrepreneurs. New kinds of networks have not changed the
underlying nature of power, just how it is exercised. Successful
businesses have always been able to evolve to succeed in new
contexts. If the new platforms for power are the places where we
connect, create and most importantly consume, successful
corporations will migrate to them. The Internet will not be tear-
ing down barriers as quickly as we think. It may even erect new
ones.

So who are the new emperors?

When hosting Google senior executives in Lebanon in 2014, I
was struck by their pulling power. Ministers who were hard to pin
down for meetings with government counterparts dropped whatever they were doing to make time. I saw the same trend at the
Hay Festival in 2013, where Google were able to gather many of
us for a dinner with the chairman, Eric Schmidt. Google were able
to hold court. As we rely more heavily on the Internet for our
social and professional lives, those who run it will become the
new emperors.

This trend alarms many. Blaming the fact that 'democracy and capitalism have both been hacked', Al Gore predicts 'the transformation of the global economy and the emergence of Earth Inc.'[11]

But I'm not so sure. Google would not be the first company in history to be ambitious and creative, with megalomaniac tendencies. Companies like them are actually creating the freedom of choice and manoeuvre that limit the power of any single institution, including their own. We are unlikely ever to see again a company as powerful as the East India Company, which ruled much of Asia, funded a massive army and set the imperial agenda.

Some of the new emperors will be NGOs. As power becomes less like a hierarchy and more like a spider web, new actors will fill some of the vacuum. The Worldwide Fund for Nature (WWF, formerly the World Wildlife Fund) has over 5 million members, and a budget three times that of the World Trade Organisation. Greenpeace has 2.8 million members, many more than any political party in the UK. Increasingly, such NGOs are punching at their weight, with advocacy arms and stronger coordination of lobbying and campaigning.

Some of the new emperors will be mayors. The rebirth of the city state is a key feature of this new landscape. More than half of the world's population live in cities, and the population of megacities has increased tenfold in forty years. By 2030, that figure will be 5 billion, or 60% of the population, and forty cities will have a population of over 10 million. By 2050, there will be more city-dwellers than the entire the population of the world in the 1990s.

Many mayors – Sadiq Khan in London, Yury Luzhkov of Moscow, Wolfgang Schuster in Stuttgart – argue that the city is already the most effective government unit. Mayors may draw strength from helping to reduce the growing trust deficit in politics, being close enough to citizens to engage, but with increasing

powers to shape lives. The hungry politician may choose municipal over national politics.

Cities will compete in the way that countries do, and that city
states used to. The Pearl River Delta in China would be a G20
member if it were a country. Our identities may become shaped
by the city of residence more than the country of origin: look at
New Yorkers, Londoners, Beirutis or Parisians. Already, cities are
often ahead of governments on urban regeneration, citizen
engagement, energy and transportation. Cities can succeed even
in failed states. But no state succeeds without successful cities.

How long before cities appoint their own diplomats, just like
their Renaissance predecessors?

The rise of the super-mayor presents other challenges. Like the
early gentleman diplomats, many require their own wealth to
succeed. The personal cost to Michael Bloomberg of his twelve
years as New York mayor was in the region of $650 million. He
flew aides at his expense, running up a $6 million bill. His
estimated tab for a multiday trip to China, with aides and security
in tow: $500,000. For the *New York Times*, 'Mr Bloomberg's
all-expense-paid mayoralty was, depending on the vantage point,
exhilarating (for his aides), infuriating (for his rivals) cost-saving
(for his constituents) or selfless (for the beneficiaries of his
largesse).'[12] Maybe we are moving back towards the age of the
public representative who can pay their own way. This might be
superficially tempting, but it will make government more distant
and impenetrable.

Power is shifting, from west to east, north to south, and from
traditional actors to newer ones. But not as fast or predictably as
many suggest. And we need to be as vigilant in establishing
checks and balances on the new emperors as the old ones.

*

But more dramatic, and I would argue exciting, are the power shifts away from states to individuals. Power is diffusing. Power as we know it has been disrupted by individuals – the likes of Steve Jobs – just as it was in the past by the likes of Alexander the Great. And by innovations – by the integrated circuit as it was by the stirrup.

This technology tsunami is changing the relationship between governments and citizens. As we have seen, this new hyper-connectivity reduces trust in traditional political and media elites, and empowers citizen commentators. We're using these devices to become creators and distributors. YouTube has more video content uploaded in a single month than the three main US channels broadcast in their first sixty years. More photos were taken in 2013 than in the rest of history. The digital generation beams out its triumphs and humiliations, not caring who is watching. As marketers have long realised, people trust the voices of their peers more than they trust elites. Increased access to information gives citizens more power than ever before, and therefore governments less. MIT's Moisés Naím characterises it not just as a shift in power but 'The End of Power'.

The generation now coming to positions of influence in much of the world is the first to have spent their entire career with the Internet. They will be even better prepared to shine a light into dark corners and comfort zones. They will get to positions of influence faster than any generation before them – but lose those positions faster too.

This shift in power is a big deal. Our comfort zones are being disrupted. New ways of thinking and living are fundamentally changing what it means to be human. The transformation of how we meet our needs for security, dignity and community will shatter the political equilibrium, and haemorrhage power away from governments towards citizens.

The printing press was the last innovation remotely compara-
ble to the Internet in its ability to diffuse and spread knowledge.
Like the Internet it reduced the entry barrier for access to information. As a result, as we've seen, it triggered the modern world.

States will still be around for some time. We haven't yet come up
with a better idea. But they are becoming weaker and less trusted.
Ironically, at a time when the world faces a more dramatic combination of change and challenge than ever before, we are overwhelmed by that change. At a time when we have the tools to
react globally, we are failing to use them. We face massive global
transition at a time when there is a lack of global leadership, and
a growing realisation that we are leaderless. No one has a plan.
We have not begun to adapt our institutions to the new realities.

If we are witnessing the birth of the first truly global, connected
civilisation, where are decisions to be taken to protect our basic
human needs? The world is becoming less like a formal traditional
British banquet and more like a Lebanese meze: unstructured,
free, sometimes chaotic.

The next fifty years are the most important in history. We are
going to need to find ways to wing it intelligently. Or as *Toy Story*'s
charismatic spaceman Buzz Lightyear puts it, 'This isn't flying,
this is falling with style.'

This is why diplomacy matters so much. These challenges are
not just about the Internet, but about how information, and the
power that goes with it, is distributed. Diplomats must help deliver
the benefits of the digital century, while helping to ease its birth
pangs. Statecraft does not get you far without states or craft. Ask
the leaders of the forgotten empires of Byblos.

Nowhere will this challenge be more evident than in the future
of work, and what that means for society. Technology has always

changed the nature of the work we do. My ancestors were arrow-makers who would have had to dust off the equivalent of their CVs when gunpowder came along. The Industrial Revolution destroyed the job prospects for weavers. We are now much more likely to be employed for our brains than our brawn.

The impact of this next phase of innovation is going to destroy jobs more quickly than we can create them, with huge implications for politics. In January 2014, *The Economist* sounded the alarm for the global labour market. Automation and robotics are driving the outsourcing of jobs in all sectors of the economy to developing countries. You are as threatened as a lawyer or sports commentator as you are on a car-assembly plant, camera film factory or security desk. Today, 47% of jobs in the US are at high risk.[13] When computers can perform more complicated tasks more cheaply and effectively than humans, the public sector should also be quaking.

We want this innovation to replace the work we don't want to do. But we don't want it to replace us altogether. We'll need to find new ways to work. Since 2008, over 333,000 people in Britain alone have registered as self-employed.[14] There will be push factors, as competition for jobs increases. And pull factors – more people will be attracted to the idea that they are masters of their own fate.

Innovation should create new and better jobs, while farmers become office workers, secretaries become computer programmers, diplomats become waiters. But less dramatic transformations of the labour market have ruptured politics and societies in the past. The costs are always felt faster than the benefits. Inequality will grow. 'Technology's impact will feel like a tornado, hitting the rich world first, but eventually sweeping through poorer countries too', *The Economist* concluded. 'No government is prepared for it.'

No government is prepared for it. These are six powerful and terrifying words for anyone in politics (and everyone outside politics).

So the bad news is that we are living in the period of fastest change in history. But that is also the good news. We have the opportunity to shape the first genuinely global community.

All this change is going to take management. The transfer of power from hierarchies to networks will generate winners and losers. Some will adjust. Others will feel threatened and disempowered. How can that transition be less brutal? If we are dealing with an accelerated Darwinism, how can we ensure that it is not just the fittest who survive? How can digital technology reduce rather than increase inequality? How can we defend societies and communities against the new threats that this massive, accelerated, disruptive change will produce? These are the themes that run through the rest of this book.

Of course, it isn't just the good guys competing in this space. Many of those now playing on the same terrain are terrorists, pirates, vandals and international crime syndicates. And we are going to have to fight them for digital territory.

The Battle for Digital Territory

This war will be a battle of ideas and values, not just weapons. It will be fought more online than offline. The enemies will not be obvious. The front lines will not be drawn on a map. On one side will be those who believe in coexistence, the ability of humans from different races and religions to live together. On the other side will be those who don't.

When I arrived in Beirut in August 2011, it was possible to feel the electrical charge of the change sweeping through the region.

I've described the way that the printing press created the modern world – it was the web of its day. But it didn't change the Arab world, because the Ottoman empire banned it, rightly fearing the implications for traditional power of the spread of information and knowledge. The Enlightenment took two centuries longer to reach much of the Middle East, the region that had done more than any to protect and develop the cause of progress when the Europeans were in their own Dark Ages.

The early years of the Arab Spring suggested that the Middle East was not going to make the same mistake twice. These were 'the Facebook and Twitter revolutions', with activists sharing news and mobilising themselves online.

The Arab Spring started in Tunisia, where technology penetration was relatively sophisticated – 40% of people had an Internet connection in 2011, and 20% were on Facebook. Social media contributed to the timing and amplification of the turmoil, undermining traditional sources of authority and repression. Activists seized on this new ability to communicate, and to organise.

There are plenty of examples from elsewhere in the world of how this works. On 12 March 2014, 100,000 people came to the Istanbul funeral of a fifteen-year-old boy, Berkin Elvan, who had been hit on the head by a police tear-gas canister while on his way to a bakery. The massive turnout was the result of the way his story had spread on Facebook and Instagram. Digital tools make it easy to build massive attention or to organise protest on an issue at lightning speed. They had such effect in Turkey during the 2014 Gezi protests that the then prime minister, Tayyip Erdogan, called Twitter a 'menace to society' (he is now president, after a campaign that included, of course, Twitter).

As I tweeted at the time, you don't have to be pro-Twitter to be pro-freedom, but I can't see how you can be anti-Twitter and pro-freedom.

Elsewhere, the Spanish Indignados movement took control of many public squares to protest against austerity. Occupy Wall Street dominated Manhattan in October 2011. And Egypt's Tahrir Square protests in January 2011 became the talismanic Arab Spring protest. In Ukraine, popular protest was accompanied by massive sharing of photos, videos and texts. Twitter became a real-time newsfeed for Venezuelan protesters, and was the venue for lively exchanges between President Nicolás Maduro and opposition leader Leopoldo López.

Just as digital technology allows for faster innovation by bringing people together, it also allows them to spread protest. This matters massively to the way we analyse the world, and the way we do diplomacy. The uprisings of the Arab Spring fed off each other. Activists could for the first time watch the simultaneous successes and failures of their counterparts in other parts of the region, document what was happening around them in real time, share it more easily, and organise themselves more effectively. Anyone can now be a broadcaster or commentator. Political action is becoming a franchise rather than a controlled party operation. Global protest politics – from WikiLeaks to Anonymous – is breaking down old power monopolies. This will be hugely empowering, but also hugely destructive.

Of course, it wasn't just about social media. In the case of the Arab Spring the underlying grievances were a mixture of economic, social and political – a desire for greater security, justice and opportunity. Those aspirations were there before Twitter, and they will probably be there after Twitter. And traditional media also still played an essential role. In the case of much of the Arab Spring, Al Jazeera, Qatar's mischievously independent TV station, spread the news of uprisings from country to country, triggering demonstrations of support and fresh uprisings.

It is too soon to tell whether the Arab Spring will generate the more enlightened government that most people want, or will be derailed by the power struggle between securocrats and Islamists, by sectarianism, or by misguided or cynical external interference. Social media revolutions also don't always work. They make it easier for activists to mobilise, organise, and to spread information – but that often means that popular protest occurs before the organisation and hard work has been done to turn it into something tangible. The Indignados, Wall Street Occupiers, Syria and Tahrir Square protesters did not in the end win. At least, not yet. The hard men fought back.

But more battles still lie ahead. Social media will continue to play a part in breaking down barriers everywhere where people are connected to the Internet. Digital media alone did not create the Arab Spring, but it made it less predictable, and more wide-spread. It is no longer possible to imagine an uprising or revolution that does not deploy social media.

We have also found that digital technology allows those opposed to basic liberties a platform to suppress them, promote their atrocities, and recruit their foot soldiers. Shrewd authoritarian regimes will crack down on digital freedom, and turn it against activists. Social media campaigns will also be used to fuel extremism and polarise debate – the modern equivalent of the use of hate radio during the Rwandan genocide, or the evil but powerful propaganda of Joseph Goebbels.

Nowhere is agile, savvy digital diplomacy needed more than in the online and offline war with ISIL and its extremist offshoots and copycats. The three cities in which I have spent most of my adult life – Paris, Beirut and Nairobi – have now all been ripped open by acts of terror. The attack on Paris in November 2015, the largest terrorist atrocity in Europe for a decade, will sear itself onto Western consciousness in the way that 9/11 did. That's what the sociopaths with smartphones wanted.

Let's not be misled about why ISIL targeted Paris. They hit what they call the 'greyzone' – places where Muslims and non-Muslims interact. In doing so, they pitched camp on the wrong side of the twenty-first century's key dividing line – not between Christianity and Islam, East and West, or even haves and have nots, but between those who want to live together, and those who don't. They have also flushed out some in our own societies, political debates and timelines who don't either. The effort to close some US and European states to refugees is a propaganda gift to ISIL.

Those who see foreigners as fundamentally different probably haven't met many. Most Syrians want what we want – to educate their children and to live in security. As anyone who has visited knows, they are among the most hospitable people in the world.

They would not be risking everything to escape unless there was no alternative. Much of the debate is reminiscent of the Twitter spats I had in 2013 in Lebanon, when it dealt with a much larger influx. 'They want our comfort.' Well, try spending a night in a refugee camp. 'They should go home.' Well, take a look at a photo of Homs. 'They are dangerous.' A tiny minority, maybe. But most are women and kids, themselves fleeing terror. We didn't blame Jewish refugees for the Nazis.

However insecure we feel, the answer is in fact more liberty, equality, fraternity, not less. And not just for those of us fortunate to have been born further, or so we thought, from the eye of the storm. The public reaction to the stories of heroism and tragedy of so many refugees has demonstrated that we have not reached the limits of our compassion. We should be proud that our countries are magnetic; generous in our support to vulnerable refugees; and smart enough to recognise the economic potential of migrants. Ask the Pilgrim Fathers.

Despite seeking to return their territory to the eleventh century, ISIL have no qualms about using the technology that embodies the modernity they claim to despise. They are box-office barbarians. They seek to monopolise the horror genre for the Internet age, and they believe they are better at social media than we are.

ISIL sent 40,000 tweets in one day as they took Mosul in June 2014. It deploys sophisticated tools to tweet hashtags at key times of the day so that they trend to a far more significant extent than their rivals. Classic propaganda using new tools. Their nimble and unstructured social media use has displaced the clumsier and lengthier speeches of al-Qaeda – even terrorists get disrupted.

As this market gets more competitive, so will terrorists. They aim to hold digital territory, not just physical territory. If ISIL claim a digital state, will people in Luton and Lagos be able to become members of that state from their bedrooms, paying taxes and pledging allegiance? In the way that children on their iPads can now inhabit imaginary worlds, we will see people spending more time in new imagined communities that increasingly resemble the offline world.

The same could apply to states that become non-states. A resistance movement driven from its territory would in the past maintain the paraphernalia of the state – flags, titles, an army. It could now take with it the digital infrastructure too – records, data, government. A state can continue without land.

I saw this battle for digital territory played out, virtual block by block, in Tripoli, northern Lebanon. Young Muslim entrepreneurs told me that what they wanted was the chance to dream big. They wanted help. But failing that, 'we'll settle for Wi-Fi and do the rest'. Local Islamists regularly disabled the Internet connections in the entrepreneurs' club, making it harder to connect with the world outside. ISIL and Co. deliberately target the places where Muslims and non-Muslims interact. They want to kill not just those coexisting, but the idea of coexistence.

Evidently, we need those entrepreneurs to win. This is the dividing line of our age, and the battle of our age.

The so-called 'Islamic State' run their digital operation like an insurgency, playing to their strengths – an ability to move fast, conduct 'drive-by' attacks, and reach out to the vulnerable and angry. We will need to build a digital counter-insurgency that plays to our strengths, including tolerance, numbers and, yes, humour. When given the choice, more people run from ISIL than are running to them. This is not a war we can lose.

Meanwhile, social media has played more of a role in the Syria conflict than any in history.

This creates opportunities for diplomats and journalists to understand what is happening on the ground, even when they have been based in Beirut or Istanbul. The flattening of the Syrian

city of Homs in 2012 was far better documented than the flattening of the nearby city of Hama in 1982, when just a few buccaneering Western journalists – Robert Fisk, Jonathan Randall,
Tom Friedman – were able to tell the world what had happened.

Those curating the information reliably become more powerful. Brown Moses is an example of an analyst who has made a
career from his sofa of being able to comment reliably on YouTube
clips of the weapons used. Groups on both sides have been able to
create waves of attention on the basis of forged videos or content
from other conflicts.

But social media creates also new challenges. Videos don't just
record conflict. They also drive it, feeding the desire for revenge or
emulation.

As part of the battle for coexistence, social media are also changing the nature of diplomatic negotiations in the Middle East and
beyond. They are now a core part of the effort to bring Iran in
from the cold, against the efforts of some hardliners in
Washington, Tel Aviv or Tehran.

After his first ever call with President Obama, President Hassan
Rouhani of Iran scooped the White House by tweeting the news
before it was announced in Washington. The negotiation between
Iran and the five permanent members of the UN Security Council
(plus Germany) was the first diplomatic breakthrough to be
announced, by John Kerry and Baroness Ashton simultaneously,
on Twitter.

Governments don't always set the agenda: Rouhani's online
messages meant that he was embraced by the Davos community
before the diplomatic and government community. The emergence of his Twitter account after his election, pumping out
much more reasonable and moderate positions than anticipated,

went a long way to change Iran's reputation and lay the ground-work for diplomacy.

Again, of course Twitter cannot take all the credit. The pieces of the kaleidoscope on a better relationship between Iran and the West were already in motion. Realignment of global forces, the impact of sanctions, and fear of the potential of further instability in the Middle East served to drive the two sides together. However, the Iran deal happened faster because of Twitter. The fact that Rouhani was enthusiastically tweeting about the potential for agreement, and retweeting those who had seemed to be his opponents, *did* change the context. This approach was part of a savvy, agile digital diplomacy plan by Iran, and made it much harder for critics of the agreement to argue that they were monolithic, closed or cynical.

I donated blood following an attack on the Iranian embassy in Beirut, and released the photo on Twitter. This was at a time when our relations were still in the freezer, and I was unsure what the reaction would be – in Iran and at home. So I was surprised but heartened to be retweeted by Rouhani, and thereafter by hundreds of Iranians. Sometimes in diplomacy, a gesture – especially when amplified widely by social media – is more important than words.

Of course the challenge for Iran now is to offer this same apparent openness to its own people, lifting controls of the Internet and allowing use of Twitter and Facebook. The government remains reluctant, knowing full well that this would provide Iranians with the access to the rest of the world that many crave. This is one to watch. Social media alone will not create democracy, but it gives those working for change a platform, connections and a voice. Their freedom is in our interest too.

The battle for digital territory doesn't just apply to non-state actors, but to wannabe-state actors. Croatia weren't getting enough recognition from the UN, so they forced Google Maps, through citizen pressure, to mark them on the map as a state. As new states emerge or return – Catalonia? Palestine? Kurdistan? – will their online presence drive their presence on the ground?

The battle for digital territory will not just be fought between ISIL and its opponents. Just as we faced fundamental questions when diplomats constructed the state-based system, there are key issues to resolve about how we share power online. We are building the plane as we fly it, but amid the cacophony I think there are three guiding principles that can help.

Firstly, technological change is unstoppable. The genie does not go back into the bottle. We can't prevent it, even if we want to. What we can do is to ask the right questions about what it means, and what we want from it. The answers should not only be about efficiency, speed and cost.

Secondly, the overall effect of the Internet is positive, and will give more people the means to understand, engage and influence the world. It is better ultimately to have too much information than too little. But it is not painless. It will also empower some whose impulses are more destructive. We should acknowledge the victims of change, and find ways to ensure that the benefits of connectivity reduce rather than increase inequality.

Third, we need a genuine public debate about our digital rights, tackling the toughest issues around trust and transparency. We need to find the balance between freedom of expression and the rights of others. We must resist the pressures towards over-sharing and relentless joining-in. We still need a smartphone-free carriage on the train, and a digital-free portion of our brain. Someone has to write the Digital Declaration of Independence. The technology works for us. We don't work for the technology.

Our envoy 2025 will need to be as responsive and creative online as her opponents. She will need to take the fight to them. To do this, in the battle of ideas, she will need to be on the side of the rational optimists.

The Case for Optimism

Never let the future disturb you. You will meet it, if you have to, with the same weapons of reason which today arm you against the present.

Marcus Aurelius, *Meditations*

Every great age is marked by innovation and daring – by the ability to meet unprecedented problems with intelligent solutions.

John F. Kennedy, 2 March 1962

People are feeling plenty of reasons to be miserable. We are no longer taking for granted that children's lives will inevitably be better than those of their parents. Early in 2014, 16,000 young adults from every continent were asked 'To what extent, if at all, do you feel that today's youth will have had a better or worse life than their parents' generation?': 42% said life would be worse, and 34% said life would be better. In China, 81% were optimistic, but in Europe the figures were abysmal – 16% in Spain, 13% in Belgium and 7% in France.[1] As French protesters I witnessed in an – I think and hope – ironic Paris 2011 demonstration, said: '*Non à 2012.*'

Pessimists look at the trends I've described, and worry about what technological advances will do to our security; to our society; and to our humanity.

Some believe we are creating new risks too fast.[2] Technology will do to twenty-first-century weaponry what it did to the musket, bayonet and pikestaff. In a hundred years, we will have cities of 140 million people. On conservative judgements the North Pole will melt by 2100. Harvests will decline in the least stable parts of the world, prompting America's National Intelligence Council to anticipate that the numbers facing shortages will rise from 600 million to 1.4 billion. Tens of millions of the angriest, hungriest people will migrate. The World Health Organisation predicts another pandemic.

The experts are not confident we can cope. Niall Fergusson fears 'a new Dark Age of waning empires and religious fanaticism; of endemic rapine in the world's no-go zones; of economic stagnation and a retreat by civilization into a few fortified enclaves'.[3] The American journalist Roger Cohen describes the present age as 'The Great Unraveling', a time of aggression, break-up, weakness and disorientation.[4]

Is this all overblown? Most experts in the 1910s, on the eve of a devastating conflict, said that a massive war was impossible – the interconnected webs of trade and finance prevented it. Now, as the US lead narrows, the risk of conflict increases, as it did when Britain declined after the Second World War. The power vacuum in the Dark Ages in Europe created space for religious fundamentalists, pirates and Vikings. Communities fell back on protecting themselves in smaller and smaller units.

Sounds familiar? The parallels are there. But some of our omens are worse. We now have twenty-five times as many people as during the Dark Ages, and vastly superior methods of destruction. When society fails to bust through moments of peril and change, we get famine, epidemic, uncontrolled migration, and state failure. We get what Winston Churchill feared in 1940, 'the abyss of a new Dark Age, made more sinister, and perhaps more protracted, by the lights of perverted science'.[5] It is why British Astronomer Royal Sir Martin Rees argues that the probability of humanity's extinction before 2100 is 50%.[6] In 1949, Einstein suggested that we don't know how World War Three will be fought. But World War Four would, he predicted, be fought with rocks.

Pessimists also worry about the impact of technology on our society. They predict that the digital economy will increase rather than decrease inequality, that human society does not know how to fight back.[7] Some fear the Internet will limit rather than advance democracy.[8] We will have a world in which we prioritise a simple consumer experience over jobs, wages, dignity and rights, with victims yet unseen.[9]

Pessimists also fear that technology destroys our humanity and creativity, what communications theorist Neil Postman calls 'the submission of all forms of cultural life to the sovereignty of technique and technology'.[10] We become addicted and enslaved.[11] The cult of the amateur prevails, culture is dumbed down and trust in authority evaporates. Imagination, idealism and creativity are replaced by economic calculation and consumerism.[12]

Maybe digitisation is even damaging our souls. Perhaps the virtual mob will become as threatening as a real one. We will be so connected that we lose our ability to truly connect. American technology expert Nicholas Carr assesses that our ability to think is decayed rather than built by the way in which we interact with the Internet.[13]

Perhaps the most powerful literary expression of this techno-pessimism is E. M. Forster's brilliant short story, 'The Machine Stops', written in 1909. This outlines a vision of an 'accelerated age' run by machines. As in Aldous Huxley's *Brave New World*, people are not coerced into allowing their senses to be controlled, but acquiesce, convinced that there are 'no new ideas'. They minimise direct human interaction, and communicate through 'The Machine', on which they can flick a switch to meet all their apparent needs: 'her room, though it contained nothing, was in touch with all that she cared for in the world'.

Some fight this. 'Cannot you see that it is we that are dying, and that down here the only thing that really lives is the Machine? We created the Machine, to do our will, but we cannot make it do our will now. It has robbed us of the sense of space and of the sense of touch, it has blurred every human relation and narrowed down love to a carnal act, it has paralysed our bodies and our wills. The Machine develops – but not on our lines. The Machine proceeds – but not to our goal.'

The story concludes with a warning that 'humanity, in its desire for comfort, had overreached itself. It had exploited the riches of nature too far. Quietly and complacently, it was sinking into decadence, and progress had come to mean the progress of the Machine ... until the body was white pap, the home of ideas as colourless, last sloshy stirrings of a spirit that had grasped the stars.'

A century later, Dave Eggers has updated Forster's prescient tale. In *The Circle* he creates a vast digital enterprise, fusing technology giants such as Google, Apple, Microsoft and Facebook, through which customers access the world around them. Its controllers merge technological and human rights idealism into their version of a perfect democracy, where public and private spheres combine and 'All that happens must be known', 'Secrets are lies', 'Sharing is caring' and 'Privacy is theft'. 'This is the ultimate transparency. No filter. See everything. Always.'[14] Success depends on the extent of your social participation.

In other words, life by Klout score.*

Of course, such pessimism about the impact of technological innovation on culture, learning, traditions, institutions, businesses or morality is not new. Breakthroughs in transport (rail, road, air), production (assembly lines), energy (steam, nuclear) or communications (telephone, radio, television) have always been accompanied by fear over the implications. So will the Digital Age.

The pessimists are right that we need to be alert and vigilant. But I think that there are more reasons for us to be hopeful about the future.

Firstly, the statistics are on our side. It is often said that a pessimist is an optimist armed with facts. In fact, it turns out that an optimist is a pessimist armed with facts. The average human lives twice as long and grows six inches taller than our great-great-grandparents. We have access to a life that they could never have imagined. The idea that human progress is inevitable is hardwired into Western history, and will always have its supporters and detractors. But the evidence so far backs it up. As nineteenth-century English historian Thomas Macaulay wondered, seeing similar pessimism spreading among his peers, 'on what principle is it, that when we see nothing but improvement behind us, we are to expect nothing but deterioration before us?'[15]

Extreme poverty has halved in the last fifteen years. We are becoming collectively richer, living longer, understanding the world better, and dying less of disease, poverty or violence. Sadly, barbarism is all too visible in a 24/7 news cycle that surrounds us

---

* Klout is an app that analyses and scores its users' online social influence.

with a sense of doom, terror and violence, but in fact it is receding. If the war death rates common in hunter-gatherer societies still prevailed, 2 billion would have been killed this century. Before states emerged, battles killed more than 500 out of every 100,000 people. In the twentieth century, including wars and genocides, it fell to 60. Today it is 0.3. So we are 200 times less likely to die in war than a century ago. The number of wars has increased by 25%, but they have been smaller.[16] Death tolls have fallen from 38,000 per conflict in the 1950s to just over 600 in the twenty-first century.

This is little consolation to a civilian in Syria, Gaza or Chad, but it is remarkable. We're becoming smarter and more literate. There were fewer than twenty democracies in 1946, but there are now 121: Churchill's 'least bad' form of government is catching on after all.

We are living in the most peaceful year since records began. That is remarkable.

Who can take credit for this? It is partly, I'm afraid, due to the decline of the Europeans. We are no longer exporting violence to all corners of the world in the way we did in the nineteenth and twentieth centuries, and seem to have found a way to stop killing each other in industrial quantities at home. The democratic, scientific, and industrial revolutions of the nineteenth century dragged the world into Europe's wars. Between 1870 and 1900, Europeans seized 10 million square miles of Africa, Asia and the Middle East, inhabited by 150 million people. We created significant violence in our wake. The European Union may not be perfect, but it aspires to something nobler than that.

The US must also take some credit – their empire has been the most benign in history. George W. Bush, much criticised for what was seen as a belligerent foreign policy, would have been perceived as a very gentle Roman emperor.

The post-1945 international system must also take some credit, whatever its flaws. Deterrence has worked, so far, up to a point.

We should also be optimistic because new technology can in fact reinvigorate our creativity and politics. Democracy will evolve, adapt and improve. The Internet brings us greater diversity, choice and opportunities for engagement. It can enable the emergence of a new political consciousness that is more participatory, more accessible and more influential, that can in Al Gore's words 'reclaim mankind's capacity to reason together to chart a safe course'.[17] We need not therefore fear what H. G. Wells predicted: a 'world brain', accessible to all as 'a sort of mental clearing house for the mind: a depot where knowledge and ideas are received, sorted, summarised, digested, clarified and compared'.[18] Instead, we can use new technology to bring more people into the political process and to build social cohesion.

The Digital Age will be less hierarchical and more liberating. It can be made to work for us, as stone and iron did when they were the currency of the day.[19]

And the empowerment of the individual is a good thing. Fewer people are being killed in conflict not just for geopolitical reasons, but because of increasing citizen power. The more that people are able to determine their own fate, the more peaceful they become.[20] Our early twenty-first-century desire to network and connect is not just a fad or blip, a short-term response to a surge in connectivity. Instead, networking is intuitive, a natural way to order the world.

Diplomats have tended to distrust the mob. Online mobs can at moments be as vicious and easily manipulated as their offline predecessors. But technology has the potential to change power for the better. We should be evangelical about citizen empowerment. Maybe we should learn to believe more in the wisdom of crowds after all.

Another reason for optimism is that we have been here before. Humanity has in the past responded to waves of change, and it can do so again. We have lived through dramatic technological revolutions. Resilience is in our DNA. We can adapt to the challenges ahead.

We have genuine form, honed over millennia, in solving problems. In 1900, 53% of humans died from infection. That figure is now just 3%. At key moments, as now, or in the West after 1200 BC, or at the end of the first century AD, we face a race between transformation and collapse. So far, we have always managed to respond: hunter-gatherers turned to domestication; farmers created cities; states created empires. When millions lost their agricultural jobs, nobody knew that they would find industrial work. At these catalytic moments, though we might not realise we're doing it at the time, we find a way to muddle through (Buzz Lightyear's 'falling with style' again).

We don't know what the next phase of evolution will deliver, but we know where to look for clues. Technology giants are investing most heavily in three areas: robotics companies; an artificial intelligence arms race; and high-altitude drones to deliver the Internet to the 5 billion people who don't yet have it.

We are already seeing how digital systems can override human instincts and alter the way that our hands and minds interact with inanimate objects – watching any three-year-old with an iPad is the twenty-first-century equivalent of watching an early Palaeolithic hominid reshaping stone tools.

These waves of technological change are going to alter basic human capacity, including how we move, communicate, store essential information and – most dramatically – think. Surveying the increased access to information in his own era, Albert Einstein counselled that we should never waste brain space memorising information we could look up in books. Now we need not remember information that we can access on our smartphone.

These rapid advances in robotics and computing are matched by those in genetics and nanotechnology. When Craig Venter, one of the first scientists to sequence the human genome, was asked if he was playing God, he allegedly replied: 'We're not playing.'[21]

We should also be optimistic because the Internet will help. Connectivity is going to be a great leveller. Deloitte studies show that expanding access to 4 billion people in developing countries will increase productivity by a quarter, GDP by almost three-quarters, create 140 million jobs and lift 160 million out of poverty. Facebook estimate that for every ten people who come online, one is lifted out of poverty.

There are many great examples of emerging economies and citizens themselves harnessing new technology for the greater good. In Rio, digital mapping using cameras on kites tracks poor sanitation and disease, and a new app helps drivers find parking spaces. 'The crowd has its own intelligence,' says Eloi, its creator. Big data is being used to track crime against children, murder and money-laundering. In a scheme run by Nandan Nilekani, founder of the IT services company Infosys, the Indian government are trying to assign every citizen a digital number and identity in order to better access state services.

———————

Late in my time at No. 10, I realised that I was unlikely ever again to be in such close proximity to extraordinary people. I was also spending too much time on the road and in airport lounges, too far from my new son, Charlie. He had become habituated to my strange life. I once spent an hour advising the prime minister on our troop numbers in Afghanistan while visiting 'Monkey World', a soft-play zone in Bromley.

By this stage Charlie had got used to me picking him up from nursery and promptly dropping him off to have a bath and dinner with the prime minister's kids in Downing Street. Having been sick all over his clothes in the car, he once turned up at Chequers completely nude. With characteristic tact and professionalism, the housekeeper commented that it was the first time a guest had arrived naked. Charlie had then interrupted a Hillary Clinton press conference by jumping around loudly. The Secretary of State asked him, 'Charlie, are you a rabbit?', and was told with a sterner voice than she was used to hearing from most leaders, 'No, I am a *monkey*.'

Partly to salve my conscience after all the weekends on the road, and partly to have something tangible to retain from that period, I began to collect advice for Charlie from the various world leaders we were meeting.

As the project gained momentum, those I asked would take more time over it. Bill Clinton wrote his advice out in draft and copied it into the book in beautiful and careful handwriting. George W. Bush took the book away with him, and returned it with his entry and a nice note about how much he had enjoyed reading what others had written. Mikhail Gorbachev got quite emotional composing his entry. Barack Obama commented that Charlie would either be very rich or very clever, depending on whether he sold the book or read it.

The advice varies from the idealistic to the practical, and in many cases reveals much about how those who wrote it saw their own leadership style, at those critical points in history. Leaders told him to dream big, give, and get to know different kinds of people. Bush counselled against sacrificing his soul for public approval. Gorbachev wrote poignantly about the fact that he would not be around by the time Charlie read his advice.

There were also plenty of entries from sportsmen, authors and celebrities. J. K. Rowling advised Charlie not to take up smoking, and to read a lot. Carla Bruni told him to play with his dad every day: '*car il à besoin de jouer, même s'il est un adulte*'.* Footballers David Beckham and Pelé and Olympians Steve Redgrave and Chris Hoy focused on the dogged persistence and hard work that had brought them such extraordinary success. Archbishop Desmond Tutu, Bill Clinton and the Dalai Lama urged him to give.

Above all, though, the advice was optimistic. The leaders who wrote in the book were genuinely excited about the world Charlie and his generation would inherit.

We are not on the verge of a digital Utopia. But neither are we about to fall into a Digital Hades. The Internet will not drag us towards a grim dystopia of online mobs, dumbing down and accelerated extinction. Nor will it be the digital equivalent of a commune in which humanity's better angels suddenly emerge triumphant.

Of course, technology will change us, and we will change technology, as we always have. It won't *always* be empowering and enlightening. But it can *often* be if we hold our nerve. Even as we become *Phono sapiens*, we can change the way we communicate without changing what it means to be human.

If digital information is the twenty-first century's most precious resource, the battle for it will be as contested as the battles for fire, axes, iron or steel. Between libertarians and control freaks.

---

* Because he needs to play, even if he is an adult.

Between sharers and exploiters. Between those who want transparency – including many individuals, companies and governments – and those who want privacy (or as its critics call it, secrecy). Between old and new sources of power.

Technological progress and the resolution of series of conflicts allowed humans to advance from tribal to feudal to industrial society. The next wave of technological disruption will be faster and greater than anything we have ever experienced.

But we can and must be ready for it.

A Progressive Foreign Policy 'To Do' List

Pile problem after problem onto mankind's shoulders, and it is easy to feel we are tottering towards the precipice of an outsized, world-shaped, earth wreck.

Chris Patten, *What Next? Surviving the Twenty-First Century* (2008)

The real problem is not whether machines think, but whether men do.

B. F. Skinner, American psychologist

So we're not finished as a globe or species yet. But we can't take it for granted.

Diplomats normally break the world down by geography. Of course the big conflicts conjoined by a slash will remain critical – North Korea/South Korea, Israel/Palestine, India/Pakistan and the many other scraps for territory or dignity that fill the foreign affairs pages of the media. As I write, we face overlapping crises – Russia's aggression in Eastern Europe, continued upheaval in the Middle East, tensions in East Asia. None are overwhelming in their own right, but taken together, they present a significant collective threat, a transition from order to disorder.

There will be a temptation to try to pull up the drawbridge, focusing purely on domestic security. We are seeing this in the return of nationalist parties such as UKIP, the Tea Party and the National Front. Yet in facing down the twenty-first century's challenges, we will need more than ever to remain engaged with the rest of the world. This is no longer the zero-sum game of great power politics. We all lose if we only pursue national interests. There is no global challenge today to which the answer is to build a bigger wall.

Whether it is convenient or practical, the major global challenges all require global solutions. There are three questions that require the most urgent attention. When and how do we go to war? How do we fix the international system? And how do we make as many people as possible less poor while conserving the planet?[1]

Firstly, when and how is it right to fight?

The debate on military interventionism versus disengagement tends to focus on America. With good reason – it is still by some way the world's superpower, even if that lead is being challenged. The irony is that the list of foreign policy challenges is growing at a time when the US is less ready to lead.

That debate has been sharpened by the Bush and Obama administrations; 52% of Americans now think that the US should 'mind its own business internationally', the highest total since the Second World War.[2] The public is drained by interventions in Iraq and Afghanistan, costly in both blood and treasure. Critics point to two decades of US-led adventures that have seemed to make the situation worse. President Obama has tended to agree, projecting a more minimalist military ambition than his predecessors. This is not just about resources or the complexity of the world out there, but national identity. Like other countries that have shouldered most of the international burden since the

Second World War, America is feeling less certain that it has an obligation to act outside its borders.

But by seeking to draw back many of the harder power instruments which were overused – some argue abused – by President George W. Bush, the US has faced charges of weakness and neglect. By deliberately stepping back, and 'leading from behind', Obama has been accused of creating the sense of a leaderless world. I hear this all the time in the Middle East, where commentators can rarely decide whether all their problems are because of too much or too little US interventionism. Most of those calling the US weak over Syria would squawk if Obama decided that it was really time to flex some muscle.

Meanwhile, public inquiries into the Iraq and Afghanistan conflicts rumble on, corroding confidence in the state and military. The media and politicians want scapegoats, someone to blame. But the link between cause and effect is never straightforward, the world is complex, and not every ideological or sectarian conflict in the world was created by the West, however convenient an explanation that can be. There won't ever be a neat answer to the question 'was military action right or wrong?' Having sat through hundreds of Cabinet committees, the answer to Iraq and Afghanistan is not more of them. And in my experience, foreign policy mistakes tend to occur when there are too few cosy chats between a prime minister and his Foreign Secretary, not when there are too many.

As well as corroding public trust, Iraq has scarred a generation of political and official foreign policymakers, creating a more risk-averse policy environment. It is right when weighing difficult foreign policy choices to draw lessons from recent experience. But we cannot allow all choices to be governed by the lessons of the last wars alone. We also have to learn from the historical experience of all the other wars – not least the NATO intervention in

Kosovo in 1999 that ended the ethnic cleansing of Albanian Muslims by the Milosevic regime in Serbia; and the military action in Sierra Leone in 2000 that prevented the overthrow of the democratic government and undoubtedly saved many lives.

We need a genuine public debate about when to use force. Part of the challenge for interventionists is to redefine for whom they are intervening. People are becoming less willing to send other people overseas to defend the nation state, let alone other nations, and they are better able to express that. We have been willing for several centuries to die for the nation state. But that entity is now in decline, and so identities are blurring.

Both the Iraq and Afghanistan interventions showed that it was not enough to simply remove a despotic regime. There needed to be a much more sustained, comprehensive strategy to rebuild the political and economic fabric of the countries concerned. Policymakers need to show sceptical publics that they can also win the peace that follows any military action. Diplomats will need to make a better case, in their own societies, for enlightened self-interest, explaining how the fate of our countries is connected to that of the world beyond our borders. Countries need to train up an army of para-diplomats, expert in post-conflict reconstruction and state-building – not commentators but fixers.

We must also find a better way to protect the most vulnerable. Middle Eastern newspapers tend to be much less squeamish than Western media. Every morning, as I worked through the Arabic newspapers over breakfast, I was bombarded by graphic images of dead children. Whether they are bombed in Gaza, Aleppo or Mosul, they look the same – small, broken, undefended. If this was happening in the town next door, we would never tolerate it. Yet in Syria, an hour's flight from Europe, almost half the population is displaced, and the casualties mount up. Despite the best efforts of so many to halt the conflict, it is as if the world has decided that the best approach is to try to quarantine it. If displaced people had a country, it would be the twenty-fourth largest in the world.

The UN's Responsibility to Protect (R2P) obligation was originally a response to Kofi Annan's idea that if a state is unwilling or unable to avert serious suffering of its civilians, the international community should intervene.[3] Supporters argue that we have a moral duty based on common identity; practical necessity; and the need to uphold international rules. The moral argument underpins the Universal Declaration of Human Rights, hammered out by the visionaries of 1948 as they surveyed a continent devastated by war. An individual's basic rights should not be defined by where they are born. The practical argument often comes down to how we deal with those who threaten international security: 'we need to fight them over there so that we don't have to fight them over here'. You can't quarantine failed states. Not to enforce rights in every country undermines them in every country.

The opponents of R2P argue against the financial and human cost of intervention. Every military intervention takes longer and costs more than predicted. Can we afford the burden of policing the world? Any intervention has unforeseen and unwelcome consequences, for which the intervening power then takes the blame and responsibility. This underlies the mantra of some in the Obama White House – 'don't do stupid shit', or the pre-watershed version, 'do no harm'. Sir John Holmes, a former British ambassador to Paris, fears that 'we have too often in recent years intervened in haste and repented at leisure'.[4]

Anti-interventionists also argue that the international system rarely delivers a clear endorsement for action. The UN Security Council permanent members wield their vetoes to protect their clients. Russia and China de-fanged the commitment to protecting the most vulnerable. And the US has also wielded its Security Council veto to protect its allies, most frequently Israel, from international law.

Facing a century of nasty wars, we should revisit the idea of a global agreement on the principles of humanitarian intervention. We can no longer rely on the Security Council to act as a neutral arbiter in shaping our approach. To insist on Security Council unanimity before any humanitarian intervention leaves a veto in the hands of authoritarian governments. In the case of Syria, it subcontracted our conscience and our foreign policy to Russia. The emerging economies must also be part of this debate – they will need to share much more of the burden.

The experience of the last two decades points the way to some guiding principles around doctrine, decisions and delivery of interventions.

On doctrine, we have what Joseph Nye calls 'Duties Beyond Borders', just as we have duties beyond the end of our garden fence. We can't intervene everywhere, all of the time. So when we do, we need to be able to show that we have picked the right fight, and that war is really the last resort. If unanimous Security Council agreement is impossible, we should act with coalitions of the willing such as the EU or NATO. Nothing gives us the right to defend a liberal world order beyond our confidence that the alternatives are worse.

On decisions, every intervention is different. We should not intervene in Iraq just because we intervened in Kosovo. We should not stay out of Syria just because we went into Iraq. So leaders should ask their experts, what is the worst-case scenario as a result of this intervention? How many civilians will die if we act, and how many if we do not act? What, to quote the much maligned Donald Rumsfeld, are the 'known unknowns', and what do we guess are the 'unknown unknowns'? Interventions should be based upon the consent, and ideally participation, of the widest possible coalition of countries. But we cannot always go at the pace of the slowest. Sometimes we will need to uphold basic humanitarian principles without clear international consent.

On delivery, interventions are not only military. They have to include the full toolkit of conflict prevention, political and humanitarian measures. Any military intervention not accompanied by a major economic and political engagement is doomed to fail – not necessarily to fail to win militarily, but certainly to fail to make the situation better. As Kofi Annan wrote in September 1999, 'When fighting stops, the international commitment to peace must be as strong as was the commitment to war.'[5] This is hard to do when public, media and political attention moves on – capacity-building projects such as Civil Service reform are less photogenic than aircraft carriers.

Once committed to an intervention, we should do it properly. But we should also always ensure that the action is proportionate. An intervention is a failure if it kills more than the action it was designed to prevent. You have to resource it. You need a credible defence and foreign affairs budget, and willingness to make tough choices about what you drop in order to deliver it. You can't be Palmerston if you don't have the gunboats.

It will never be neat and tidy. No plan survives contact with the enemy. War is foggy. There are not always good guys and bad guys (though some sides are less bad than others). Even to consider intervention is to recognise that the options are all bad.

Amid the worst conflicts it is always possible to find the most inspirational responses. In Lebanon, I often spent time with Syrian and Palestinian refugees, and those who are hosting them with such generosity. One told me the story of a boy picking up shellfish on the beach, and carrying them back to the sea. An adult passes by and asks why he is doing it. How can it matter when there are so many millions of shellfish washed up? The boy replies that, to the shellfish in his hand, it matters.

We will still be shocked and horrified by photos of dead children. We will see more of them as digital cameras and connectivity spread. We are not always going to be able to protect all of them. But we can do much better.

The Universal Declaration of Human Rights is mankind's greatest text, the most powerful and revolutionary document of all time. The problem is not that we don't understand our duty to our fellow citizens, but that we don't have the will to deliver it.

As well as *when* we can fight, we need a clearer sense of *how* we should fight.

Drones make warfare easier and cleaner, and reduce the public's ability to constrain governments. They are popular at home while governments are using them against their enemies. They will be less popular when those enemies turn them on us. Psychologists have assessed that military personnel operating drones are as likely to suffer post-traumatic stress disorder as those firing conventional weapons from nearer their targets.

The rules for cyber warfare and the use of drones are dangerously opaque, creating a free-for-all. We have developed strong international systems on nuclear weapons, chemical weapons, cluster bombs and the arms trade, but as yet we have nothing to manage this new area of rapid growth. As in the past, this risks remaining the case while a few countries have the technological advantage, and therefore lack the incentive to agree restraints. But that will not be the reality for long. These new weapons won't fit into existing international legal systems. They will have to redefine them.

*

The second great challenge for the global community is how do we build international institutions that are fit for purpose.

We have devised systems of national government that are dynamic and evolving. We must never assume a static international architecture. As Henry Kissinger puts it, 'intellectuals analyse the operations of international systems; statesmen build them'.[6]

Yet the last serious attempt to agree rules for international governance was after the Second World War, with the creation of the United Nations and Bretton Woods institutions. Those bodies, now almost seventy years old, are full of hard-working, usually well-meaning professionals, but in an age requiring global solutions to global problems, they are no longer fit for purpose. Fixing them will take serious creativity, determination and patience. Austerity has a tendency to make countries look inward, yet historical precedent suggests that times of political and economic challenge are those when it is most important to look outward.

The UN is much maligned, though Chris Patten rightly asks how things would have been without it.[7] It was set up as the answer to a different set of problems. And the reality is that there is no forcing moment where pressure for change or reform comes to a head, where the national politics are aligned in the right way. Most international institutions are going through cumbersome and slow reform processes, but none are likely to conclude that their time is up. Turkeys do not vote for Christmas, and bureaucracies do not volunteer for the axe.

As a result, cumbersome regional blocks such as the Arab League, African Union or European Union have spread like treacle over a keyboard, their bureaucratic inertia gumming up the management of international relations. Transnational challenges such as jihadism or epidemics such as Ebola are therefore harder to respond to. It is recklessly irresponsible of us to subcontract global problems on this scale to institutions that can't manage them.

We may feel less able, culturally and politically, to remodel this architecture. We don't have the patience or time to build systems, at a time when the fun is in breaking them up.

Any discussion of reform of the international architecture has to begin with a debate over where we need to pool sovereignty in order to respond more effectively to the threats facing us. Fighting infectious disease; migration; the health of the global economy; climate change; terrorism – these are all issues that cannot be tackled within national borders alone.

The effort towards reshaping the international architecture was shot in the paddock by the world economic crisis of 2008–9 as many countries inevitably turned inwards. We now need to take up this challenge again. We will have to ensure that these institutions, or whatever replaces them, are more representative. They must involve a louder voice for the emerging powers. But we also need to escape from global governance as being the equivalent of an annual promotion or relegation battle from a sports league, where the strongest nations of the day try to lock in that position, as we did in 1815 and 1945. More importantly now, these institutions need to be representative of wider society, not nation states alone. We have to find ways to enfranchise more of the world's population.

There also needs to be a much harder-headed debate on national responsibilities. Emerging economies can't use an excuse for massive carbon emissions that it is 'their turn' to burn fossil fuel. China is going to need to have its own debate about when it is right to intervene militarily in other countries – it has not been shy of doing so economically. It is not in the long-term interest of rising powers to have killed off the early Doha trade rounds and the 2009 Copenhagen climate negotiations. Meanwhile, big weapons exporters such as the US have to accept that their role is not to deliver the right to bear arms on a global scale. At some point Russia has to rediscover its obligations as a permanent member of the Security Council, not the rebel at the back of the class. And both Russia and the US have to see that their UN veto is not just for protecting their client states.

An urgent task for governments and their diplomats, therefore, is to take a step back from the competing national agendas, shortening political and media attention spans and immediate day-to-day challenges, and to redesign, refocus and reboot the international system. In the absence of such a debate, and such leadership, we will find that the institutions we have created to deliver a measure of humanity's collective governance cease to retain any influence or relevance, leaving a dangerous vacuum.

The third pressing challenge we face is how to reduce global inequality without destroying the planet.

The Intergovernmental Panel on Climate Change, a United Nations group that monitors climate science, published a dramatic and sobering report in October 2014. Failure to reduce emissions will create water and food shortages, natural disasters, refugee crises, flooding and mass extinction of plants and animals.

We have seen the emergence of an overdue and essential understanding that our fate is deeply connected with the ecology of the planet. The Paris Agreement of 2015 is a big step forward. Yet our collective actions to date are barely scratching the surface of the response necessary. I'm struck by how many ecologists already say that we are too late to manage, let alone turn back, the devastating environmental consequences of the industrial age.

We have to win the argument that green growth does not mean slower growth, but rather increases productivity and efficiency, creates space for innovation and new markets, and reduces long-term risks of negative economic shocks.

Every world leader can give the speech about why climate change matters so much, the metaphorical hot air to match the hot air that their travel to climate summits pumps out. But the rhetoric is not matched by any seriousness of intent. Diplomacy must be more assertively part of the effort to set the right global rules, including how best to balance the developing world's legitimate energy needs and aspirations with the long-term health of the planet.

We have to manage the end of the fossil-fuel era without triggering the kind of major conflict that energy transitions have created in the past. The Middle East creates 31% of the world's oil, and has 65% of the world's reserves. Oil is not as much of a factor in policymaking as the conspiracy theorists like to claim, but it is clearly another complicating issue in a region that already has plenty of its own already.

Austerity, insecurity and the decline of nation states have all served to take our minds away from rethinking our energy needs. They should have the opposite effect.

There is also a compelling humanitarian and security case for reducing the gap between rich and poor. The bottom half of the world's population own less than 1% of total wealth. The top 1% has just under half of the world wealth.[8] Without action, the twenty-first century will be the Greatest Migration, with millions more hungry and angry people heading north and west. The annual World Economic Forum global-risk report lists growing inequality as the biggest geopolitical risk today.

Inequality is a serious problem within as well as between countries. In the US, the richest 1% earns more than the poorest 90%, and there are more inherited fortunes than a decade ago on the Forbes 400 list of the wealthiest Americans. But the bad news is that inequality is increasing faster in China and India than the US and Europe. It has reached a twenty-eight-year high in thirty-two developing economies.[9]

The better news is that new technology can help us to reduce those gaps.

There are countless examples of individuals or communities in the poorest parts of the world using smartphones to track weather or market conditions, or to secure small-scale investment or banking services, to improve their economic prospects. I spent time with farmers in northern Kenya whose livelihoods had been transformed by an ability to get text messages with weather forecasts and market conditions in nearby trading centres. Global Pulse monitors discussion of food on Twitter in Indonesia to spot shortages and price hikes. Deloitte estimate that expansion of Internet access could increase personal income levels in the developing world by 15%.[10] But this will require a greater concert of effort between governments, NGOs and the companies involved. Coalitions of the willing again.

It used to be said that you could give a man a fish and he would not be hungry that day, but give him a fishing rod and teach him to fish and he will never be hungry again. Perhaps the modern equivalent is that we need to give him a smartphone and an Internet connection.

Whether we like it or not, aid is a security issue, at a time when global inequality and insecurity are becoming more of a direct threat to our populations. That means we will need to be firmer in insisting that we do spend on aid, but harder-headed in deciding *how* we spend on aid.

*

These issues all require much broader coalitions and debates than has happened in the past – they cannot be fixed simply by summit diplomacy or governments talking to governments.

So I want now to conclude this book to the point at which social media, coexistence and diplomacy collide.

There is lots of talk about citizen journalists, but not enough about citizen diplomats. Behind the 'Excellencies' and the protocol, diplomacy is not a mysterious cult. It doesn't require years of training like medicine or law. Anyone can do it, and many people do so through small acts of resistance against apathy, division, corruption and fatalism.

If we are to get through a century of significant peril and uncertainty, we need the coexisters to fight back. We need citizen diplomacy to kick in.

18

Citizen Diplomacy

To see the world, things dangerous to come to, to see behind
walls, to draw closer, to find each other and to feel.
That is the purpose of life.

Fictional *Life Magazine* motto, quoted in James Thurber's
'The Secret Life of Walter Mitty' (1939)

I have described in this book the transformation and disruption
of everything we thought we knew. I have considered what this
means for power, hierarchy and traditional authority, including
statecraft and diplomacy, and how technology can help us
promote coexistence.

Two hundred years after the Congress of Vienna tackled the
huge questions of the day, we need another Congress of Vienna
moment. But this time it cannot be diplomats working for months
behind palace doors, nor a great-powers stitch-up – it is harder
being a great power than it used to be. We need to find a more
inclusive, empowering and effective way of marshalling the best
instincts of humanity against the worst.

I have argued that diplomacy at its essence is about promoting
coexistence – or, to put it more starkly, stopping violence. We are
trying to provide the lubricant in the system as continents, states,

armies and ideas rub up against each other. We are trying to find ways to agree how best to distribute resources and power without fighting. We are trying to bring reason to an unreasonable world. Technology is disrupting established notions of what is and isn't political. This requires compromise and debate, and diplomats need to be in those arguments.

But so does everyone else. In the Digital Age, anyone can be a diplomat. Increasingly, everyone will *need* to be a diplomat. You don't have to be working for a foreign ministry to do the vital work I've described. Indeed most of the people doing it have never crossed the threshold. They are working in communities, in NGOs, in the media, in business, elsewhere in government. They are all, without knowing it, diplomats – citizen diplomats.

Diplomacy is not a creed or a code. It is a basic human reflex. Negotiating access and distribution of resources is as essential to the survival of the species as finding the resources in the first place. A little more conversation, a little less action.

We'll now need to think harder about how we create citizen diplomats. How can we influence how pupils are taught in schools in order that they are more likely to think diplomatically? Can we learn more about the costs of failure of diplomacy, i.e. wars? Anthony Seldon, the political biographer and former headmaster of Wellington College, has pioneered the teaching of happiness, character, resilience. When teaching the next generation of citizen diplomats, we should be thinking less about how to write a treaty than how humanity has managed to find ways, throughout history, to coexist.

For me, Lebanon was a test case for that idea, a front line for coexistence. If we cannot live together there, across a plethora of races, competing ideologies and religions, we will fail to live together in Madrid, Paris and London. If we cannot better manage the Middle East's transition towards security, justice and opportunity, we will face a generation of upheaval, with more empty life jackets on our shores, and more suicide vests in our shopping malls. In the end, politics will prevail. The job of diplomats, and therefore all of us, is to help it do so without decades of bloodshed.

So can we summon up a period of citizen diplomacy? Socrates claimed to be 'not a citizen of Athens or Greece, but of the world'. This sounds naive to our more cynical and worldly twenty-first-century ears, and few leaders get elected by proclaiming themselves global citizens. Yet technology is making it a more imaginable reality. We won't always need to put our nationality before common humanity. We are going to find ourselves with the ability to organise ourselves in new ways, consistent with John Locke's definition of community as a state of perfect freedom, with the power to act as one body.

I have argued in this book that the gradual democratisation of making foreign policy, the result of political advancement and technological innovation, has proven positive. The world is, despite plenty of media coverage to the contrary, becoming safer for its citizens.

But if that basic hypothesis on the positive effect of greater public participation is true, we *depend* as a species on those participating to understand their increased power, and to engage with the issues that they can now shape to such an extent. Only half a century ago, 'diplomatist' Harold Nicolson could write with bemused disdain that 'Now the man in the street is expected to have a view on international problems, yet the complexities are too great.'[1] Any diplomat or politician who dared to utter such words now would be pilloried as elitist and out of touch. And rightly so.

The man or woman on the Clapham omnibus, Tokyo bullet train or Dubai monorail now has three things that have never existed in the same way before.

They have the means to disentangle the complexities of international problems, through access to information that was previously either out of reach or confined only to policymakers or elites.

They have access to networks that allow them to form an unmediated view on the information they receive. The public no longer need to wait for a *Times* editorial or government statement to form an opinion on the latest atrocity in Syria. Indeed, by the time the thunderous denunciation or timid bleat of concern arrives on their television screen or in their newspaper – for the rapidly declining proportion of people who use either – they will normally have moved on to forming a view on the next crisis or debate.

And they have an unprecedented ability to influence and shape how humanity responds. This is what I have described as the smartphone superpower in our pockets.

Economic forces will accelerate this trend. The numbers of economically productive and connected people will continue to rise dramatically, as will their aspirations and expectations. The triumph of the individual.

Yet factors are getting in the way of this vision of diplomatic and therefore social Utopia.

One is our hardwired tendency to form gangs. Already, social media users are migrating towards closed or tribal platforms. Indeed several countries are aiming to create them, dividing and nationalising the Internet.

More corrosive than this desire to retreat into smaller or more exclusive groups are disinterest, apathy and distraction. As anyone with an iPad knows, it can unlock extraordinary and exciting potential. But it can also make us idler, whether through the temptations of cute cats, celebrity churn or 'FOMO', the fear of missing out that leads us to need to follow every twist and turn of today's trend or story. We crave the buzz of the phone in our pocket, and the validation of the Facebook like. I tweet, therefore I am.

On this basis, some of the greatest threats to the coexistence and creativity we need to survive are now banality, extremism, short attention spans, disorder and alienation. Tyrannies have worked this out. They always have – look back at the Romans and their provision of 'bread and circuses' to keep the masses amused, fed and subservient. If we really are in the age of the 'slacktivist', the bad guys still win.

The world is fiendishly complicated. It is all too easy not to care, to see it all as too difficult, to swallow the easy Internet conspiracy, or simply oppose. It becomes harder to find those ready to fight for something, rather than against something. It is easier to destroy than to build.

How do we ensure, then, that more people use technology to become Theodore Roosevelt's 'man in the arena', not just his 'critic'?*

The reality is of course that we don't have to know everything about everything. We don't need to have an emotional reaction to everything. But, with the world getting smaller, we do need to care.

Why? Because the people in the news are also human. We cannot allow ourselves to be removed from a sense of community with the poorest or most oppressed, just because they happen to be born in a different country or have a different passport.[2] It should not just be the world's billionaires who commit a propor-

---

* 'It is not the critic who counts; not the man who points out how the strong man stumbles, or where the doer of deeds could have done them better. The credit belongs to the man who is actually in the arena, whose face is marred by dust and sweat and blood; who strives valiantly; who errs, who comes short again and again, because there is no effort without error and shortcoming; but who does actually strive to do the deeds; who knows great enthusiasms, the great devotions; who spends himself in a worthy cause; who at the best knows in the end the triumph of high achievement, and who at the worst, if he fails, at least fails while daring greatly, so that his place shall never be with those cold and timid souls who neither know victory nor defeat.' (Speech, 'Citizenship in a Republic', 23 April 1910.)

tion of their income to humanitarian causes. History suggests that walls and checkpoints don't last long.

We also need to care because it is pragmatic. We have got to find creative and ingenious ways to fix the twenty-first century's mounting challenges if we are to thrive as a species. As a global civilisation emerges, our survival will depend to a greater extent to our ability to innovate across traditional boundaries. The threats no longer take the form that they did in the nineteenth and twentieth centuries. Neither therefore must our responses.

And we need to care because history hasn't finished. War has shown itself exceptionally resilient,[3] and able to survive technological innovation and globalisation. Technology is not just empowering the good guy: look at the selfies of beheadings by the self-declared 'Islamic State'. We read the histories of the past thinking that we know how it ends. But we don't know how it ends. We're not finished.[4] We have not had the last world war, nor reached a plateau where everyone broadly agrees that liberal democratic values are as good as it gets. We have not got to a final destination. That should fill us with fear. But it should also fill us with hope.

The most influential generation in history will need to summon up fresh will to defend the progress, rule of law and freedoms we take for granted. Those ideas will only survive if we fight for them. We cannot be complacent, put these challenges in the 'too difficult' tray, nor wait for someone else to come up with the answers.

We also need to care because we haven't yet worked out how to convert our incredible new access to information and potential influence into genuine influence. Like all superpowers, the smartphone depends on what we choose to do with it. We can download pictures of cute cats, follow the twists and turns of Justin Bieber's hairstyle, 'like' something on Facebook and flirt with the girl in the class next door. Or we can use it to shape the environment around us.

Citizens can now control the public square, literally and digitally, in a way they never could before. But leaderless programmes, too often against something rather than for something, have so far fallen well short of their expectations. Citizen diplomats must convert that disparate energy into genuine and lasting positive change. As governments become more attuned to online digital opinion, citizen campaigns will matter more. But they must be accompanied by a real effort, by getting outside our comfort zones. They require backbone – organisers and institutions to turn the energy that they generate into something better than we inherited.

At other moments when technological innovation or historical changes have been most acute, leaders have seen the potential to use that change for common good. In President Harry Truman's inaugural address of his second term in 1949, he argued that, 'for the first time in history the counsels of mankind are to be drawn together and concerted for the purpose of defending the rights and improving the conditions of working people – men, women, and children – all over the world. Such a thing as that was never dreamed of before.' President Kennedy saw the same potential in his own inaugural address in 1961. 'More than half the people of the world are living in conditions approaching misery ... For the first time in history, humanity possesses the knowledge and the skill to relieve the suffering of these people.'

We also need to summon up that idealism. Aristotle was not necessarily a diplomat. He counselled his pupil Alexander, in his brief period pre-Greatness, to 'be a despot' to his enemies, dealing with them 'as with beasts or plants'. Yet Aristotle's concept of *eudaimonia*, 'human flourishing', was more diplomatic: it was about combining virtue or excellence with reason and practical wisdom to live a better life. He saw this as a natural aim not just of philosophy but of politics and society.

Aristotle was also history's first great scientist. I think that he would have acknowledged that in the twenty-first century the reason he aspired to is increasingly dependent on the digital tools we are creating. He would have seen access to more and better information as a positive, exciting trend. But he would also have been adamant, and probably tweeted it, that reason is not the property of the tools with which we access it. Our exploration, and the human development it must create, should still be driven by virtue. Otherwise, we're just the wrong kind of mob.[5]

Twitter did not create democracy, democracy created Twitter. Facebook did not create liberty. Liberty created Facebook. Google did not create choice. Choice created Google.

This is not a new debate. Pre-smartphone and at a time when different threats seemed to be overwhelming mankind and different technologies changing the world, Charlie Chaplin's reluctant demagogue changes the script in the final scene of *The Great Dictator*, telling his listeners that:

> We have developed speed, but we have shut ourselves in. Machinery that gives abundance has left us in want. Our knowledge has made us cynical. Our cleverness, hard and unkind. We think too much and feel too little. More than machinery we need humanity ... The aeroplane and the radio have brought us closer together. The very nature of these inventions cries out for the goodness in men – cries out for universal brotherhood – for the unity of us all ... You, the people, have the power – the power to create machines. The power to create happiness! You, the people, have the power to make this life free and beautiful, to make this life a wonderful adventure ... Let us fight for a world of reason, a world where science and progress will lead to all men's happiness.

Steve Jobs transformed much about the world. Before that he

changed marketing with his first campaign at Apple. He told his team that they needed to find the essence of who they were as a company – not about selling boxes that help people to work more effectively, but something much bigger. The result was the epic 'Crazy People' campaign, with its brilliant conclusion: 'The people who are crazy enough to think they can change the world are the ones who do.' Apple placed themselves in a line of pioneers and innovators, rebels and dreamers from Charlie Chaplin to Albert Einstein, Francis Crick and Martin Luther King.

With or without diplomats, those crazy people will continue to change the world. The gadgets and apps that this book has talked about will quickly become as comical as the huge mobile phones heaved around by characters in 1990s sitcoms. It is in our restless nature not to be satisfied with what we create – we go from novelty must-have to car-boot sale (or now eBay) at lightning speed. The ideas, gadgets, changes and predictions that startle us today will not be startling for long.

What we do as humans, and how we do it, is changing at a faster pace than any time in history. I've argued that this should be cause for optimism. Yet that optimism requires hard-headed realism.

It must be based on our success in the past to prepare for and manage these apocalyptic moments of change.

It must be based on our ability to master new tools and ways of interaction.

It must be based on a fundamental belief that, like Chaplin, 'more than machinery we need humanity'.

It requires ceaseless creativity and innovation: the Stone Age didn't end because we ran out of stones.

It requires the courage to try to bend the arc of history, to write our own epitaphs. But also – in the pursuit of justice and coexistence, or what some of us call diplomacy – to be on the right side of that history. This will test our heads and hearts.

Jacob Bronowski's work on the nuclear bomb in the 1940s drove him from the most complex corners of the destructive power of mathematics and science towards a profound understanding of this simple but vital challenge. He concludes his television series *The Ascent of Man*, an extraordinarily powerful account of human development, standing knee-deep in a muddy pond at Auschwitz, with the slime of the Holocaust – in which many of his own family were killed – running through his fingers. He talks about the danger of certainty. We need, he exhorts us in the final shot, 'to reach out and touch people'.

There is an amazing gadget for citizen diplomacy. It allows us to take in masses of information, process it, engage with people, listen, communicate, connect, influence. It has been honed over centuries, and is constantly improving. It is not the smartphone. It is that instinctive ability to reach out and touch people.

So perhaps the greatest danger is not actually the nuclear bomb, environmental catastrophe, the robot age or the crazed terrorist, frightening as they all are. The greatest danger is in fact the loss of the curiosity to learn from each other, the loss of the desire to live together.

Armed with technology, citizen diplomacy must enhance rather than remove that vital and creative part of our DNA, as important to Ug as competition for survival. Not because of fluffy platitudes about warm relations, but because our ability to find ways to coexist is what makes us survive.

This is going to be an exhilarating century. We had better not screw it up. Let's not fail for lack of ingenuity, creativity or curiosity. Let's not fail for lack of courage.

If diplomacy did not exist, we would indeed need to invent it. But it is now much too important to leave to diplomats.

Over to you, Your Excellencies.

EPILOGUE

Valedictory

There used to be a Foreign Office tradition that departing ambassadors would send a 'valedictory', in which they described their career highlights, complained about the Foreign Office, hinted that they still had a bigger job in them, and thanked their wives for their patience. The practice was culled in the last decade, because too many of the telegrams leaked – indeed several were probably written solely for that purpose. Several that didn't leak fell victim to enterprising Freedom of Information requests and so found their way to the public domain anyway.[1]

I decided that I would mark my departure from Lebanon differently. I wrote a private and classified valedictory for ministers. In it, I suggested that this followed several of the classic traits of the genre: rhetoric, unverifiable boasts, harrumphing, alliteration, rewriting the past, risky predictions, genuine thanks and affection. Despite all that, I had to explain this was of course not a valedictory, since those were banned.

The telegram was not written to be shared publicly. Instead it aimed to speak truth unto power on some of the mistakes we had made in the Middle East. I tried to make the case for some politically difficult decisions, including talking to people with whom we disagreed. I praised the extraordinary, purposeful, courageous public servants I had worked with from across Her Majesty's

Government. 'They marched towards the sound of gunfire, often literally.' I tried to set out what we had aimed to achieve, and where we had succeeded and failed. I made the case for more digital work to sceptical colleagues.

It was a love letter to diplomacy – a shorter version of this book. Ironic, since this book was also the reason I had to leave mainstream diplomacy.

In making my Flexit, I hoped that I would be back at some point in that imperfect, purposeful, brave, funny, humble, committed, well-meaning, wonderful business. I hoped to not write another valedictory one day.

But I also wanted to find a more public way to mark the end for what had been for me a huge adventure, to try to connect to the people to whom I wanted to explain what modern diplomacy is, and why it matters. So I released a public valedictory, another open letter to Lebanon. It went viral, and spawned a BBC documentary. Here it is:

So ... Yalla, Bye

Dear Lebanon,

Sorry to write again. But I'm leaving your extraordinary country after four years. Unlike your politicians, I can't extend my own term.

When I arrived, my first email said 'welcome to Lebanon, your files have been corrupted'. It should have continued: never think you understand it, never think you can fix it, never think you can leave unscathed. I dreamt of Beirutopia and #Leb2020, but lived the grim reality of the Syria war.

Bullets and Botox. Dictators and divas. Warlords and *wasta*. Machiavellis and mafia. Guns, greed and God. *Game of Thrones* with RPGs. Human rights and hummus rights. Four marathons,

100 blogs, 10,000 tweets, 59 calls on prime ministers, 600+ long dinners, 52 graduation speeches, two #OneLebanon rock concerts, 43 grey hairs, a job swap with a domestic worker, a walk the length of the coast. I got to fly a Red Arrow upside down. I was even offered a free buttock lift – its value exceeded our £140 gift limit, so that daunting task is left undone.

Your politics are also daunting, for ambassadors as well as Lebanese citizens. When we think we've hit bottom, we hear a faint knocking sound below. Some oligarchs tell us they agree on change but can't. They flatter and feed us. They needlessly over-complicate issues with layers of conspiracy, creative fixes, intrigue. They undermine leaders working in the national interest. Then do nothing, and blame opponents/another sect/Sykes–Picot/Israel/Iran/Saudi (delete as applicable). They then ask us to move their cousin's friend in front of people applying for a visa. It is Orwellian, infuriating and destructive of the Lebanese citizens they're supposed to serve.

But this frustration beats the alternative – given potential for mishap, terror or invasion, there is no substitute for unrelenting, maddening, political process.

Khalil Gibran said 'you have your Lebanon, I have mine'. When the Middle East was in flames, and its people caught between tyrants and terrorists, the Lebanon I will remember sent its soldiers to protect the borders; confronted daily frustrations to build businesses and to educate its children; and showed extraordinary generosity to outsiders, be they ambassadors or refugees. The Lebanon I will remember is not asking for help, but for oxygen. It is not arguing over the past, but over the future. It is not debating which countries hold it back, but how to move forward. It is not blaming the world, but embracing it.

People will look back at what we have come through and ask how Lebanon survived. But we already know the answer: never underestimate the most resilient people on the planet. A people that has, for millennia, beaten the odds.

I hope you will also look back and say that the Brits helped you to hold your corner. Giving those soldiers the training and equipment to match their courage. Giving those pupils the books to match their aspiration. Giving those businesses the networks to match their ambition. Building international conspiracies for Lebanon, not against it. And above all, believing you would beat the odds. Four years: 100 times the financial support, ten times the military support, double the trade. We even helped Walid Joumblatt join Twitter.

What could the West have done differently? Many of you have a long list. We are at last feeling our way to a serious conversation with Iran, and a credible political process that leaves Syrians with more than the barrel bomber and the box-office brutality of ISIL. I hope President Obama can deliver his aim of a Palestinian state with security and dignity. I hope we can talk to our enemies as well as our friends – aka diplomacy.

I hope we can also rediscover an international system that aspires to protect the most vulnerable: Syria must not be RIP R2P. The driving quest of diplomacy is for imperfect ways to help people not kill each other. Let's not give up on the idea that the Middle East can find security, justice and opportunity. I hope other countries reflect on what they could do differently too.

They say that Lebanon is a graveyard for idealism. Not mine. It has been a privilege to share this struggle with you. I believe you can defy the history, the geography, even the politics. You can build the country you deserve. Maybe even move from importing problems to exporting solutions. The transition from the civil-war generation lies ahead, and will be tough. You can't just party and pray over the cracks. But you can make it, if you have an idea of Lebanon to believe in. You need to be stronger than the forces pulling you apart. Fight for the idea of Lebanon, not over it.

And we need you to fight hard. Reading your history in a musty Oxford library over four years ago, I realised that if we cannot win the argument for tolerance and diversity in Lebanon, we will lose it everywhere. That's why we've helped – it is in our national interest too. This is the front line for a much bigger battle. The real dividing line is not between Christianity and Islam, Sunni and Shia, East and West. It is between people who believe in coexistence, and those who don't.

So if the Internet doesn't work, build a new Internet. If the power supply doesn't work, build a new power supply. If the politics don't work, build a new politics. If the economy is mired in corruption and garbage piles up, build a new economy. If Lebanon doesn't work, build a new Lebanon. It is time to thrive, not just survive.

I worried I was too young for this job. I discovered I was too old. We experimented on Twitter – first tweetup with a PM, with a diva, first RT of a Western diplomat by the president of Iran, online scraps with terrorists and satirists, #Leb2020 and much more. I hope it amplified our impact in an authentic, engaging and purposeful way. I have banged on about how digital will change diplomacy. Someone should write a book about how it will also change power, and how we can marshal it to confront the threats to our existence. Now there's an idea.

You gave me Bekaa Valley sunrises and Cedars sunsets. You gave me the adventure of my life, and plenty of reasons to fear for it. You gave me extraordinary friends, and you took some away. I loved your hopeless causes and hopeful hearts, shared your tearful depths and your breathless heights.

There are eight stages of life as an ambassador here. Seduction. Frustration. Exhilaration. Exhaustion. Disaffection. Infatuation. Addiction. Resignation. I knew them all, often simultaneously. I wouldn't have swapped it for anywhere in the world. I and the brilliant embassy team are still buying shares in Lebanon 2020. I'm finishing my time as an ambassador to Lebanon, but with your permission I'll always be an ambassador for Lebanon.

Many of you ask me why I remain positive about this country. All I ever tried to do was hold a mirror up and show you how beautiful you really are. Shine on, you crazy diamond.

Please stay in touch.

Yalla, bye

Tom

Acknowledgements

I first realised I wanted to write a book when I found – deep below Rhodes House in Oxford – my grandfather's handwritten letters to my grandmother, written daily over fifty years. He described them as their 'indestructible links'. His son, my uncle Anthony, was the source of the 'Only Connect' theme, from the title of his memoirs. My parents did the rest, and no acknowledgement can do them justice.

Several people tried to teach me to write, including Marj Francis, Joy Arathoon, David Dickinson, Pat Argar, Nigel Thomas, Martin Hydes and Edward Clay. Professor Christopher Tyerman at Hertford College, Oxford gave me a break, and then pressed me to have the curiosity of a fellow rebel. The late Patrick Seale gave me advice on writing 'with mischief'. The late Sir Martin Gilbert infected me with his ceaseless enthusiasm for discovery.

Three prime ministers gave me the immense privilege of serving in 10 Downing Street. As they dislike me saying, they have much more in common than they realise, not least a deep and profound drive to make Britain better. Politics is not a popular profession, but I wish that people could see more of the vital work that goes on behind the scenes. Being at No. 10 also allowed me to work with some of the most extraordinary public servants around, starting with the duty clerks, 'garden girls', security officers and switchboard operators who see us all in and out of the black door. As Bonnie Tyler puts it, we were living in a powder keg and giving off sparks.

I'm also grateful to many diplomatic pioneers, online and offline. Former UK Foreign Secretaries David Miliband and William Hague were sounding boards, as were many HMG colleagues, including particularly John Casson, Christian Turner, Hugh Elliott, Jane Marriott, Menna Rawlings, Peter Hill, Simon McDonald, Hugh Powell, Mark Lowcock and Mark Sedwill. Alec Ross and Jared Cohen are the Lennon and McCartney of twenty-first-century statecraft. Ambassadors like Mike McFall blazed a trail long before most of us had logged on. Sarah Brown was my Twitter fairy godmother, and had made the connection between social media and humanitarian campaigns before most of us even had a handle. UK diplomats like Jon Benjamin, Frances Guy and Leigh Turner made the first steps into this new terrain, taking risks on behalf of all of us. Angela Solomon was a great communications partner in crime in Beirut, and helped shape much of this book.

Many others took time to amend, cajole, challenge and correct these ideas, or just to argue with me about the world. They included Jules Chappell, Khaled Mouzanar, Nadine Labaki, John Kampfner (on a kayak on the Wye), Lara Setrekian, Valerie Amos, Anthony Seldon, Tomos Grace, Katrin Bennhold, Sam Coates, Kirsty McNeil, Jonathan Luff, Ben Brogan, Arminka Helic, Doug McAndrew, Andy Ross, Jeremy Bowen, Bernadino Leon, Guy Winter, Mishaal Gargawi, Jeremy Chivers, Chloe Dalton, Lord Stewart Wood, Alex Asseily, Sir Graeme Lamb, Jonathan McClory, Kirsty McNeil, Nick Jefferson, Uli Willhelm, Nicolas Galey, Manuel Lafont-Rapnouil, Najib Salha, David Cvach, Renaud Salins, Walid Joumblatt, Ziyad Barroud, Ewan Foster, Amel Karboul, my feisty class at New York University, Alastair Campbell, Andy Coulson and Justin Forsyth.

And last but not least, the core team. I was blessed with two brilliant editors, Martin Redfern and Arabella Pike; two unflagging agents in Charlie Campbell and Charlie Brotherstone; the expertise and patience of copy-editor David Milner and project editor Stephen Guise; and Rebecca Cox, who kept the whole show on the road. All that under the wise, invigorating and reinforcing guidance of the inestimable Don Corleone of the literary world, Ed Victor.

I am grateful to so many people on and beyond this list for the inspiration, ideas and idealism that underpin what I have tried to write. The errors, self-indulgence and naivety are all mine.

Further Reading

For more on the business of diplomacy:

G. R. Berridge, Maurice Keens-Soper and T. G. Otte, *Diplomatic Theory from Machiavelli to Kissinger* (2001)

John Colville, *The Fringes of Power: Downing Street Diaries 1939–1955* (1985)

Daryl Copeland, *Guerrilla Diplomacy* (2009)

François de Callières, *On the Manner of Negotiating with Princes* (1963)

James der Derian, *On Diplomacy, a Genealogy of Western Estrangement* (1987)

R. G. Feltham, *Diplomatic Handbook* (1970)

Keith Hamilton and Richard Langhorne, *The Practice of Diplomacy* (1995)

Nico Henderson, *Inside the Private Office* (1987)

Katie Hickman, *Daughters of Britannia* (1999)

Geoffrey Jackson, *Concorde Diplomacy: The Ambassador's Role in the World Today* (1981)

Maurice Keens-Soper, *Abraham de Wicquefort and Diplomatic Theory* (1997)

Henry Kissinger, *Diplomacy* (1994)

Garrett Mattingly, *Renaissance Diplomacy* (2015 edition; first published in 1955)

Harold Nicolson, *On Diplomacy* (1961)

Carne Ross, *Independent Diplomat* (2007)

Andreas Sandre, *Twitter for Diplomats* (online)

Ernest Satow, *Guide to Diplomatic Practice* (2009 edition; first published in 1917)

True Brits (book of the BBC series)

John Ure, *Diplomatic Bag* (1994)

For more on power, and the future:

Jared Diamond, *Guns, Germs and Steel* (1997)

Niall Fergusson, *Civilisation: The West and the Rest* (2011)

Al Gore, *The Future: Six Drivers of Global Change* (2013)

Ian Morris, *Why the West Rules – For Now* (2010)

Moisés Naím, *The End of Power* (2013)

Joseph Nye, *The Future of Power* (2011)

Chris Patten, *What Next? Surviving the Twenty-First Century* (2008)

Stephen Pinker, *The Better Angels of Our Nature: A History of Violence and Humanity* (2011)

Kenneth Pomeranz, *The Great Divergence* (2000)

Alec Ross, *Industries of the Future* (2016)

Eric Schmidt and Jared Cohen, *The New Digital Age* (2013)

For more on tech:

Nicholas Carr, *The Big Switch: Rewiring the World, from Edison to Google* (2008)

Nicholas Carr, *The Shallows: What the Internet Is Doing to Our Brains* (2011)

Mark Helprin, *Digital Barbarism: A Writer's Manifesto* (2009)

Jaron Lanier, *You Are Not a Gadget* (2010)

Philippe Legraine, *Aftershock: Reshaping the World Economy After the Crisis* (2010)

Lewis Mumford, *Technics and Civilization* (2010)

Nicholas Negroponte, *Being Digital* (1995)

Neil Postman, *Technopoly: The Surrender of Culture to Technology* (1992)

Adam Thierer, *The Case for Internet Optimism Part 1: Saving the Net From Its Detractors* (2008)

Sherry Turkle, *Alone Together* (2011)

Tim Wu, *The Master Switch: The Rise and Fall of Information Empires* (2011)

Notes

Introduction to the Paperback Edition

1. See Epilogue.
2. Early in Obama's presidency, the UK press obsessed about the removal of the Churchill bust from his office. The story was completely overblown – the bust had been loaned by Blair to Bush for the duration of his term. But it is a nice early example of post-truth politics.
3. David Cameron's first G8 summit was in Muskoka (Canada). To show his political virility, he and I went swimming in a freezing lake, and I briefed the other delegations. When we got to the main meeting, his fellow leaders were all suitably impressed. Except Berlusconi, who stormed off in a strop, and came back with eight photos of himself in very tight swimming trunks, which he then handed out to the baffled leaders. I have never seen them all so perturbed.
4. W. B. Yeats, 'The Second Coming', 1919.
5. World Economic Forum Global Risk Report, 11 January 2017.
6. Save the Children, Report on Global Refugee Crisis, 14 September 2016.
7. See Chapter 18.

Preface

1. The then Turkish prime minister Recep Tayyip Erdogan was the first leader I observed bringing an iPad into a G20 meeting, to great effect. David Cameron was the first to do so at a G8. Erdogan subsequently lost his tech credentials when he tried to ban Twitter.

2. *The Economist*, September 2012.

Introduction to the First Edition

1. *New York Times*, 21 January 2013.

2. See R. P. Barston and Hans Morgenthau on the academic debates on representation.

3. See 2014 Policy Exchange report on digital governance.

4. See the University of Pennsylvania's 2014 Global Go-To Think Tank Index for the full league table.

5. See Robert Phillips, *Trust Me, PR Is Dead* (2015) for a similar critique of public relations.

6. Garrett Mattingly, *Renaissance Diplomacy* (2015 edition).

Chapter 1

1. For more on caveman diplomacy, see Finnish diplomat and anthropologist Ragnar Numelin's work on the early evolution of diplomacy (1950).

2. I recommend Yuval Noah Harari's 2015 TED Talk on what sets humans apart.

3. For more on this magnum opus, see Roger Boesche, *The First Great Political Realist: Kautilya and his Arthashastra* (2002).

4. Joshua Mark, *Ancient History Encyclopedia* (2009).

5. See James Montgomery, *History of Yaballaha III* (1927).

Chapter 2

1. Edward Dreyer, *Zheng He, China and the Oceans of the Early Ming* (2007).

2. See Jared Diamond, *Guns, Germs and Steel* (1997).

3. For more on the competition between East and West, see Ian Morris's brilliant *Why the West Rules – For Now* (2010).

4. See Pierre Chaplais, *English Diplomatic Practice in the Middle Ages* (2003) for more on the intrigues and espionage of the court.

5. Wellington Society of Madrid, *Wellington Anecdotes* (2008).

Chapter 3

1. Harold Nicolson, *On Diplomacy* (1961).

2. David Brown, *Palmerston: A Biography* (2010).

3. Letter to Lord Gower, 2 October 1807, quoted in Boyd Hilton, *A Mad, Bad and Dangerous People? England, 1783–1846* (2006).

4. James Mill, quoted in *The Cambridge History of the British Empire, Volume 4* (1990).

5. Ernest Satow, *Guide to Diplomatic Practice* (2009 edition).

6. Uncle Matthew, in Nancy Mitford, *The Pursuit of Love* (1945).

7. F. S. Pepper (ed), *Twentieth-Century Anecdotes* (1990).

8. Robert Tucker and David Hendrickson, *Empire of Liberty: The Statecraft of Thomas Jefferson* (1990).

9. Independence Day speech, House of Representatives, 4 July 1821.

10. Quoted in John Ure, *Diplomatic Bag* (1994).

Chapter 4

1. F. P. Walters, *A History of the League of Nations* (1986).

2. Goldsworthy Lowes Dickinson, 'War: Its Nature, Cause and Cure' (1923).

3. US commentator Reinhold Neibuhr, April 1943.

4. See Cita Stelzer, *Dinner with Churchill* (2011), for more on how Churchill used culinary diplomacy.

5. Arnold Toynbee, *A Study of History* (1934).

6. Peter Preston, *Guardian*, 15 June 2014.

7. For more on this extraordinary event, see Ed Conway's *The Summit: The Biggest Battle of the Second World War* (2014).

8. Wilson P. Dizzard, 'Digital Diplomacy', Center for Strategic and International Studies (2001).

9. Quoted in Alex Barker, 'Britain's First Female Diplomats', *Financial Times*, 6 November 2009.

10. Ibid.

11. For more on women in diplomacy, see Helen McCarthy, 'The Rise of the Female Diplomat', *Prospect*, 20 October 2014.

12. FCO, 'Guidance on the Do's and Don't's of Etiquette and Other Relevant Matters' (1965).

13. For more on diplomatic spouses, see Katie Hickman, *Daughters of Britannia* (1999)

14. *Guardian*, 5 February 2011.

15. See Geoffrey Jackson, *Concorde Diplomacy: The Ambassador's Role in the World Today* (1981). Jackson was kidnapped for eight months in 1971 by Uruguayan guerillas. Maybe the diplomatic experience had not changed so much after all.

16. John Colville, *The Fringes of Power: Downing Street Diaries 1939–1955* (1985).

17. *Memoirs of the Prince de Talleyrand* (1891).

18. Quoted in John Ure, *Diplomatic Bag* (1994).

19. Al Gore, *The Future: Six Drivers of Global Change* (2013).

20. Chris Patten, *What Next? Surviving the Twenty-First Century* (2008).

Chapter 5

1. Burson-Marsteller, July 2013.
2. *New York Times*, 4 February 2014.
3. Anne Marie Slaughter, former State Department Director of Policy Planning.
4. Jimmy Leach, 'In the Digital Diplomacy Battle, the Upstarts Will Start to Win Out', *Huffington Post*, 6 October 2014.
5. Oliver Miles, 'Stop the blogging ambassadors', *Guardian*, 12 July 2010.
6. Sir Leslie Fielding, 'Is Diplomacy Dead?', VIII Adforton Lecture, Oxford University, June 2010.

Chapter 6

1. Sir Leslie Fielding, 'Is Diplomacy Dead?', VIII Adforton Lecture, Oxford University, June 2010.
2. Harold Nicolson, *On Diplomacy* (1961).
3. Ibid.
4. BBC Radio, *Desert Island Discs*, 13 November 1968.
5. Sir Christopher Meyer, 'The Secrets of my Success', *Daily Mail*, 6 February 2010. The title of the article suggests that modesty was less important to the skill set.
6. Oliver Miles, 'The job of an ambassador', *Guardian*, 14 July 2010.
7. Nicolson, op. cit.
8. Ernest Satow, *Guide to Diplomatic Practice* (2009 edition). Satow's book is still a good read.
9. Ibid.
10. *Bloomsbury Anthology of Quotations* (2002).
11. Quoted in John Ure, *Diplomatic Bag* (1994).
12. Quoted in Stephen Lee, *Aspects of European History, 1789–1980* (2008). For more on Cavour's effective but often

unscrupulous diplomacy, see Edgar Holt, *Risorgimento: The Making of Italy, 1815–1870* (1970).

13. Charles Hill, *Grand Strategies: Literature, Statecraft and World Order* (2010).

14. Tony Blair, *A Journey* (2010).

15. Fielding, 'Is Diplomacy Dead?', op. cit.

16. Miles, 'The job of an ambassador', op. cit.

17. Quoted in Richard Armitage and Joseph Nye (eds), Commission on Smart Power, Center for Strategic and International Studies (2007).

18. Nicolson, op. cit.

19. Quoted in George Egerton, *Political Memoir: Essays on the Politics of Memory* (1994).

20. Richard Stengel, *Mandela's Way: Fifteen Lessons on Life, Love and Courage* (2010).

21. BBC News Magazine, 10 October 2006.

22. R. G. Feltham, *Diplomatic Handbook* (1970).

23. Rosemarie Jarski (ed), *Words from the Wise* (2013).

24. BBC News Magazine, 10 October 2006.

25. Nicolson, op. cit.

26. Foreign Affairs Committee report, January 2014.

27. Quoted in Raymond Jones, *The British Diplomatic Service, 1815–1914* (1983).

Chapter 7

1. Harold Nicolson, *On Diplomacy* (1961).

2. See Malcolm Gladwell's brilliant description of co-creation during the Industrial Revolution in *Blink: The Power of Thinking Without Thinking* (2005).

3. Al Gore, *The Future: Six Drivers of Global Change* (2013).

4. *Independent*, 17 August 2010.

5. Office for National Statistics, 2013.

6. See Daniel Levitin, *The Organized Mind* (2014).

7. Quoted in Martin Ford, *The Rise of the Robots: Technology and the Threat of a Jobless Future* (2015).

8. Minqing Hu and Bing Liu, *Mining Opinion Features in Customer Reviews* (2004).

9. Kalev Leetaru, *Culturomics 2.0* (2011). The term 'culturomics' and the form of analysis it refers to were pioneered by Harvard academics Jean-Baptiste Michel and Erez Lieberman Aiden in 2010.

10. McKinsey, 'Big Data – The next frontier for innovation, competition and productivity', May 2011.

Chapter 8

1. For more on the heavy drinking, ferociously deceptive master traitor, I highly recommend Ben Macintyre's riveting *A Spy Among Friends* (2014), given to me by an impressed Lebanese warlord.

2. CNN, 30 November 2010.

3. *Guardian*, 5 February 2011.

4. Michael V. Hayden, 'The Future of Surveillance in a Post-Snowden World', *Huffington Post*, 18 March 2014.

5. Gerald Martin, *Gabriel García Márquez: A Life* (2008).

6. *Financial Times*, 13 February 2014.

7. *Financial Times*, 3 November 2014.

8. Hayden, 'The Future of Surveillance in a Post-Snowden World', op. cit.

9. Sir David Omand, Jamie Bartlett and Carl Miller, *#Intelligence*, Demos, April 2012.

10. *Guardian*, 28 February 2014.

Chapter 9

1. Quoted in Henry Kissinger, *Diplomacy* (1994).
2. Durham Global Security Institute.
3. Richard Armitage and Joseph Nye (eds), Commission on Smart Power, Center for Strategic and International Studies (2007).
4. IfG-Monocle Soft Power Index, www.instrumentfor government.org.uk.
5. Many of the quotes in this chapter are from the excellent 2013 House of Lords report on smart power, 'Persuasion and Power in the Modern World' (online).
6. Quoted in ibid.
7. Quoted in ibid.
8. Armitage and Nye (eds), Commission on Smart Power, op. cit.
9. See James Barr's brilliant *A Line in the Sand: Britain, France and the Struggle for the Mastery of the Middle East* (2011) for more on this controversial period. The grandson of Sykes, Christopher Simon Sykes, is also writing a book on this period.
10. Quoted in Keith Hamilton, *Bertie of Thame* (1990).

Chapter 10

1. Quoted in José Calvet de Magalhães, *The Pure Concept of Diplomacy* (1988).
2. Douglas Rushkoff, *Present Shock: When Everything Happens Now* (2013).
3. Garrett Mattingly, *Renaissance Diplomacy* (2015 edition).
4. See the scene in the movie *Love Actually* (2003) when the British prime minister, played by Hugh Grant, lays into his American counterpart.
5. Quoted in Richard Wigg, *Churchill and Spain* (2011).

6. Massolution report, 2013.

7. TED talk, 2013.

Chapter 11

1. See Anthony Seldon and Peter Snowdon, *Cameron at 10* (2015) for the full account.

2. See Jonathan Powell, *Great Hatred, Little Room: Making Peace in Northern Ireland* (2008) for a more detailed discussion.

3. For more of Jonathan Powell's vital thoughts on audacious peacemaking, see his book *Talking to Terrorists* (2014).

4. John Ure, *Diplomatic Bag* (1994).

5. Sue Monk Kidd, *The Secret Life of Bees* (2013).

6. Gareth Evans, blogpost 'Sorry Is The Hardest Word' for Project Syndicate, 28 January 2014.

7. President F. D. Roosevelt is reported to have said in 1939 of Uruguayan dictator Anastasio Somoza, 'He may be a son of a bitch, but he's our son of a bitch', although there is no official record of this.

8. Interview, 'The Work of Diplomacy – Conversation with Philip Habib' (1982).

Chapter 14

1. Bob Zoellick, 'The Currency of Power', *Foreign Policy Magazine*, October 2012.

2. For more on theories of power, see Ian Morris, *Why the West Rules – For Now* (2010).

3. TED talk, January 2011.

4. Philippe Legraine, *Aftershock: Reshaping the World Economy After the Crisis* (2010).

5. West Point speech, May 2014.

6. *Daily Telegraph*, 20 November 2003.

7. See the Economist Intelligence Unit's annual Democracy Index.

8. International Institute for Strategic Studies.

9. Quoted in 2013 House of Lords report on smart power, 'Persuasion and Power in the Modern World' (online).

10. Again see James Barr's *A Line in the Sand: Britain, France and the Struggle for the Mastery of the Middle East* (2011), on British and French perfidy in the region.

11. Al Gore, *The Future: Six Drivers of Global Change* (2013).

12. *New York Times*, 29 December 2013.

13. Carl Benedickt Frey and Michael A. Osborne, 'The Future of Employment: How Susceptible are Jobs to Computerisation?', Oxford Martin School working paper, September 2013.

14. Office for National Statistics.

Chapter 16

1. Ipsos MORI.

2. Fermi's Paradox asked why, if there is such a high probability of alien life somewhere in the universe, on planets billions of years older than ours, have they not yet come to find us? Fermi, a physicist, wondered 'where is everybody?' It is a fair question. Maybe these other forms of life do not exist. Maybe the conditions for life are unique on earth, or life elsewhere is periodically destroyed by natural disasters. Or maybe it is because civilisations end up destroying themselves before they can develop sophisticated space travel – they get to a point where they overheat, where they cannot control the pace of their own development. In this theory the fact that we haven't heard from older and more developed planets is because they wipe themselves out. Or maybe because they are all online, having lost the will to innovate and explore.

3. Niall Ferguson, 'A World Without Power', *Foreign Policy Magazine*, October 2009.

4. *New York Times*, 15 September 2014.

5. Speech to Parliament, 18 June 1940.

6. Martin Rees, *Our Final Century* (2003).

7. See Thomas Piketty, *Capital in the Twenty-First Century* (2014), or Jaron Lanier, *You Are Not a Gadget* (2010).

8. See, for example, Evgeny Morozov, *The Net Delusion: The Dark Side of Internet Freedom* (2011).

9. Simon Head, on 'Amazonia', in *Mindless: Why Smarter Machines are Making Dumber Humans* (2014).

10. Neil Postman, *Technopoly: The Surrender of Culture to Technology* (1992).

11. See Jonathan Franzen, *How to be Alone* (2002).

12. See Francis Fukuyama, *The End of History and the Last Man* (1992).

13. Nicholas Carr, *The Shallows: What the Internet is Doing to Our Brains* (2011).

14. Dave Eggers, *The Circle* (2013).

15. Thomas Macaulay, *The History of England from the Accession of James II, Volume 1* (1849).

16. 2009–10 Human Security Report.

17. Al Gore, *The Future: Six Drivers of Global Change* (2013).

18. Lecture to the Royal Institution of Great Britain, 20 November 1936.

19. See Nicholas Negroponte, *Being Digital* (1995) for some uber-optimism.

20. See Jonathan Schell, *The Unconquerable World: Power, Non-Violence and the Will of the People* (2003).

21. Ray Kurzweil's 'Singularity' is the concept that by 2045, computers will be able to host all minds in the world, merging carbon and silicon intelligence into a single

consciousness. See his book *The Singularity is Near: When Humans Transcend Biology* (2006).

Chapter 17

1. See Lucy Parker and Jon Miller, *Everybody's Business* (2013), for their take on the eleven conversations people are having globally.
2. Pew Research Center, 2013.
3. The Canadian government established the International Commission on Intervention and State Sovereignty (ICISS) in September 2000 in response to Kofi Annan's idea.
4. Speech at The Hague Institute for Global Justice, 14 November 2013.
5. *The Economist*, 16 September 1999.
6. Henry Kissinger, *Diplomacy* (1994).
7. See Chris Patten, *What Next? Surviving the Twenty-First Century* (2008).
8. Global Annual Wealth Report, Credit Suisse, 2014.
9. Save the Children.
10. Deloitte, 'Value of Connectivity', February 2014.

Chapter 18

1. Harold Nicolson, *On Diplomacy* (1961).
2. For more on this, see Peter Singer, *The Life You Can Save* (2009).
3. Despite what Norman Angell argued in *The Great Illusion* (1909).
4. Or as Harvard's Dan Gilbert put it at TED 2014, 'Human beings are works in progress who mistakenly think they're finished.'
5. See Jaron Lanier, *You Are Not a Gadget* (2010) for the case for us to fight against the danger that we are defined by our

technology: we must 'avoid reducing people to mere devices. The best way to do that is to believe that the gadgets I can provide are inert tools and are only useful because people have the magical ability to communicate meaning through them.'

Epilogue

1. See Matthew Parris and Andrew Bryson's entertaining *Parting Shots* (2010) for a selection of the best.

Index